101 CALMNESS Coloring Book

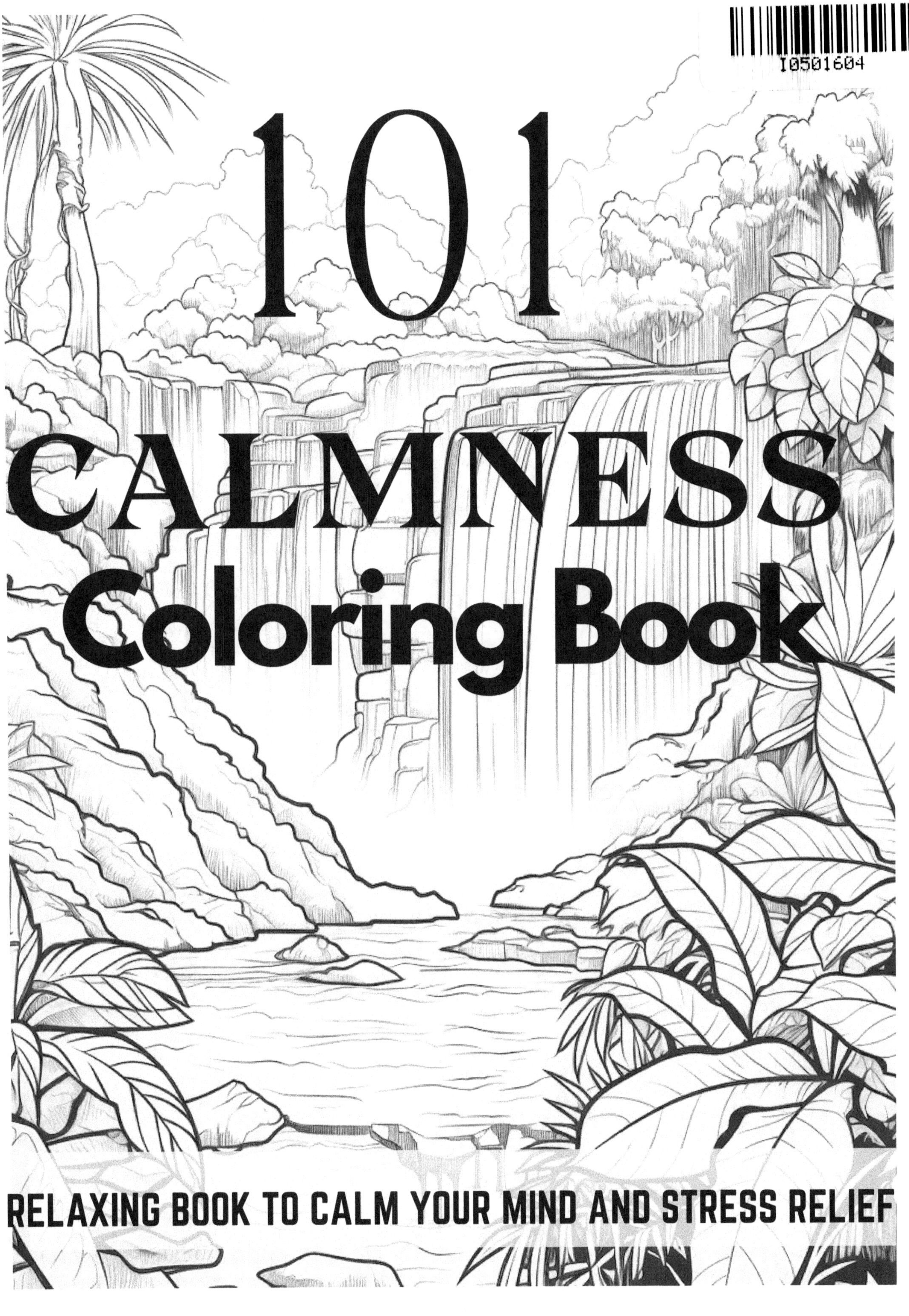

RELAXING BOOK TO CALM YOUR MIND AND STRESS RELIEF

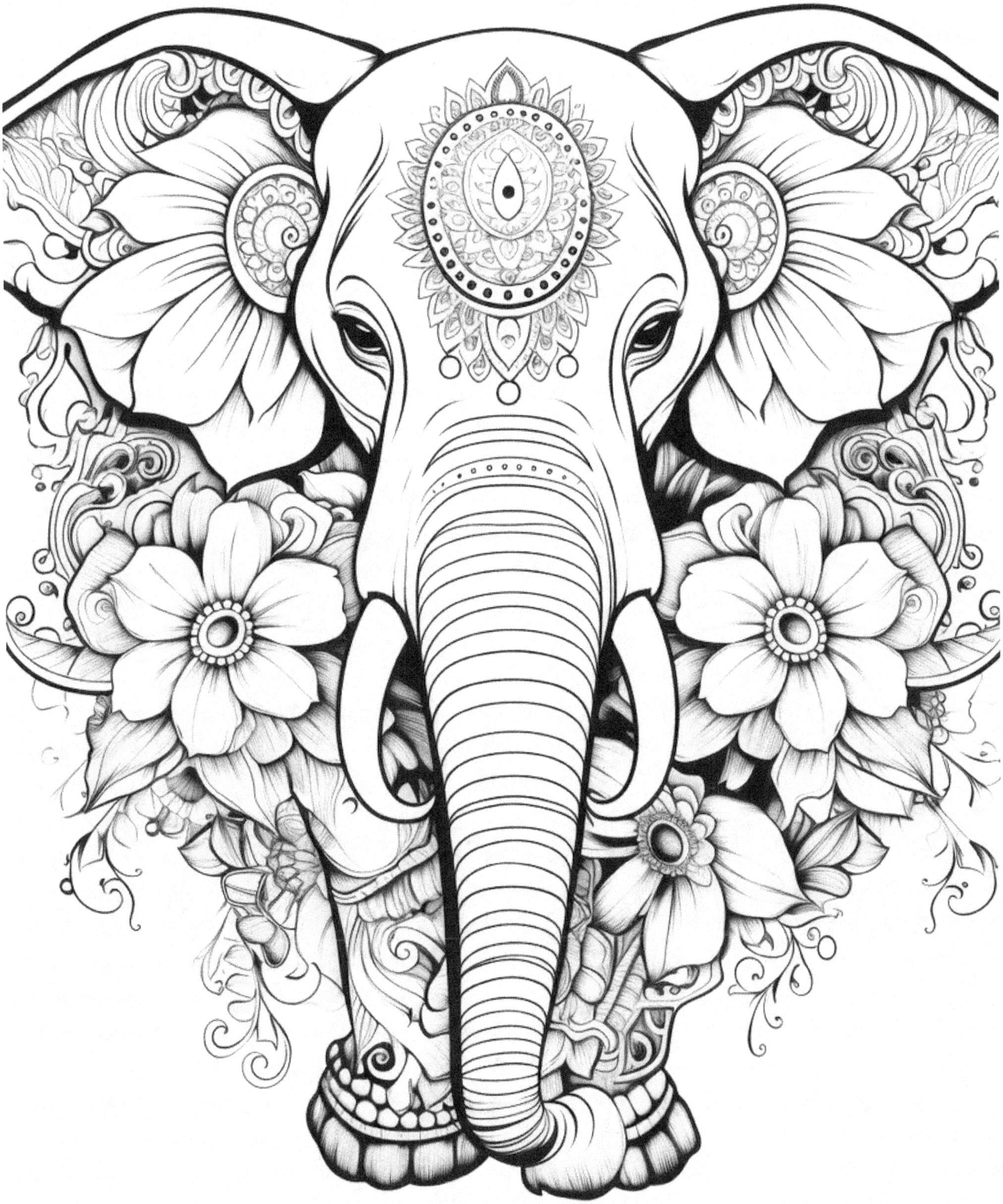

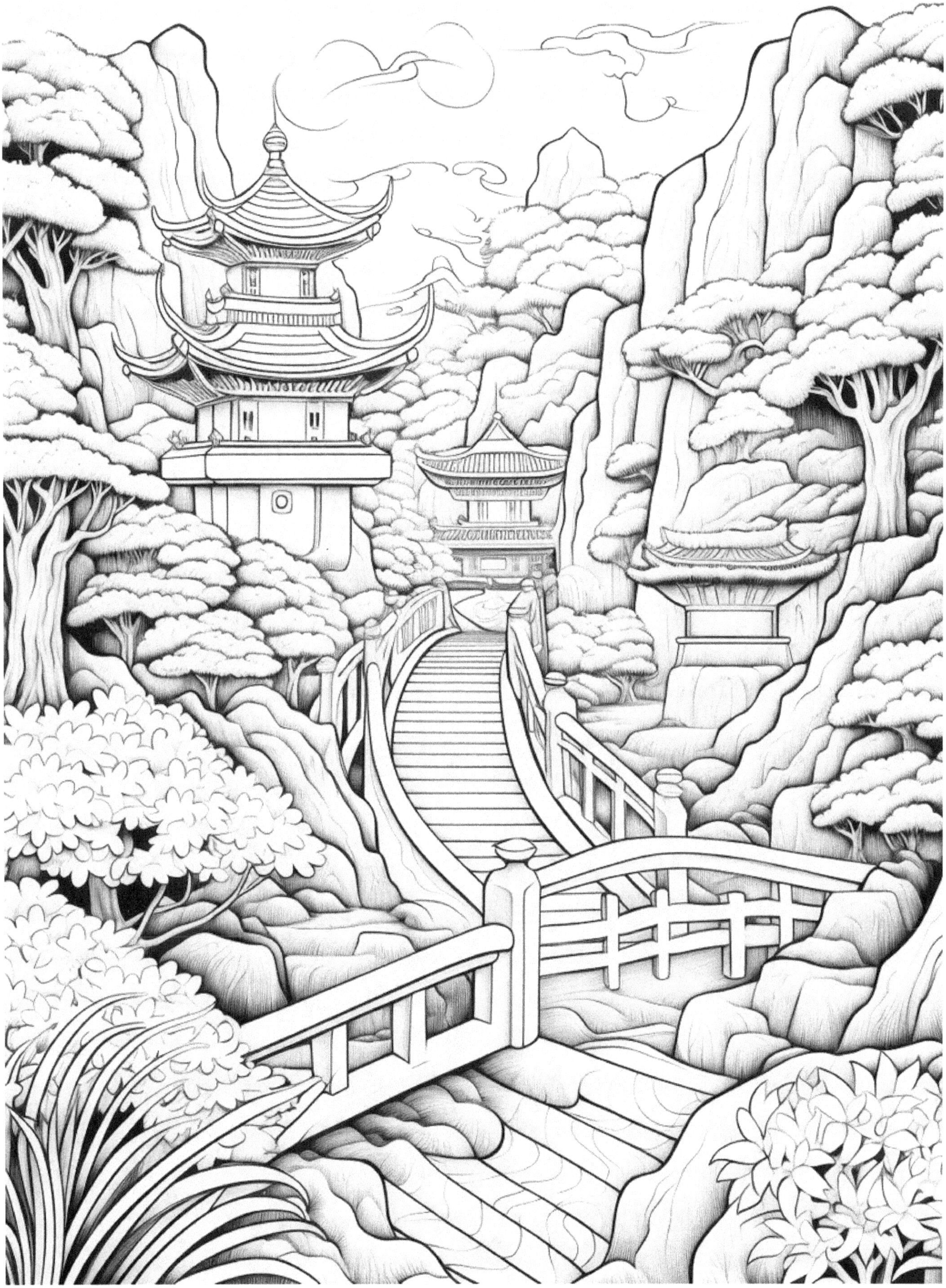

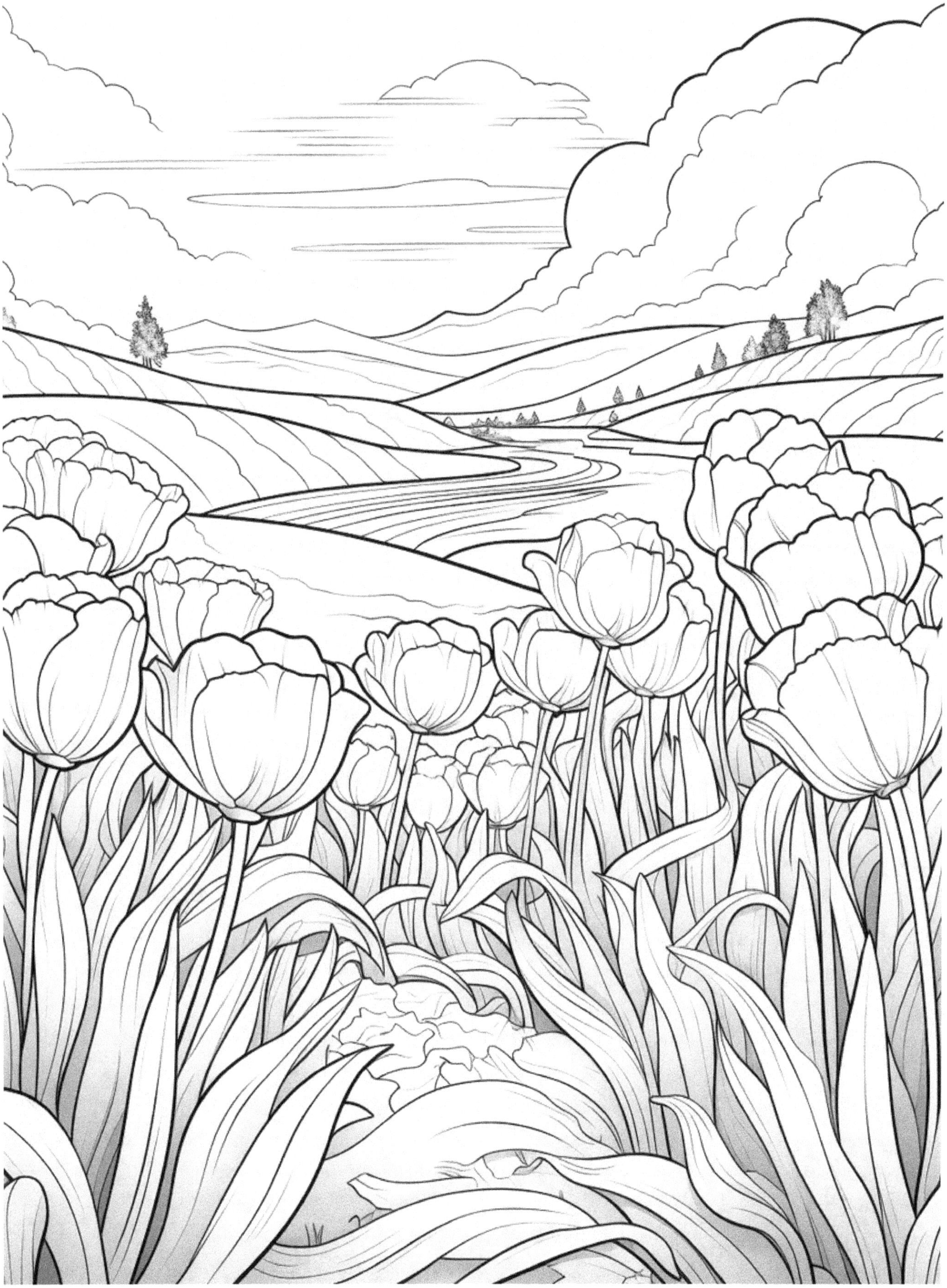

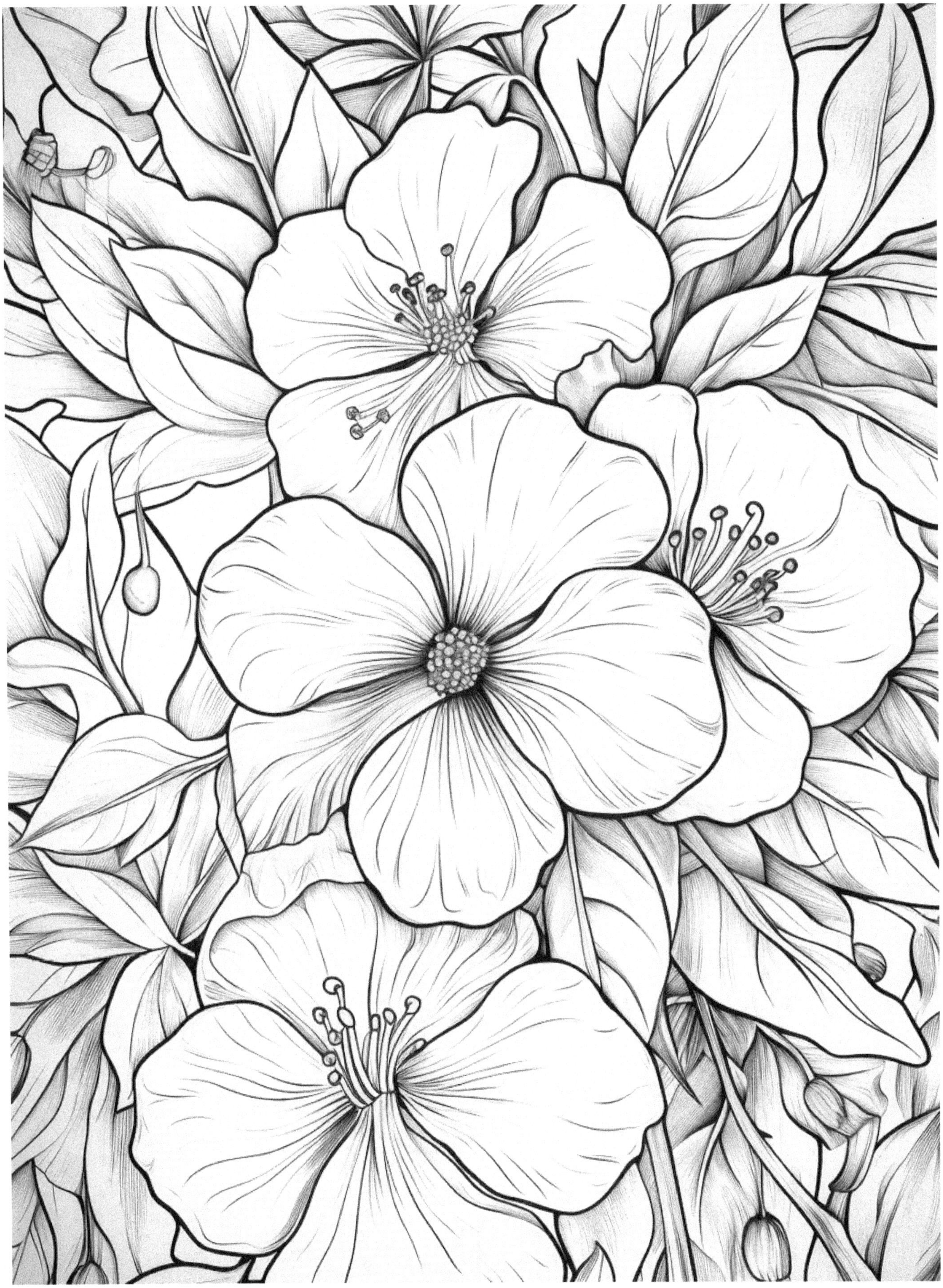

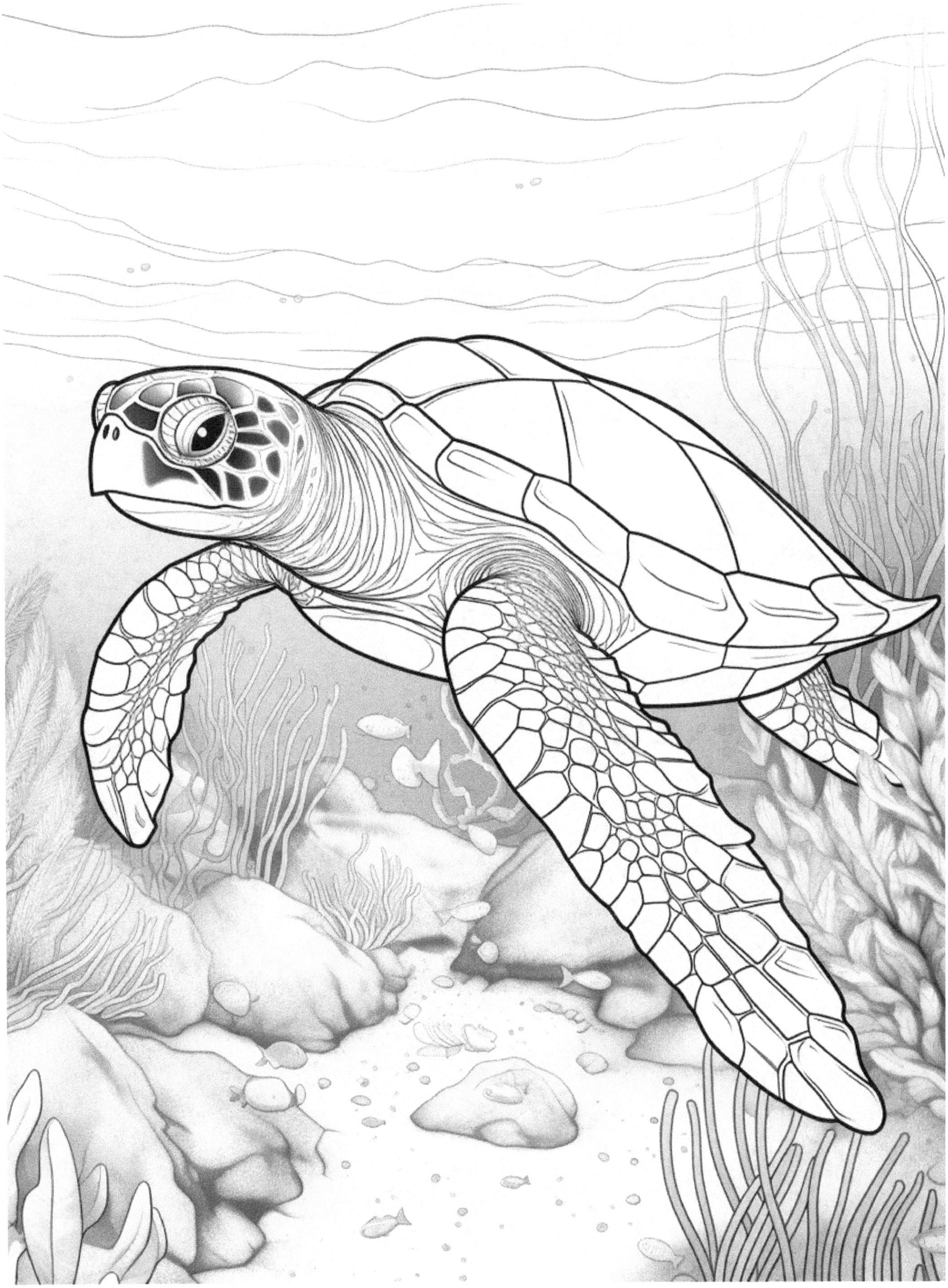

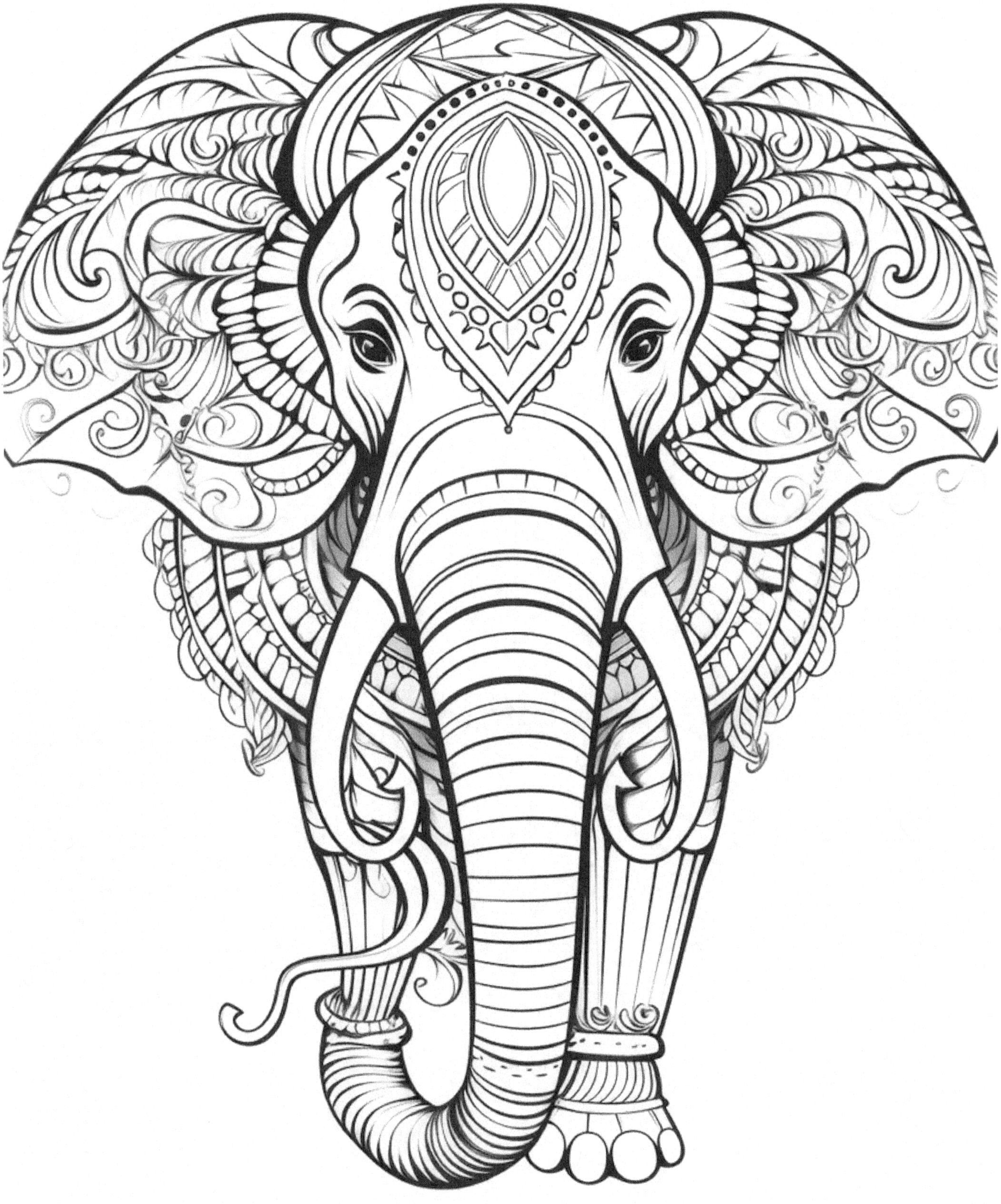

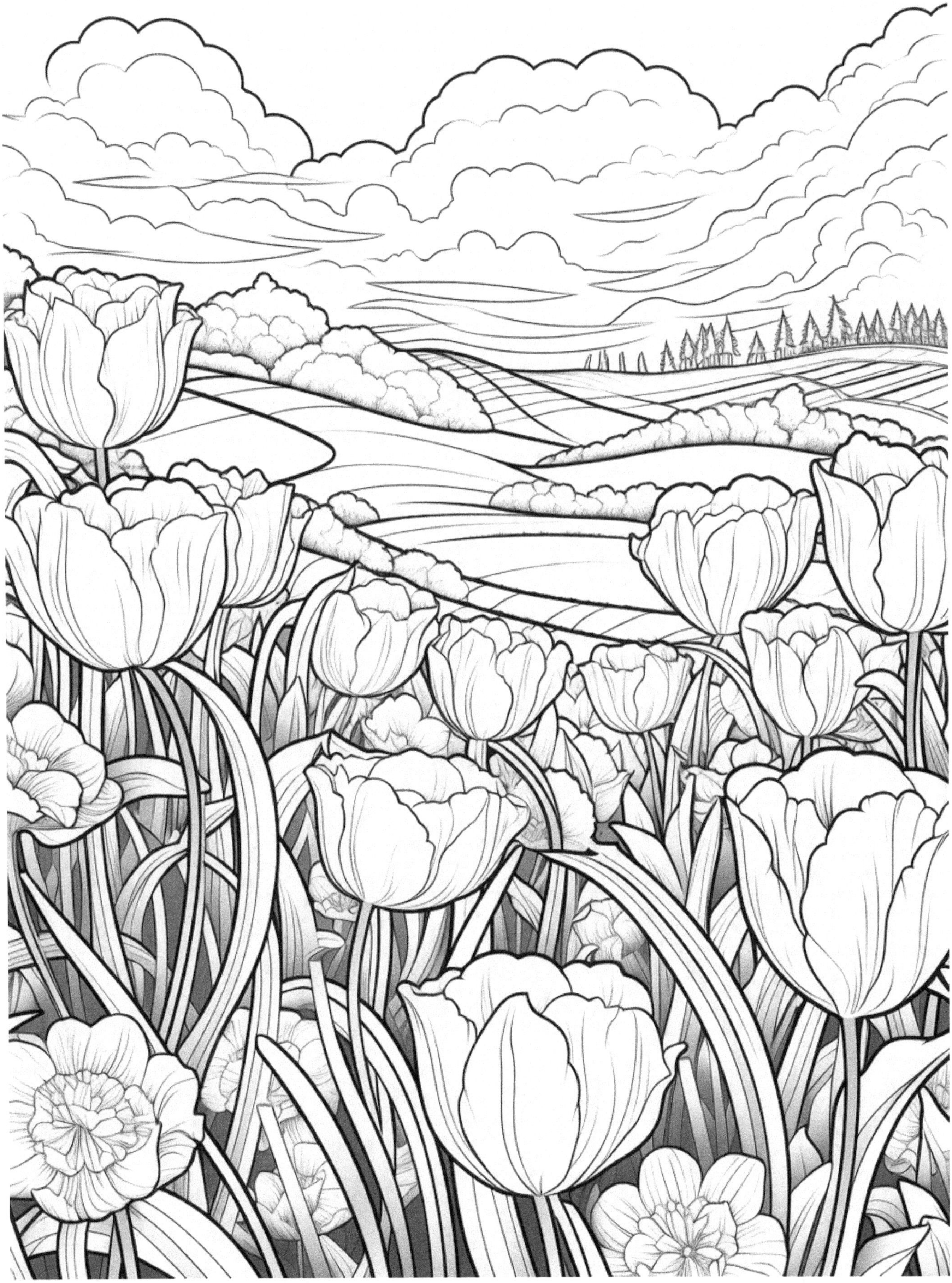

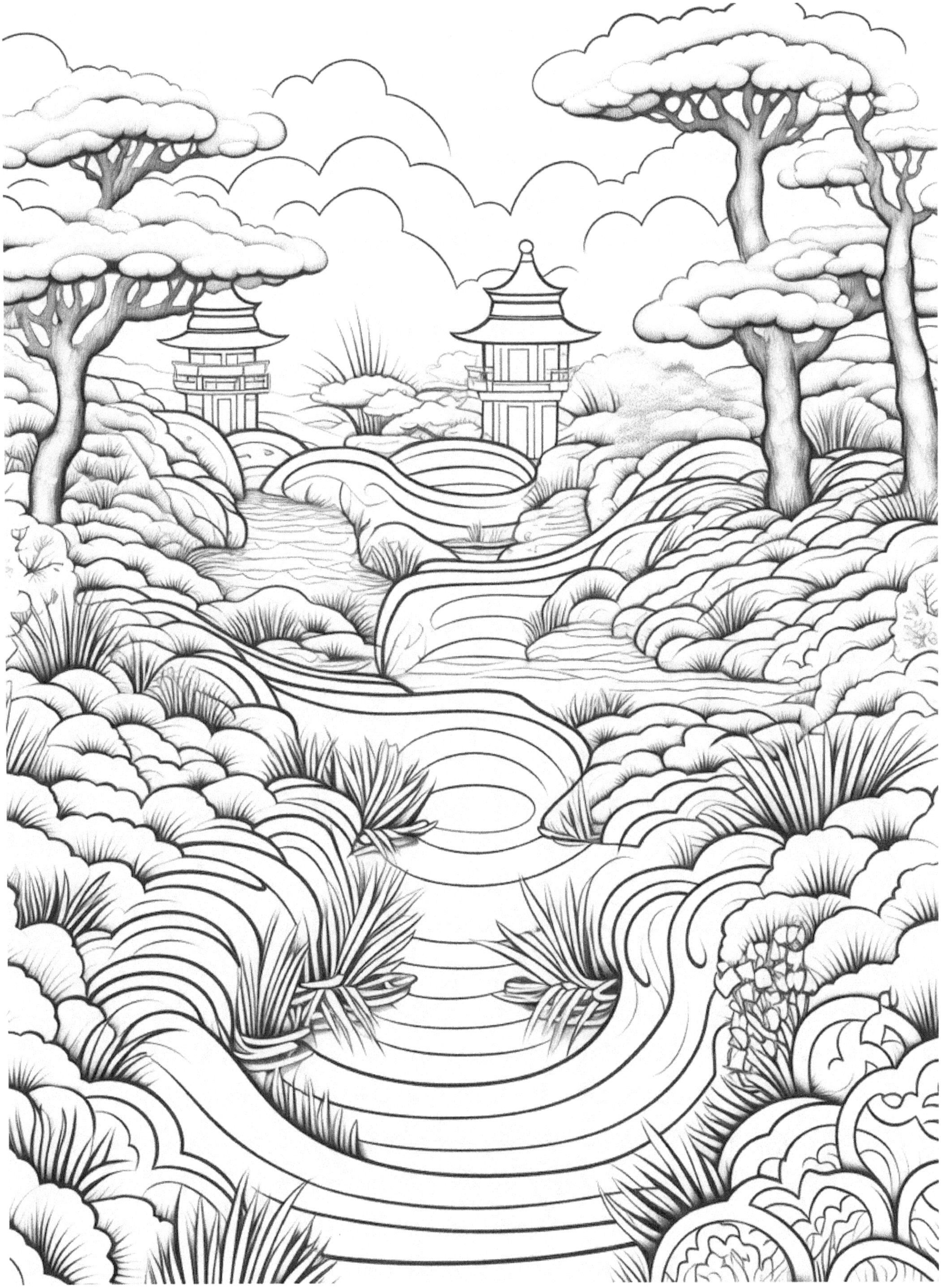

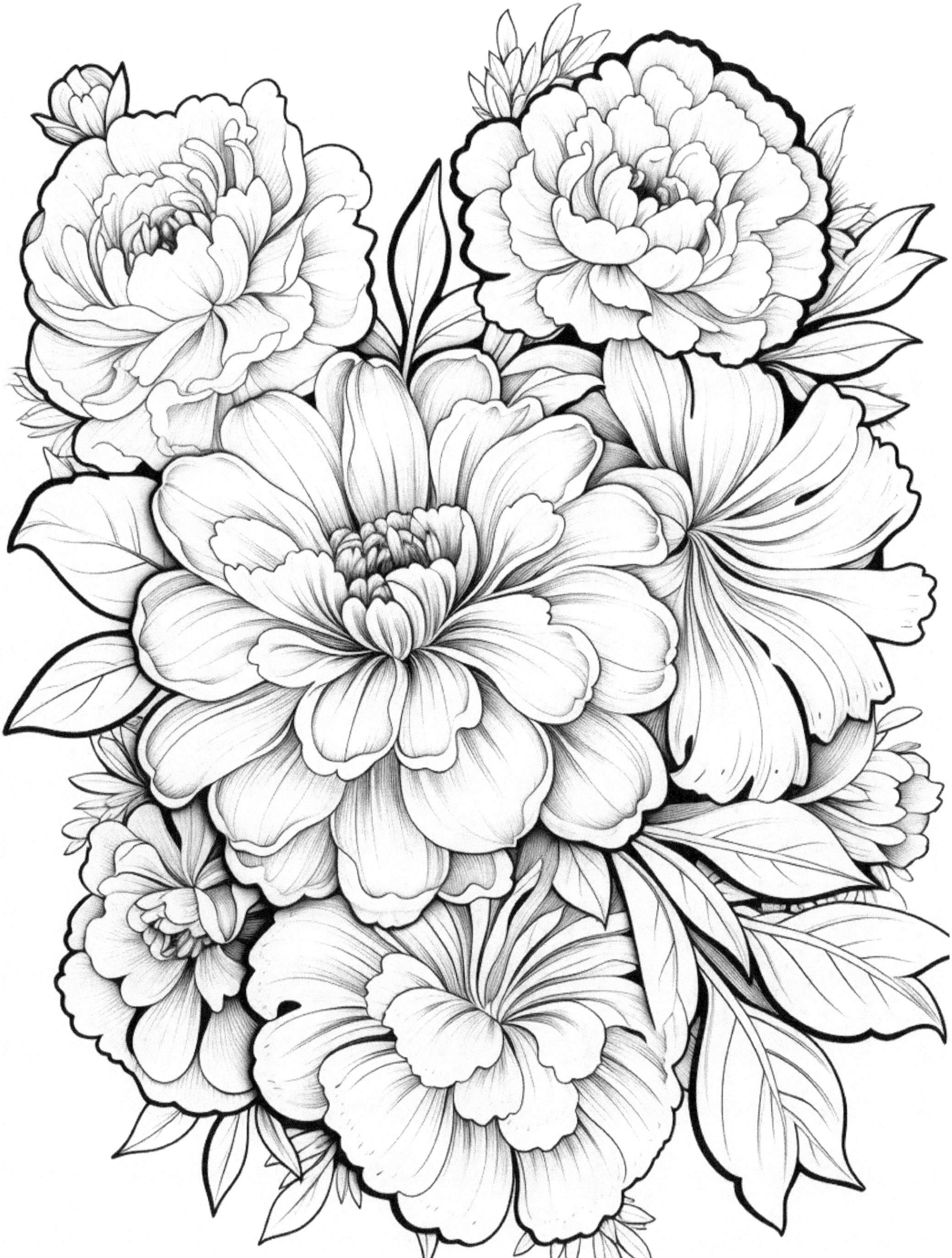

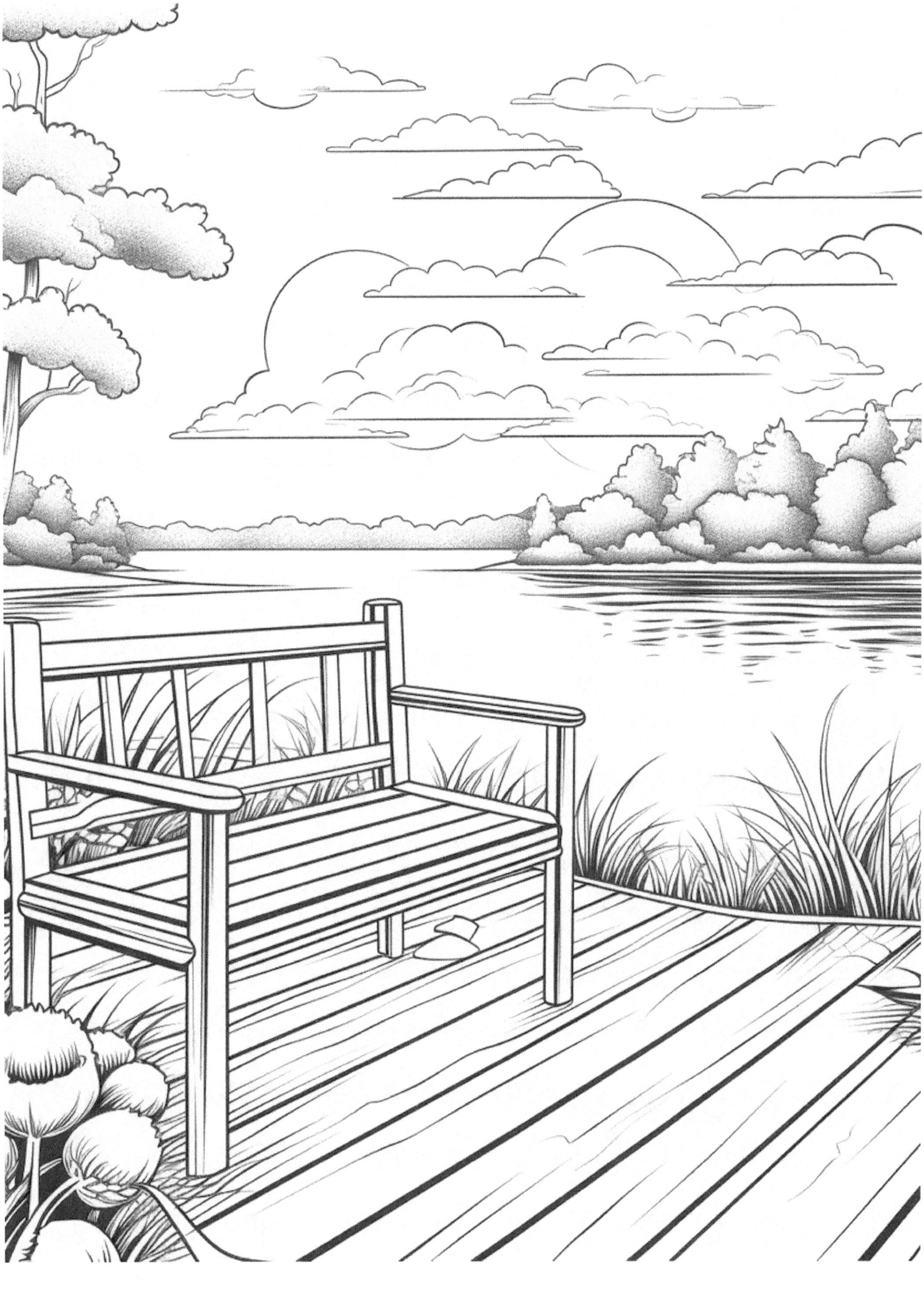

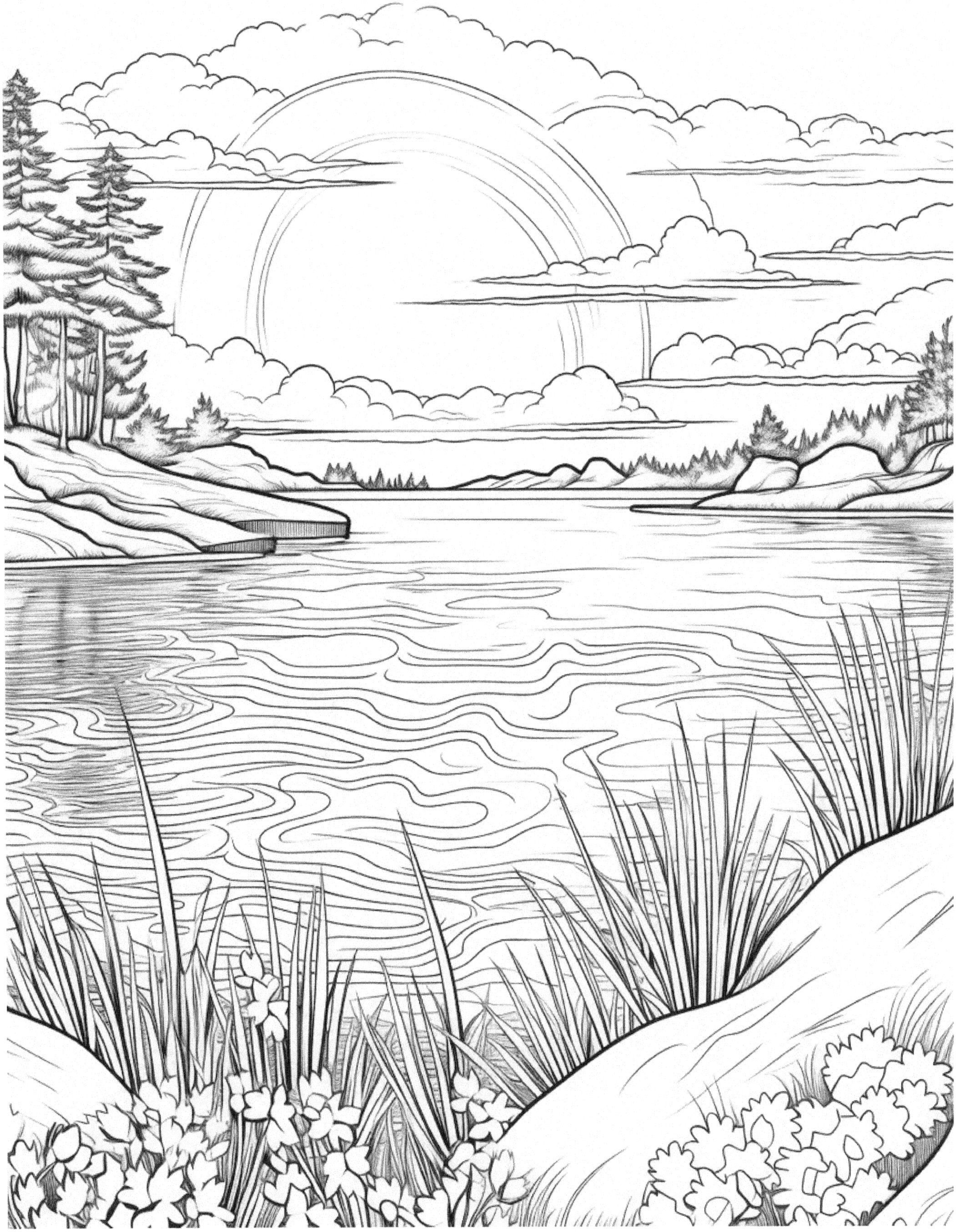

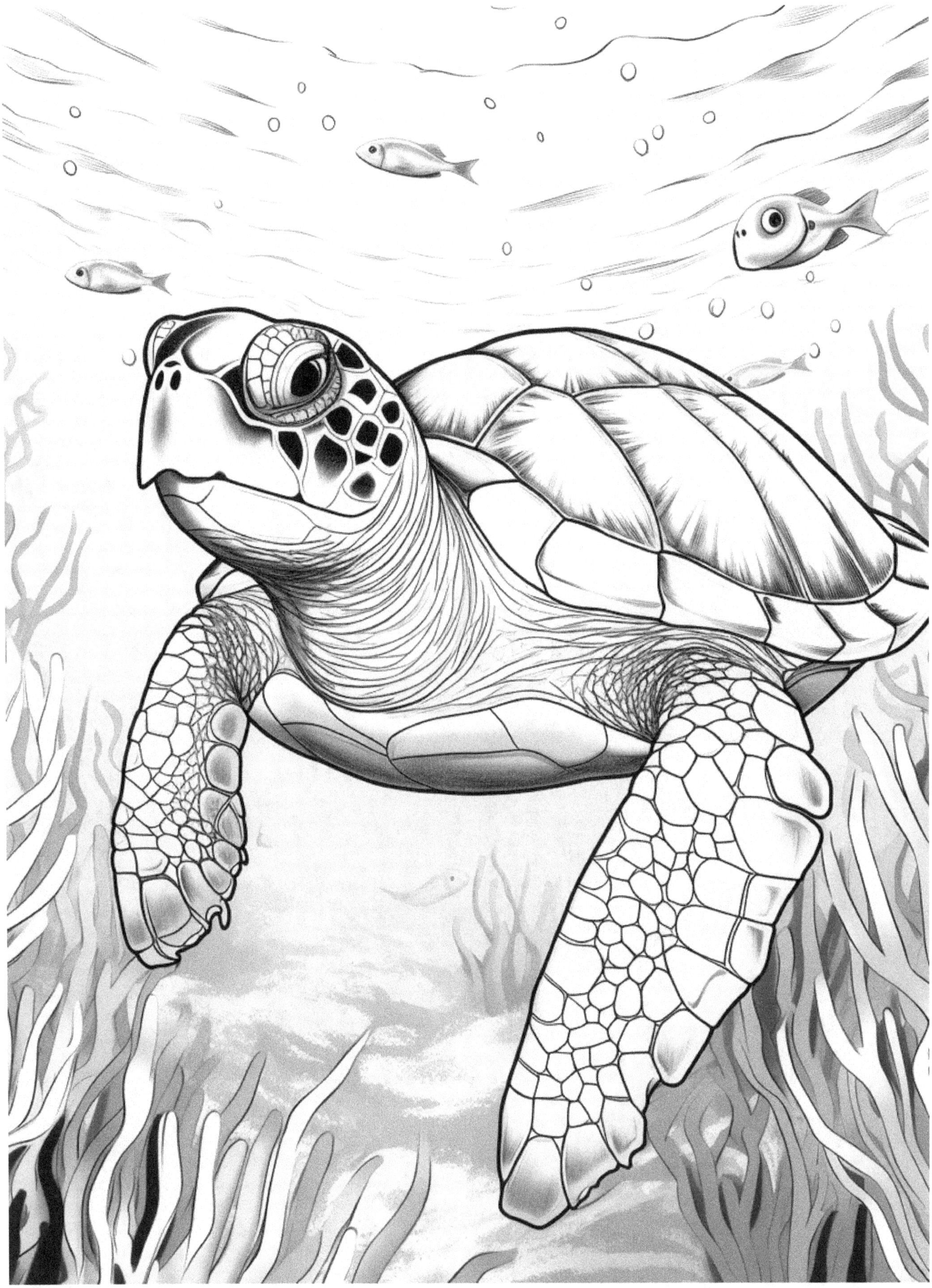

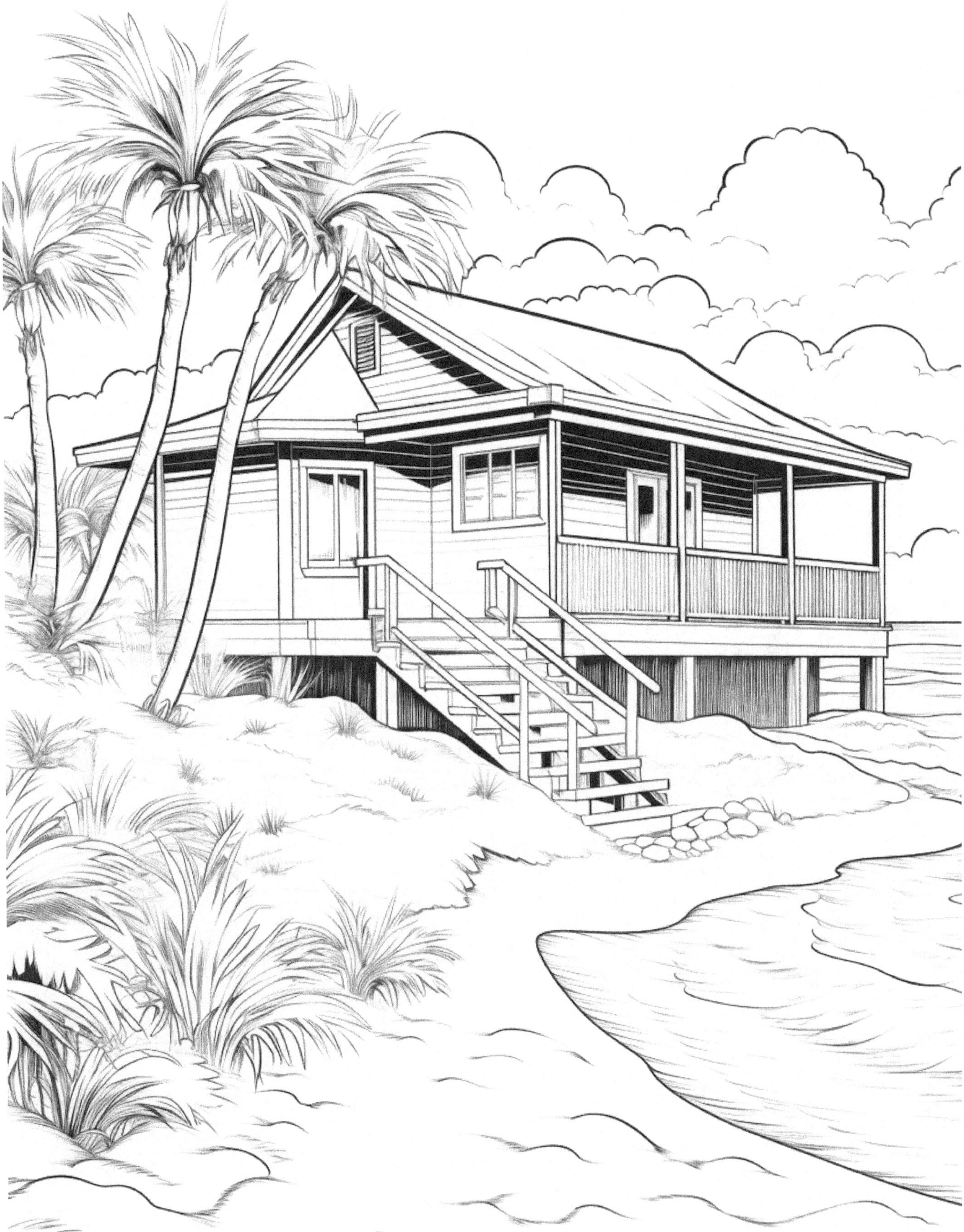

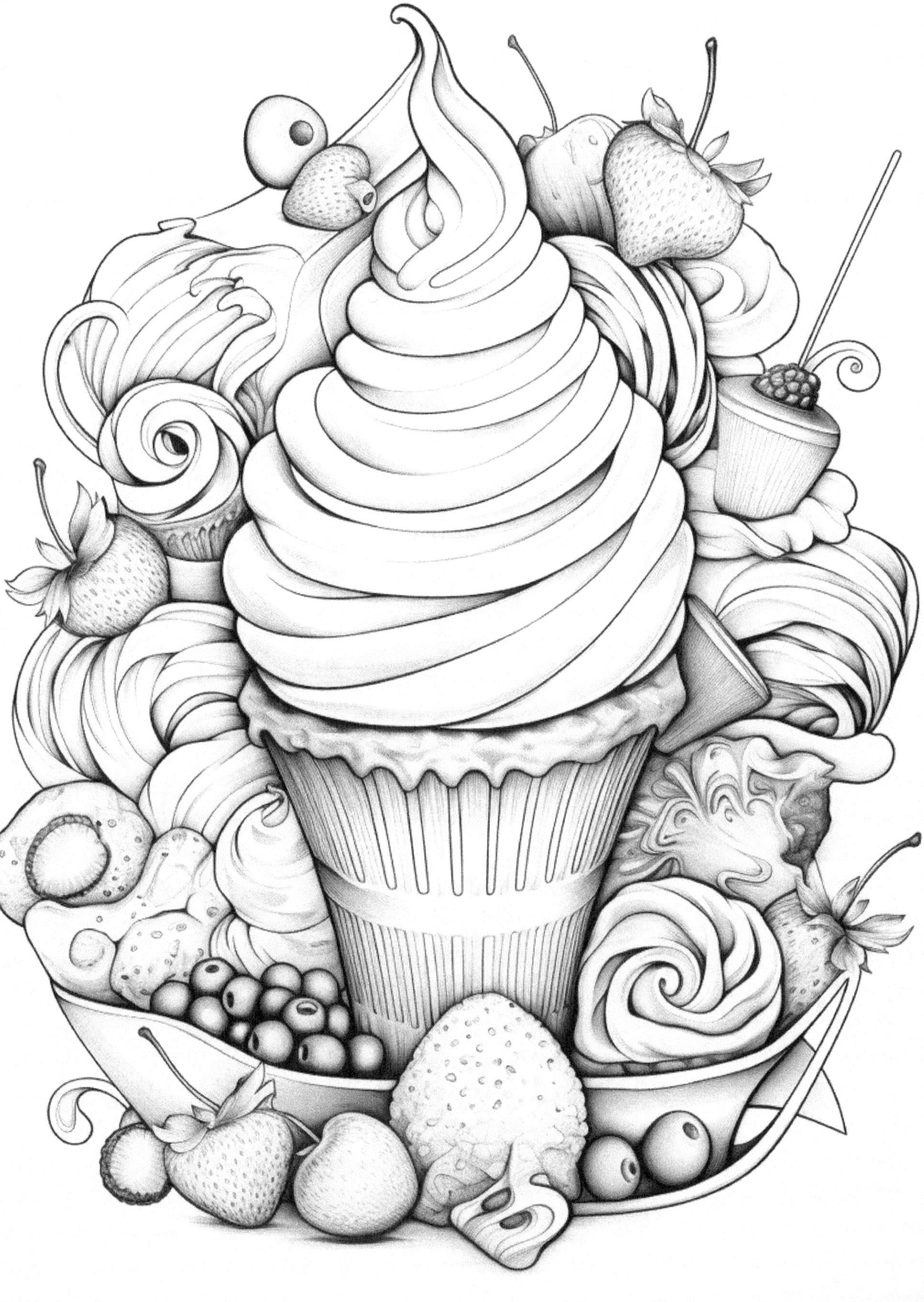

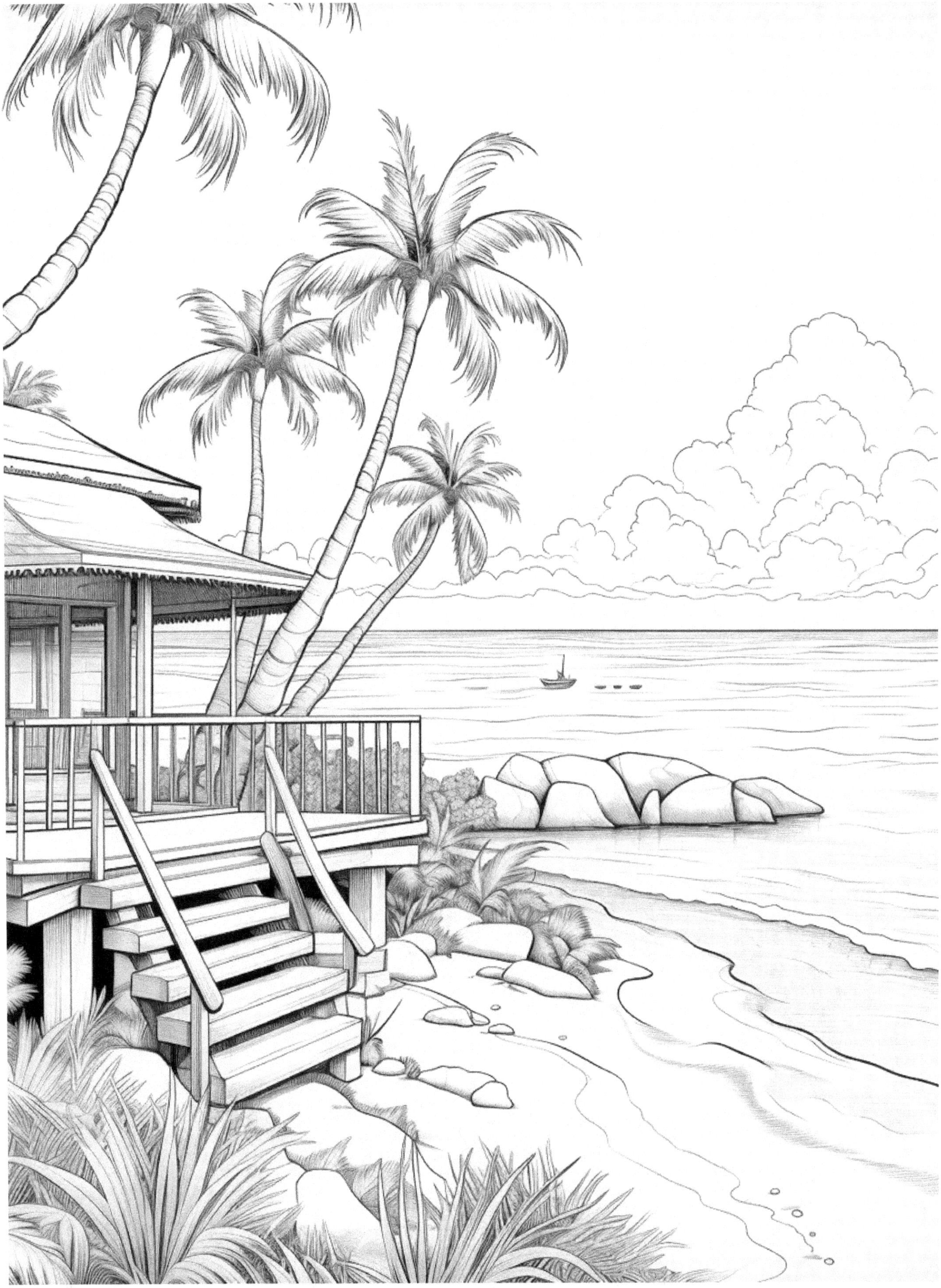

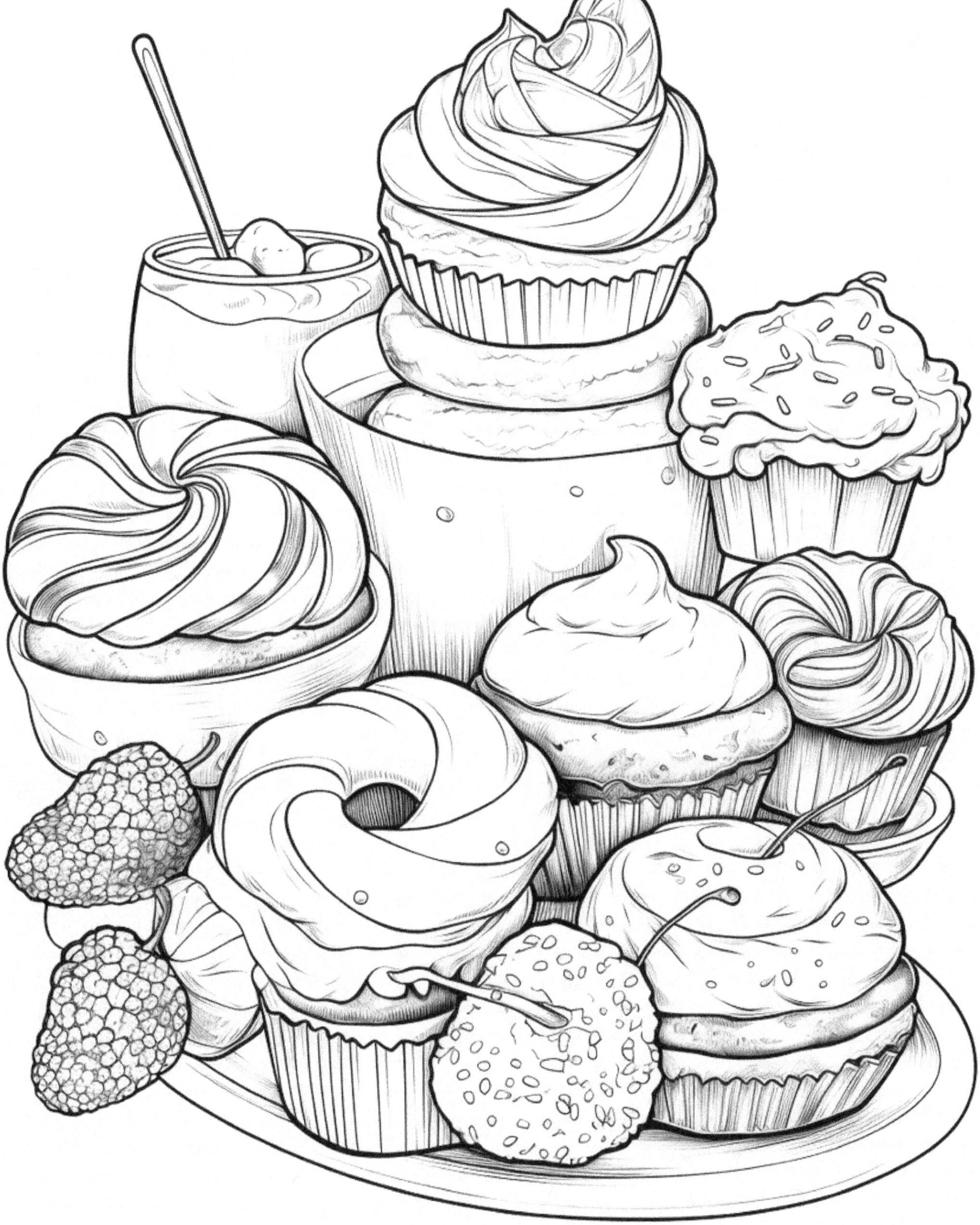

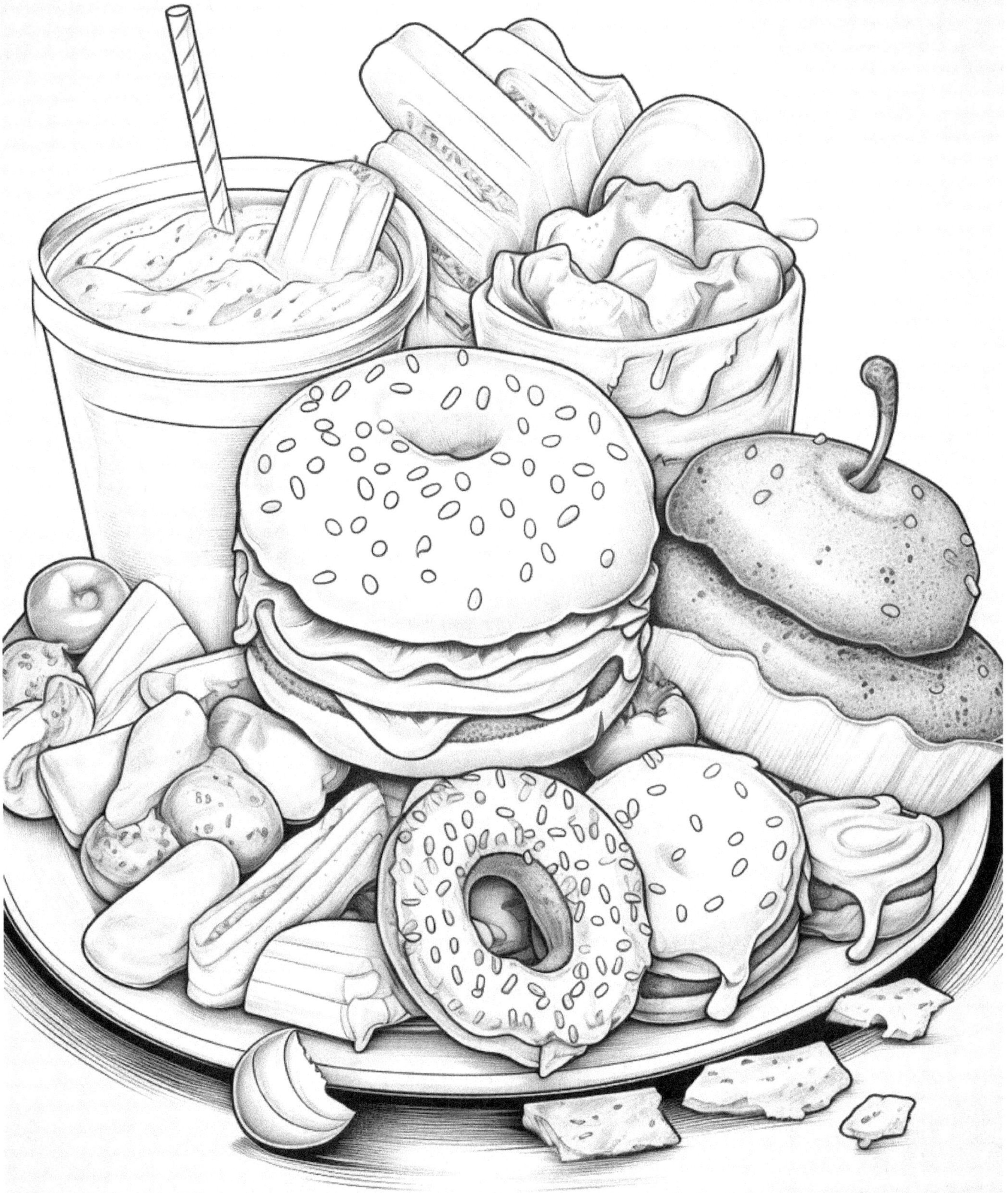

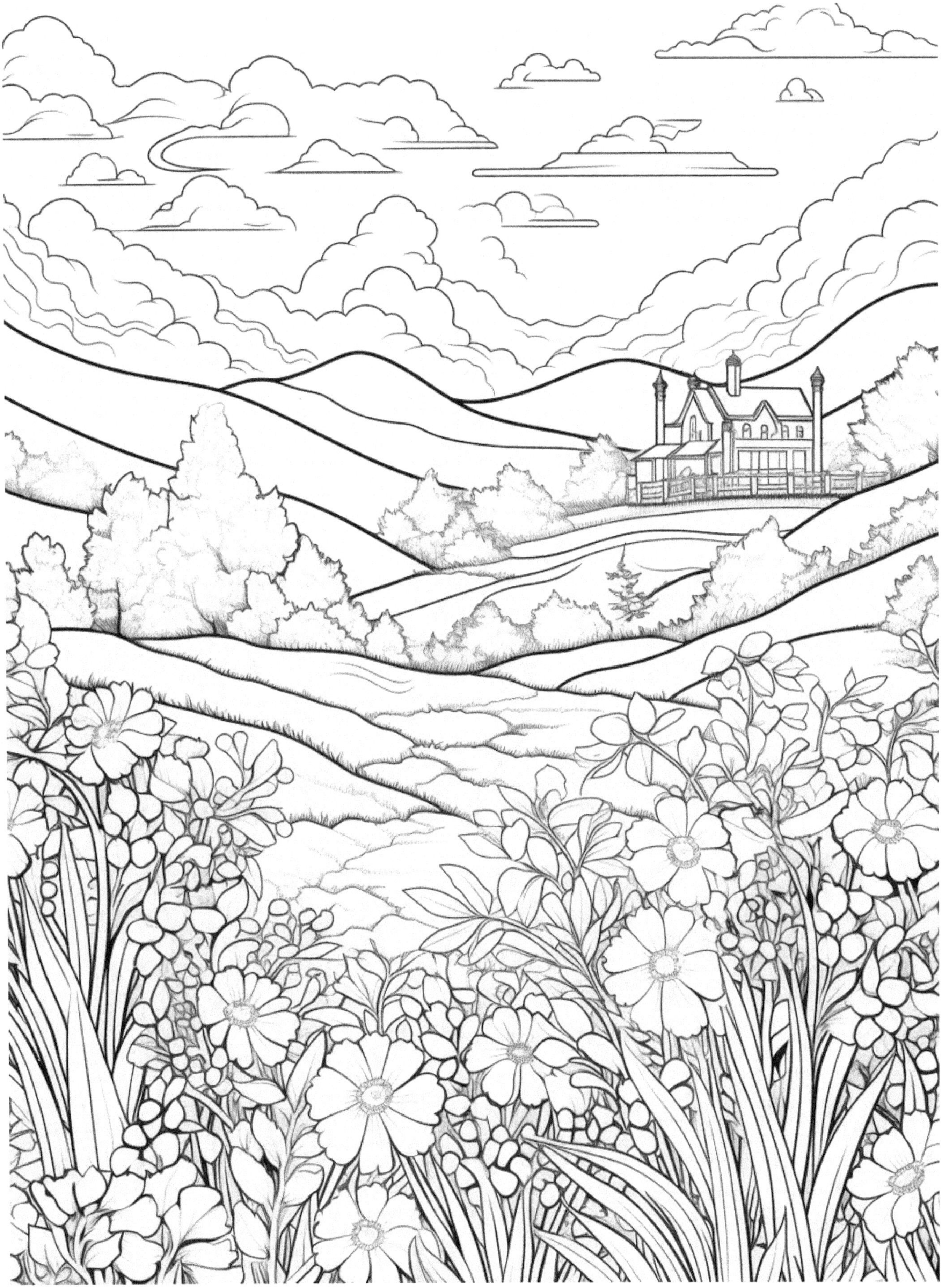

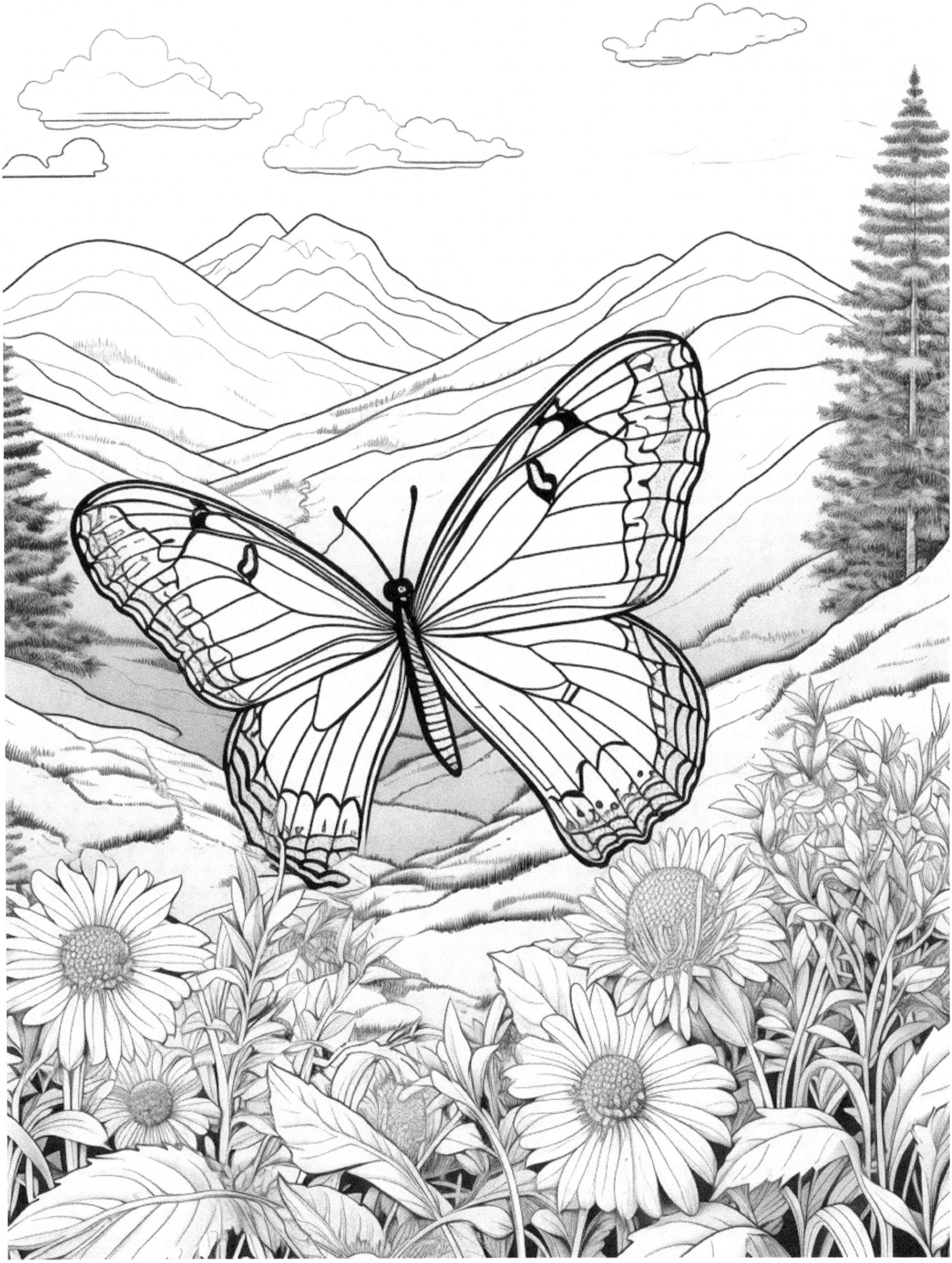

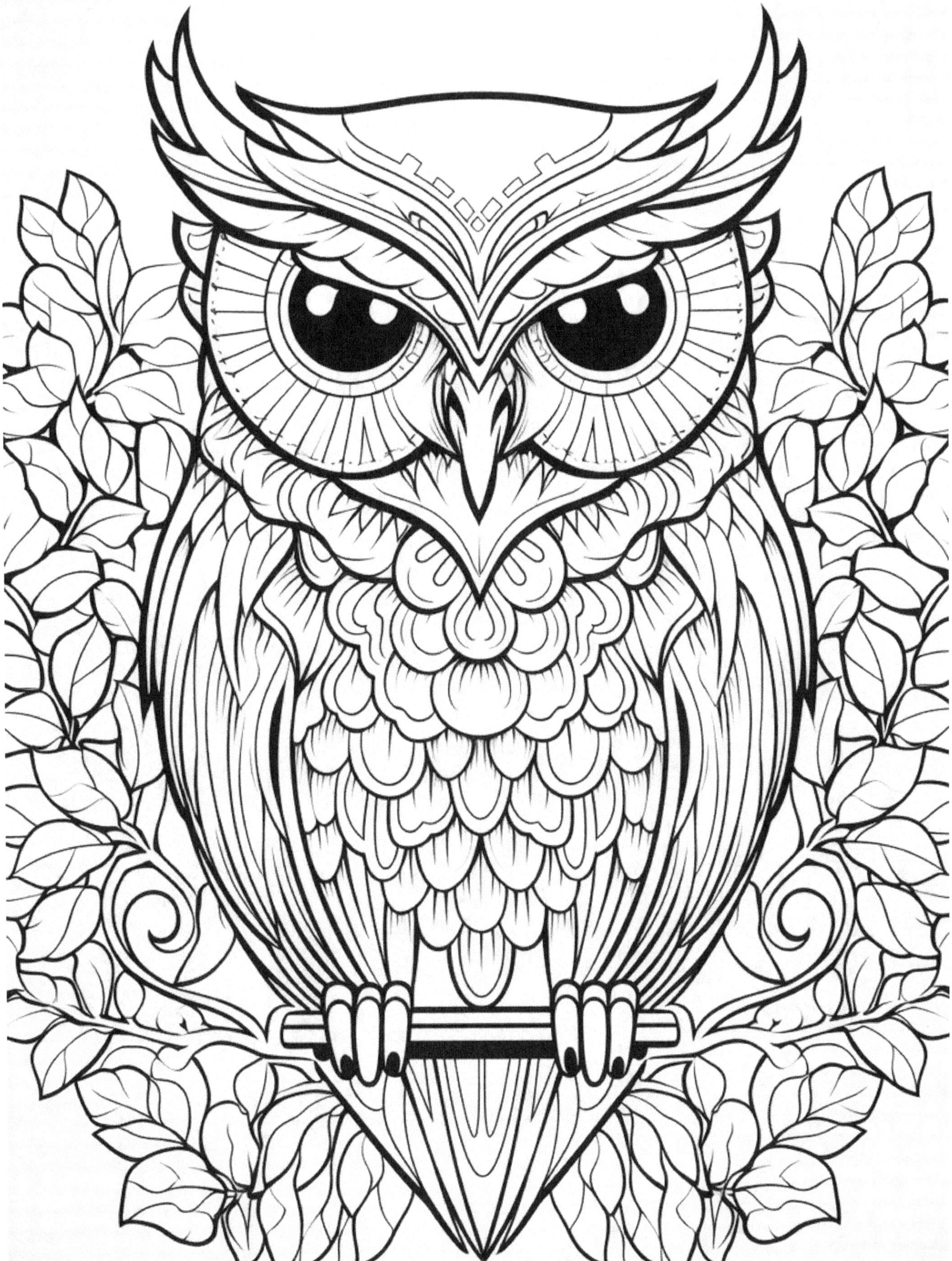

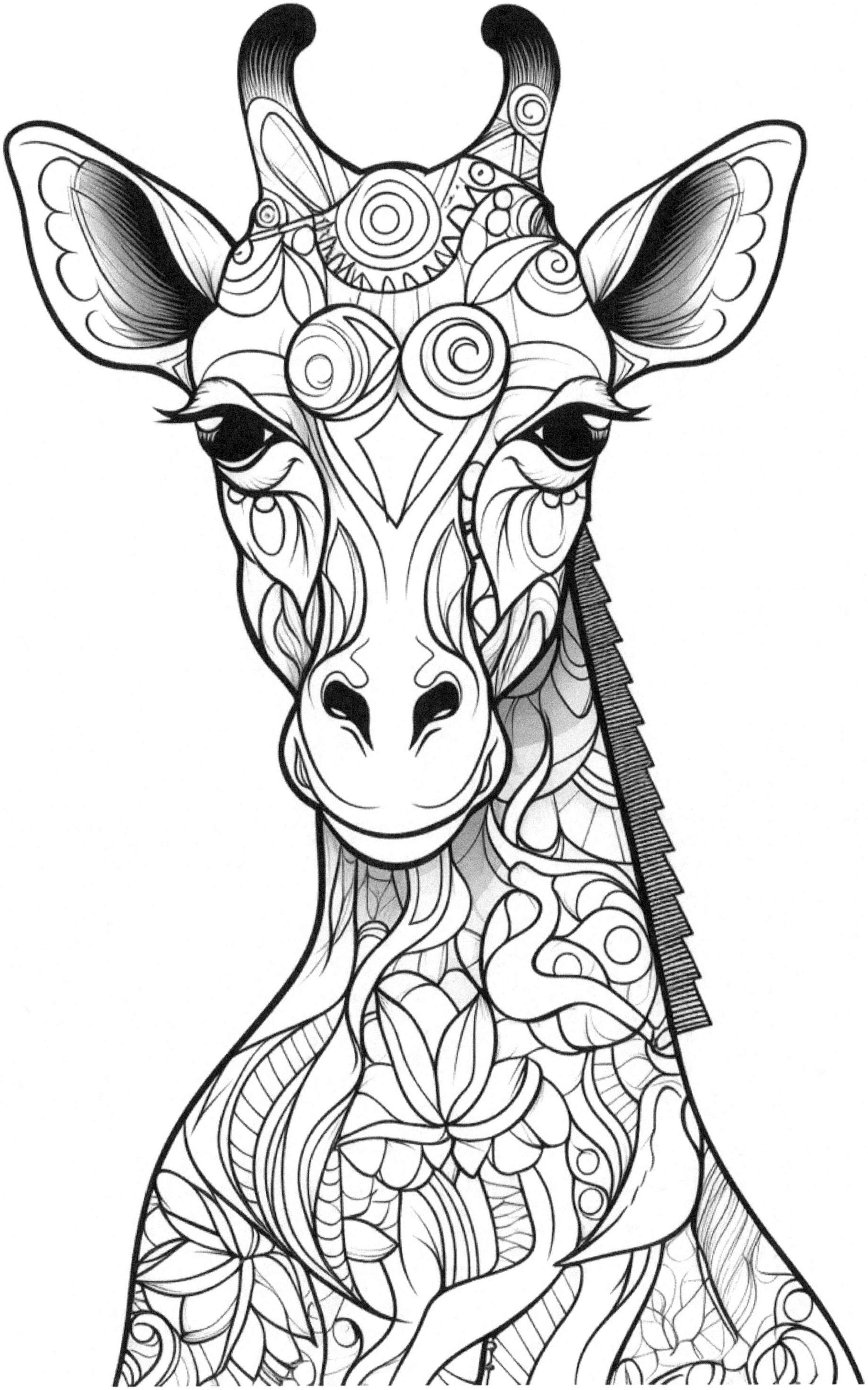

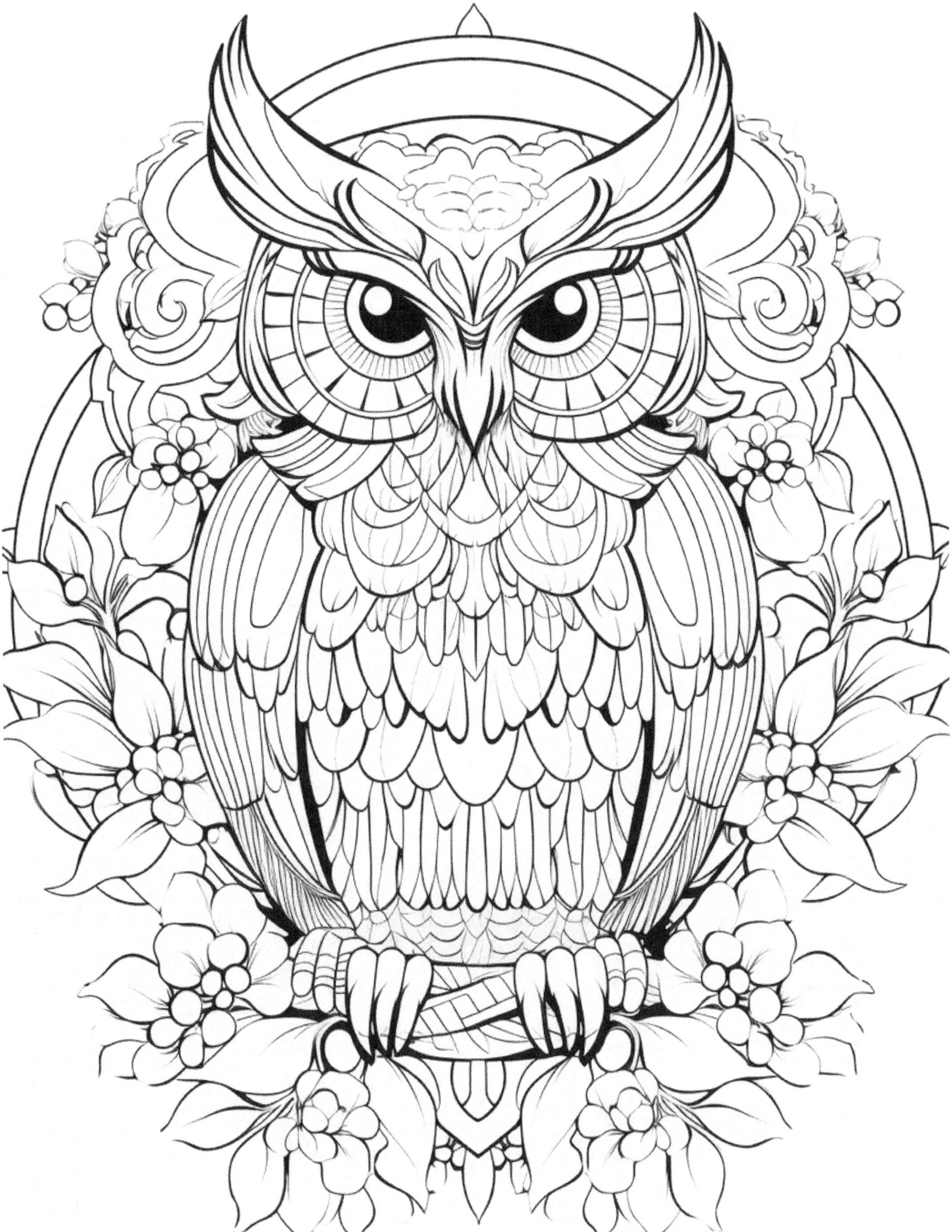

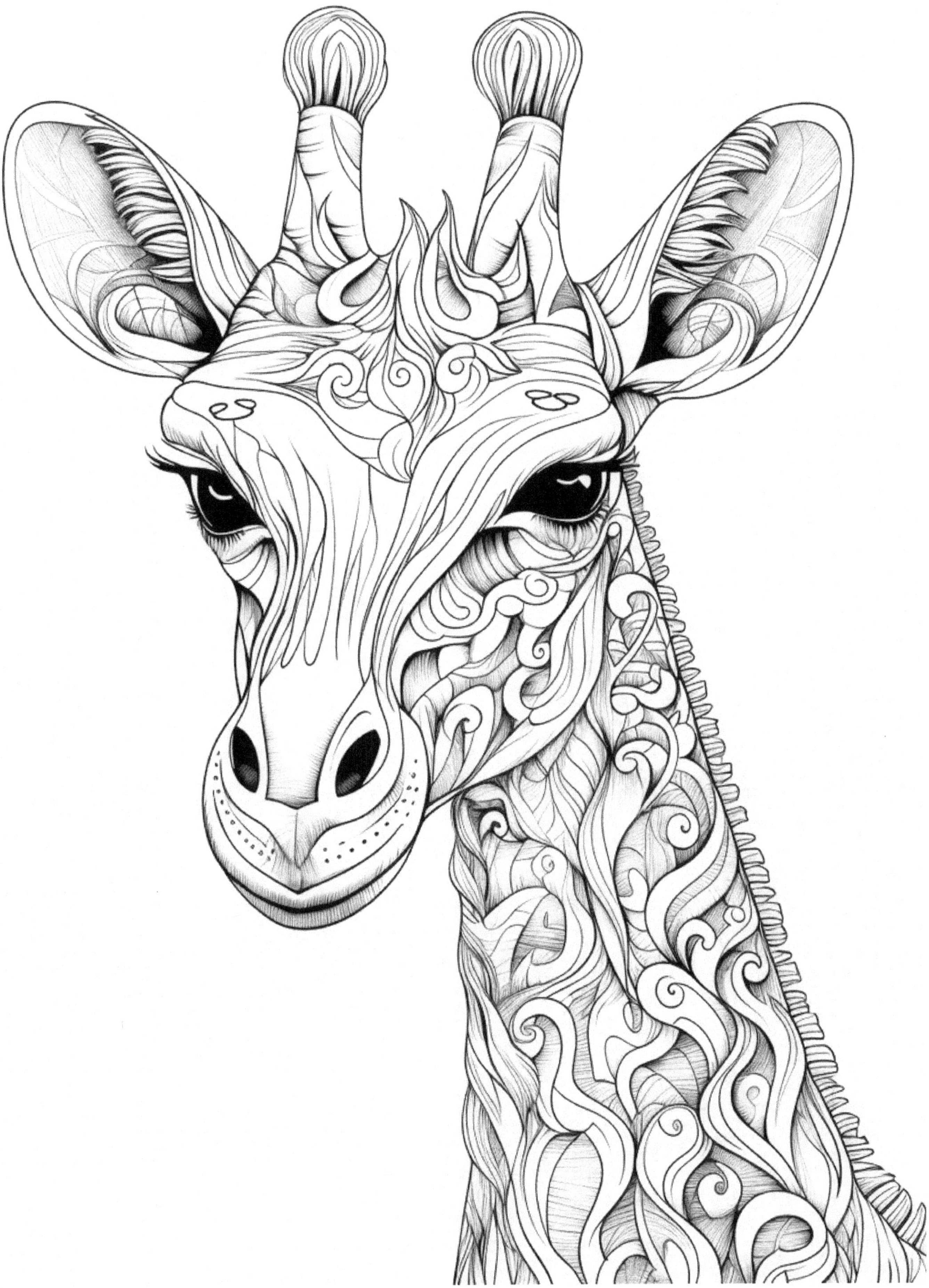

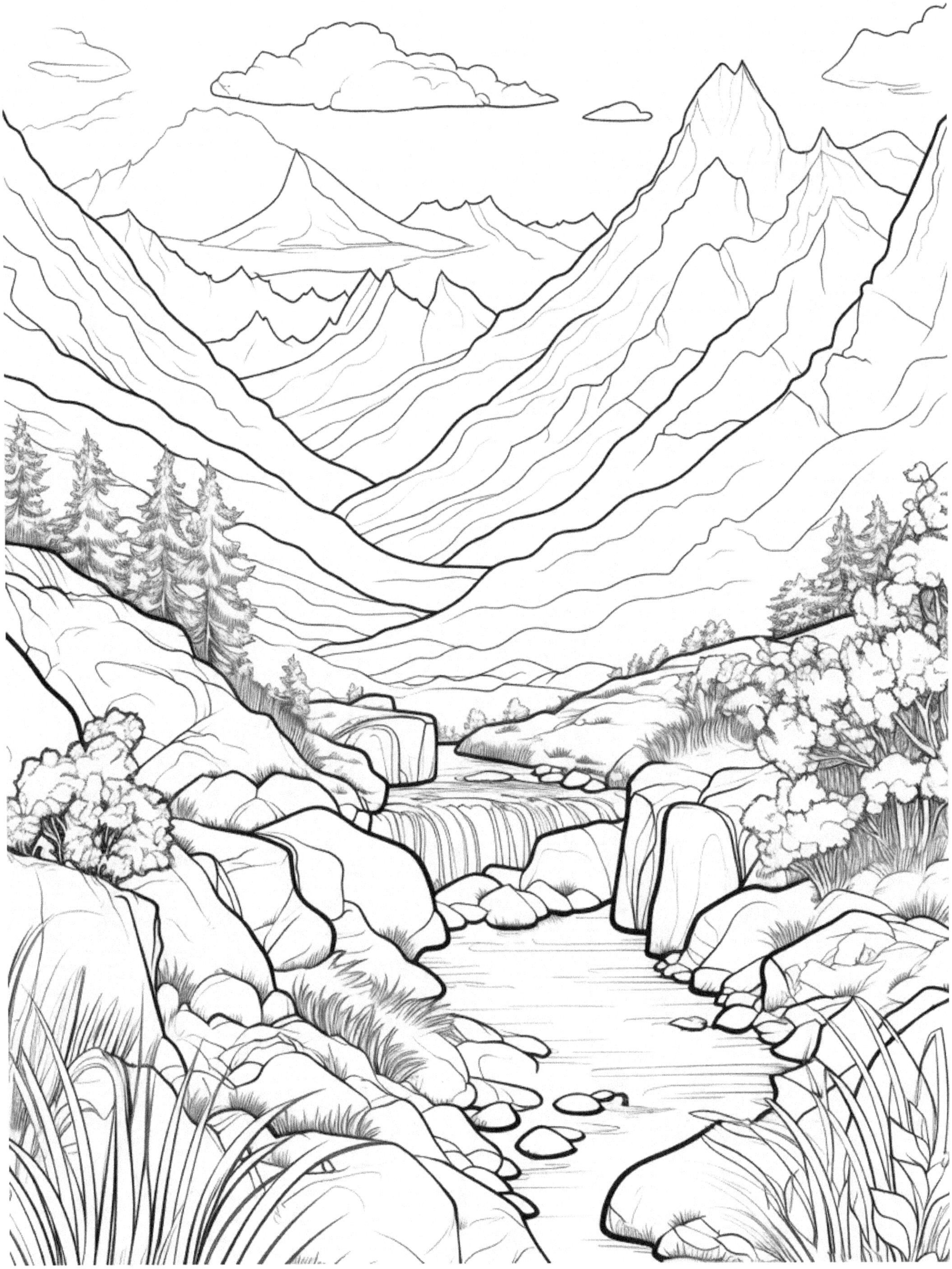

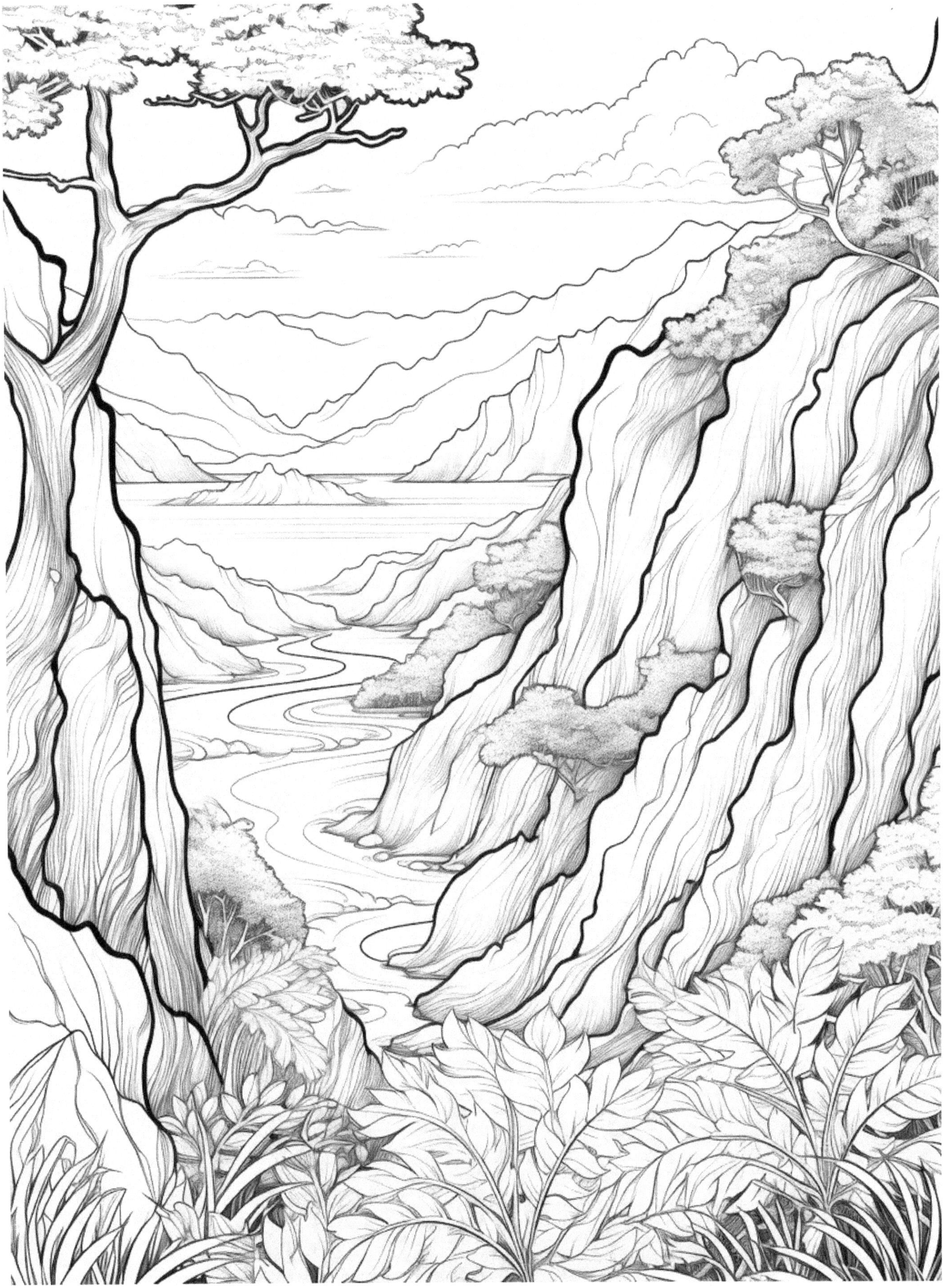

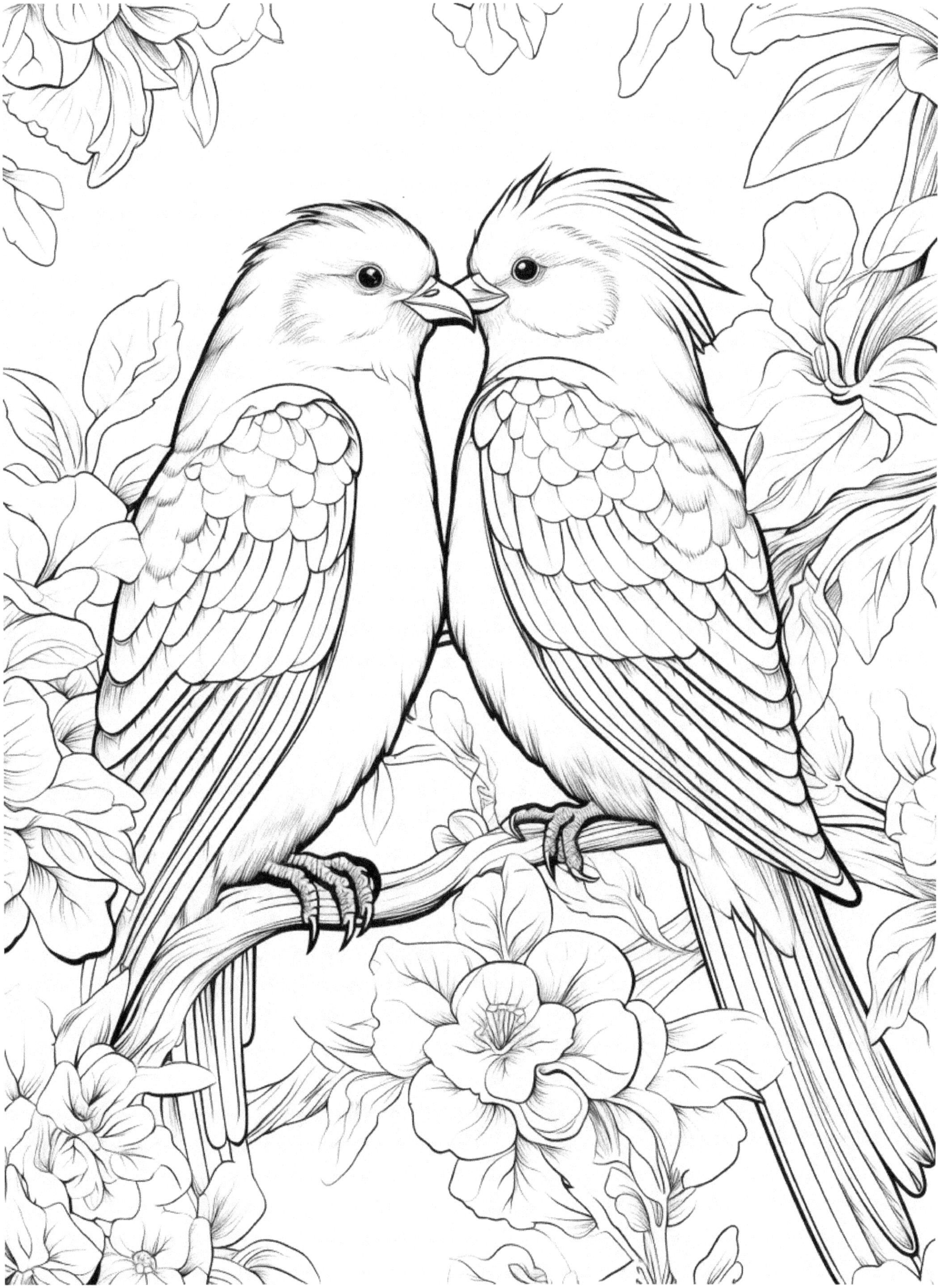

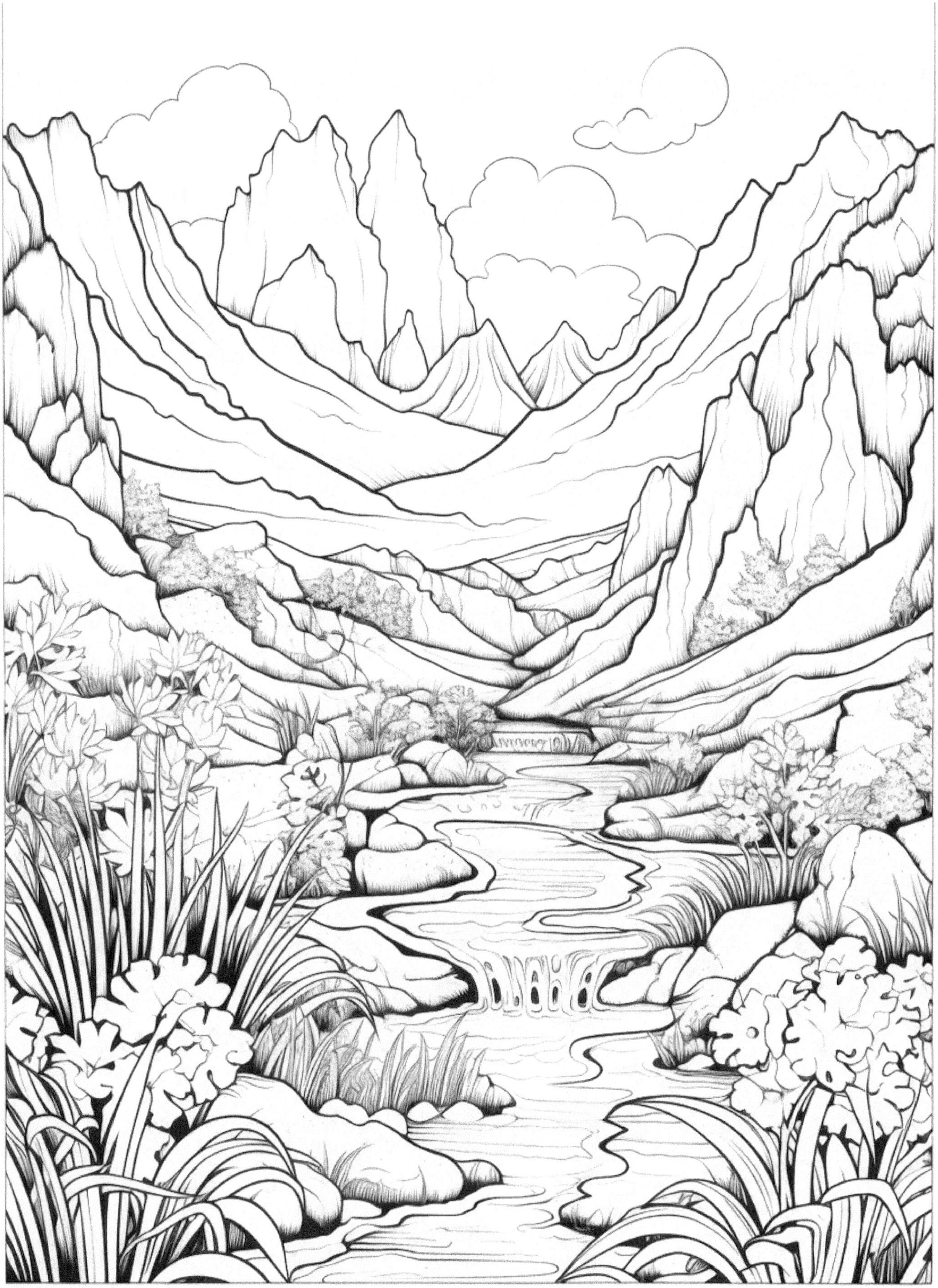

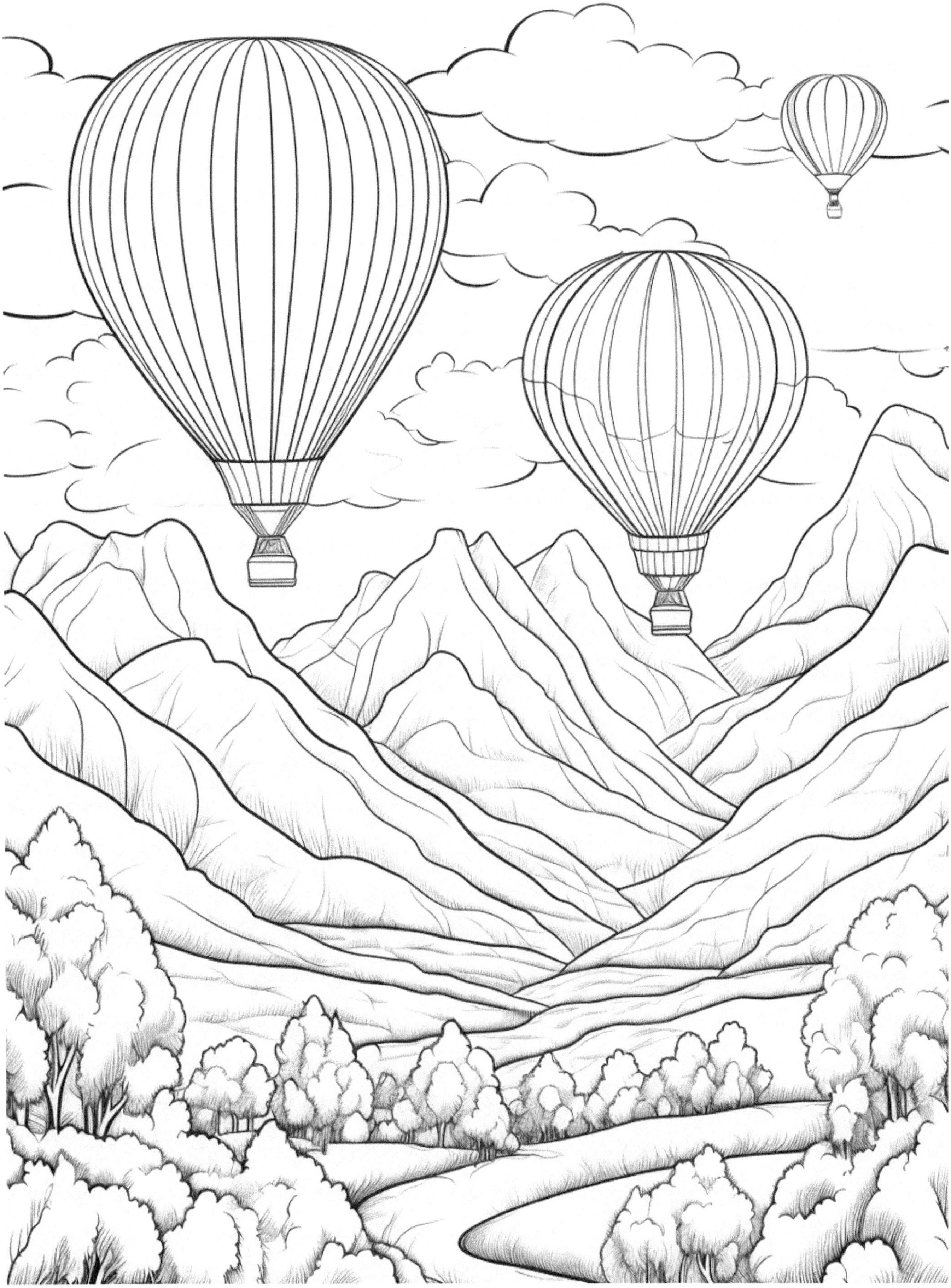

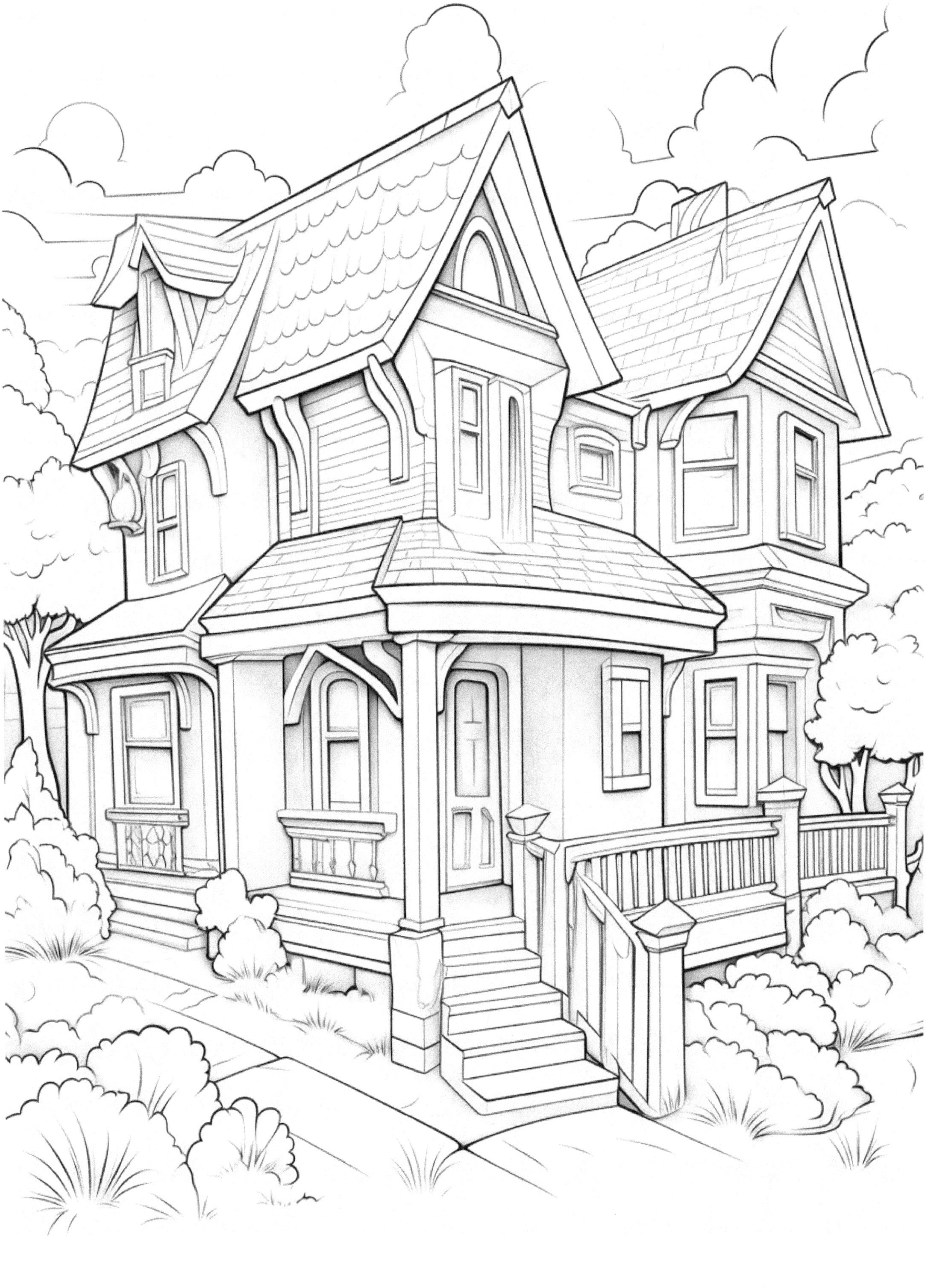

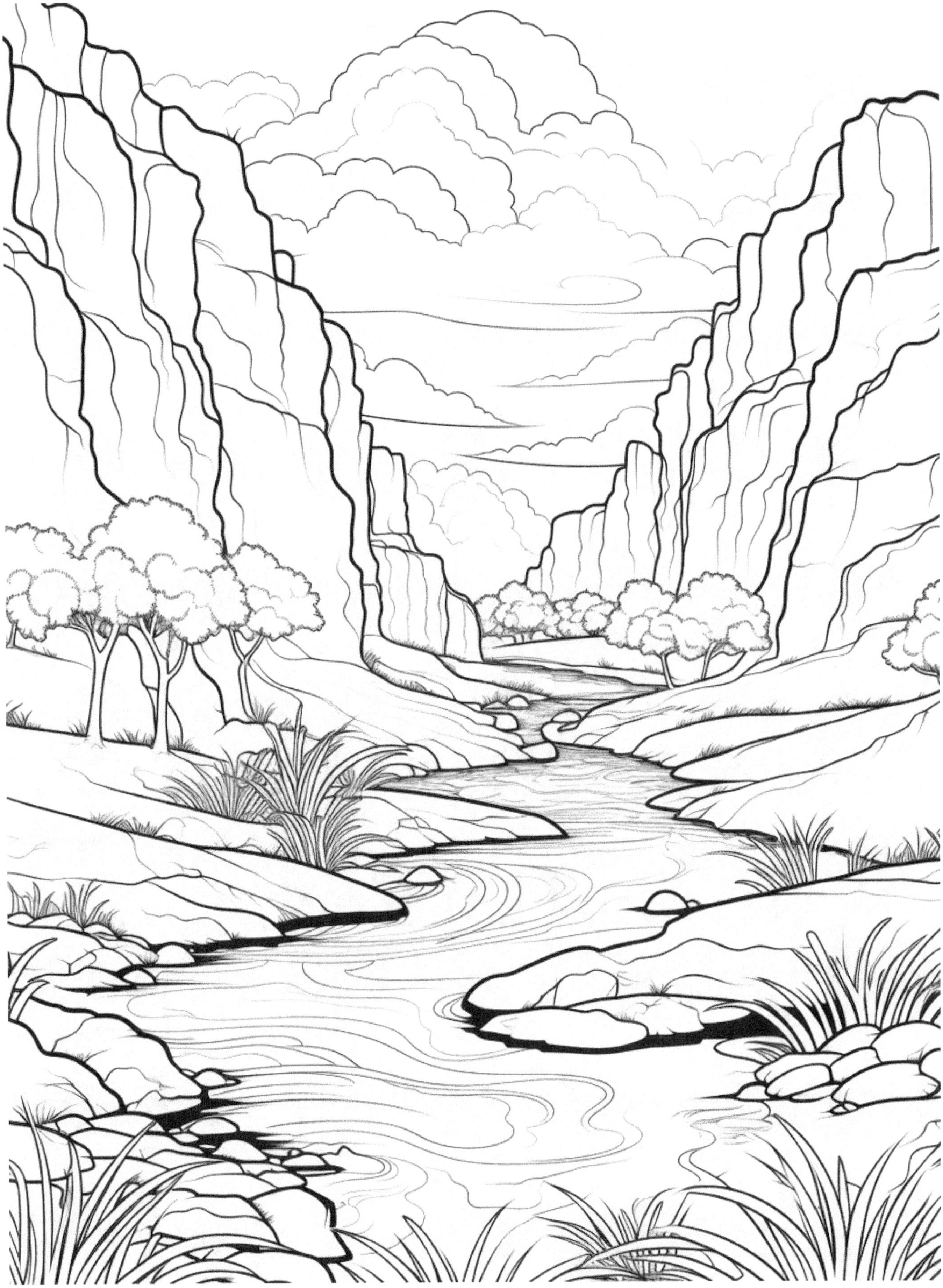

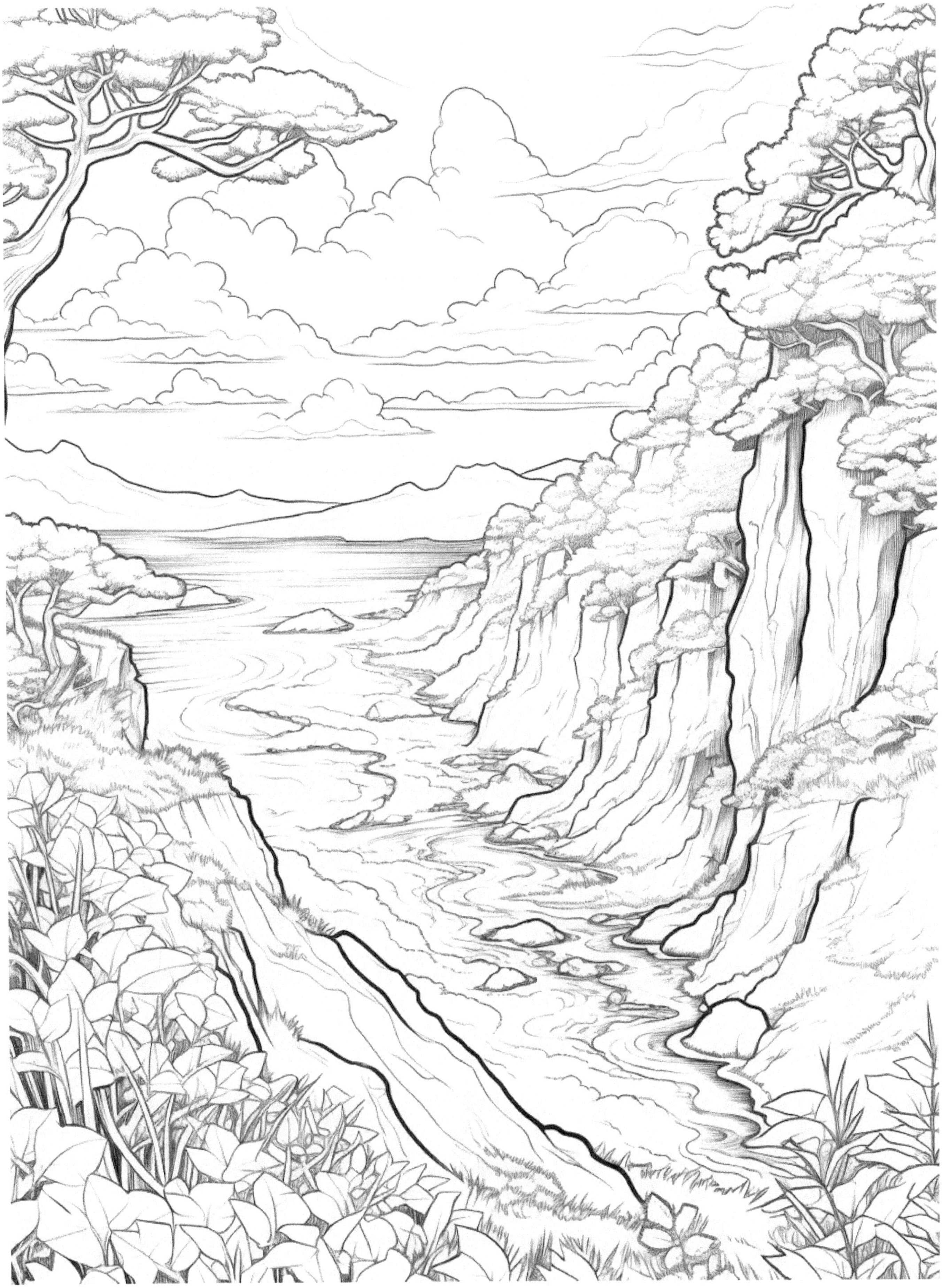

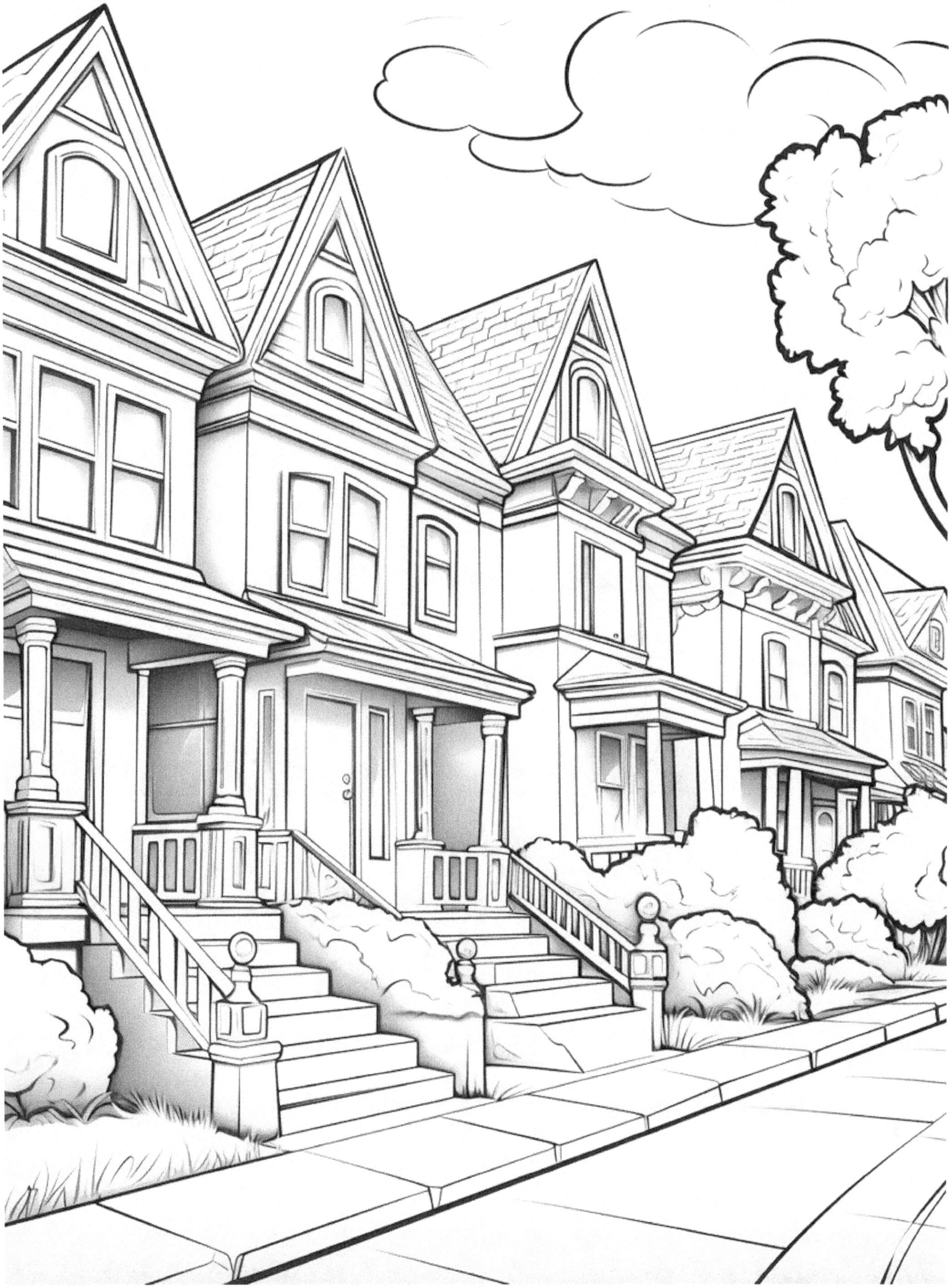

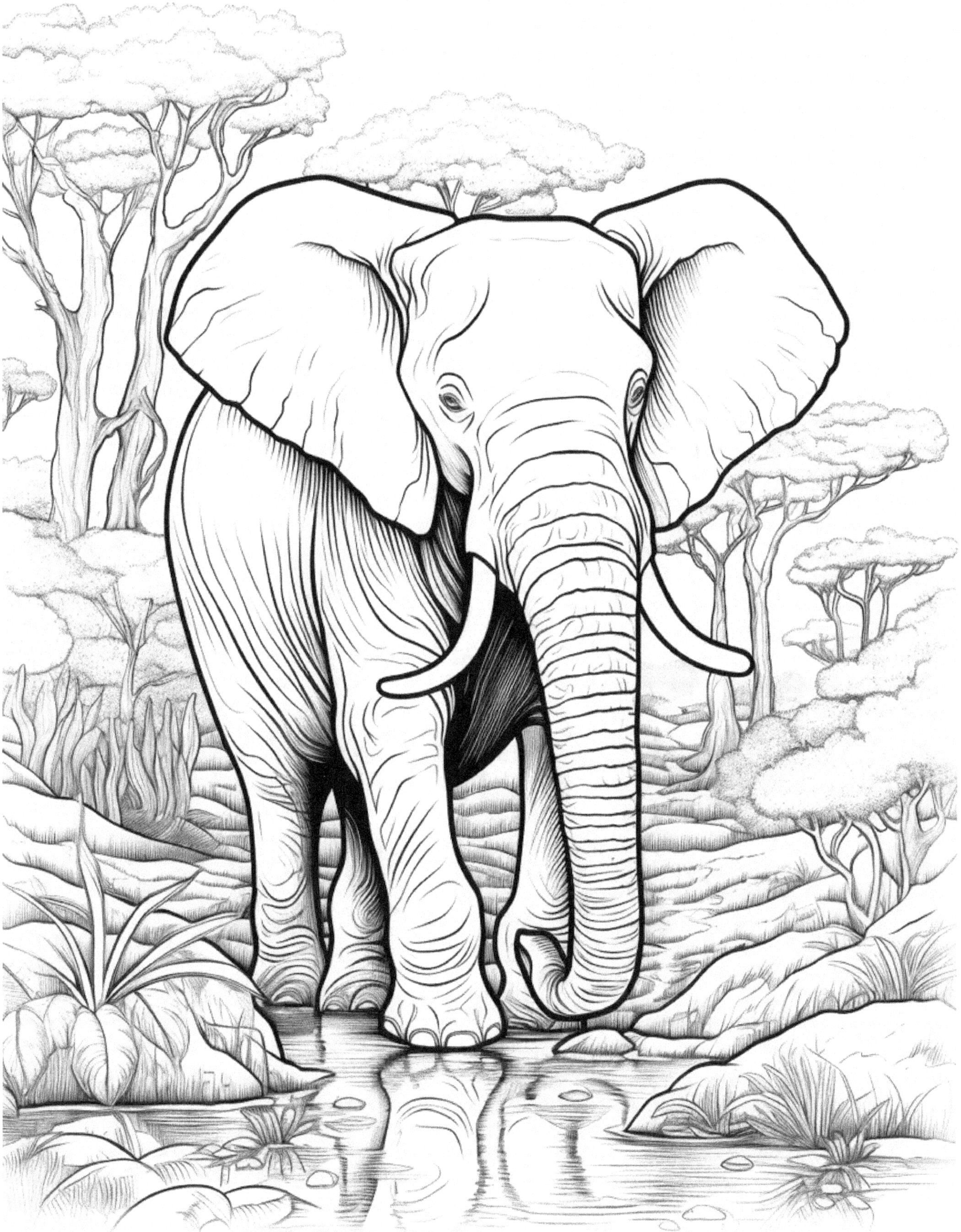

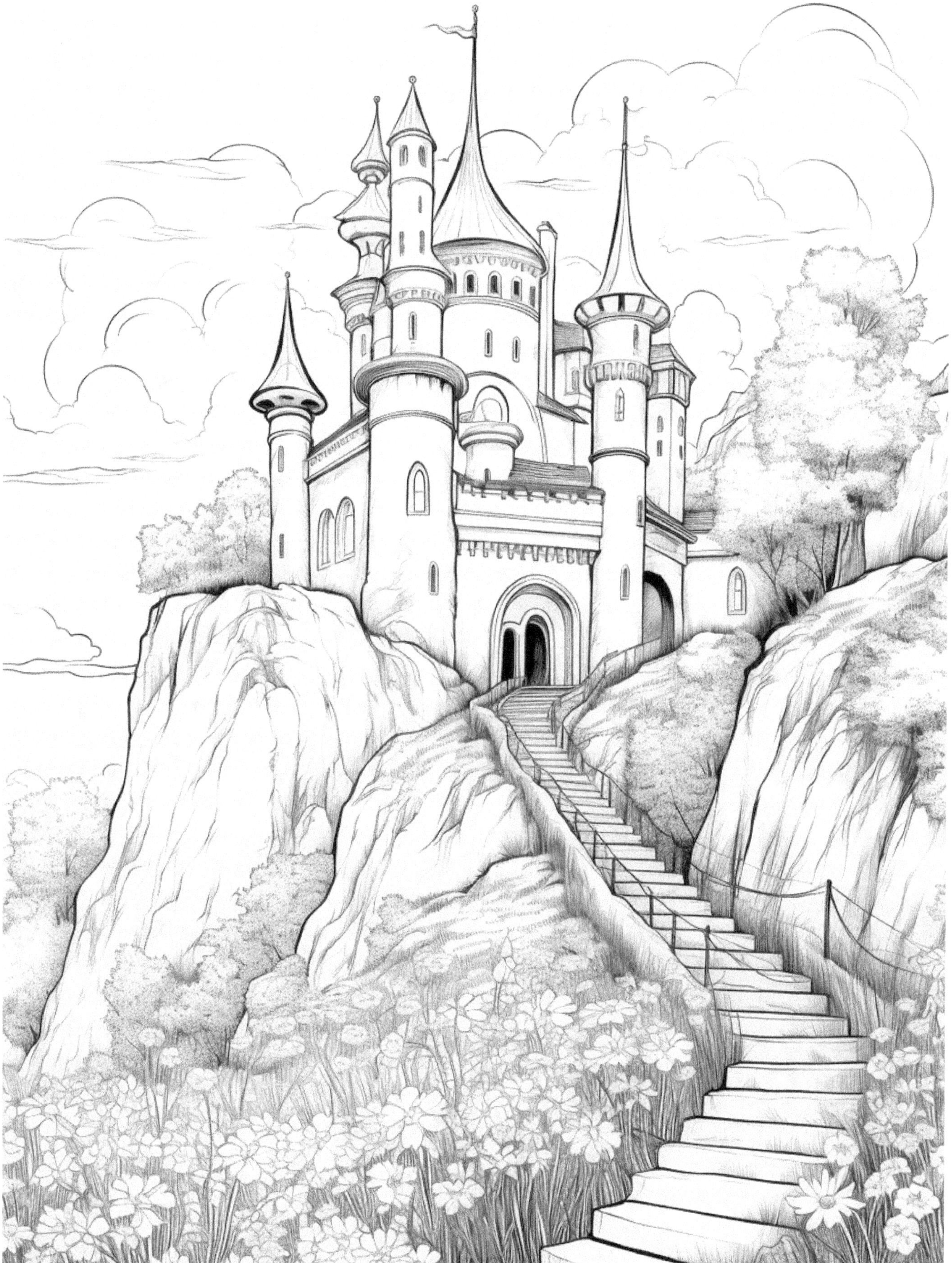

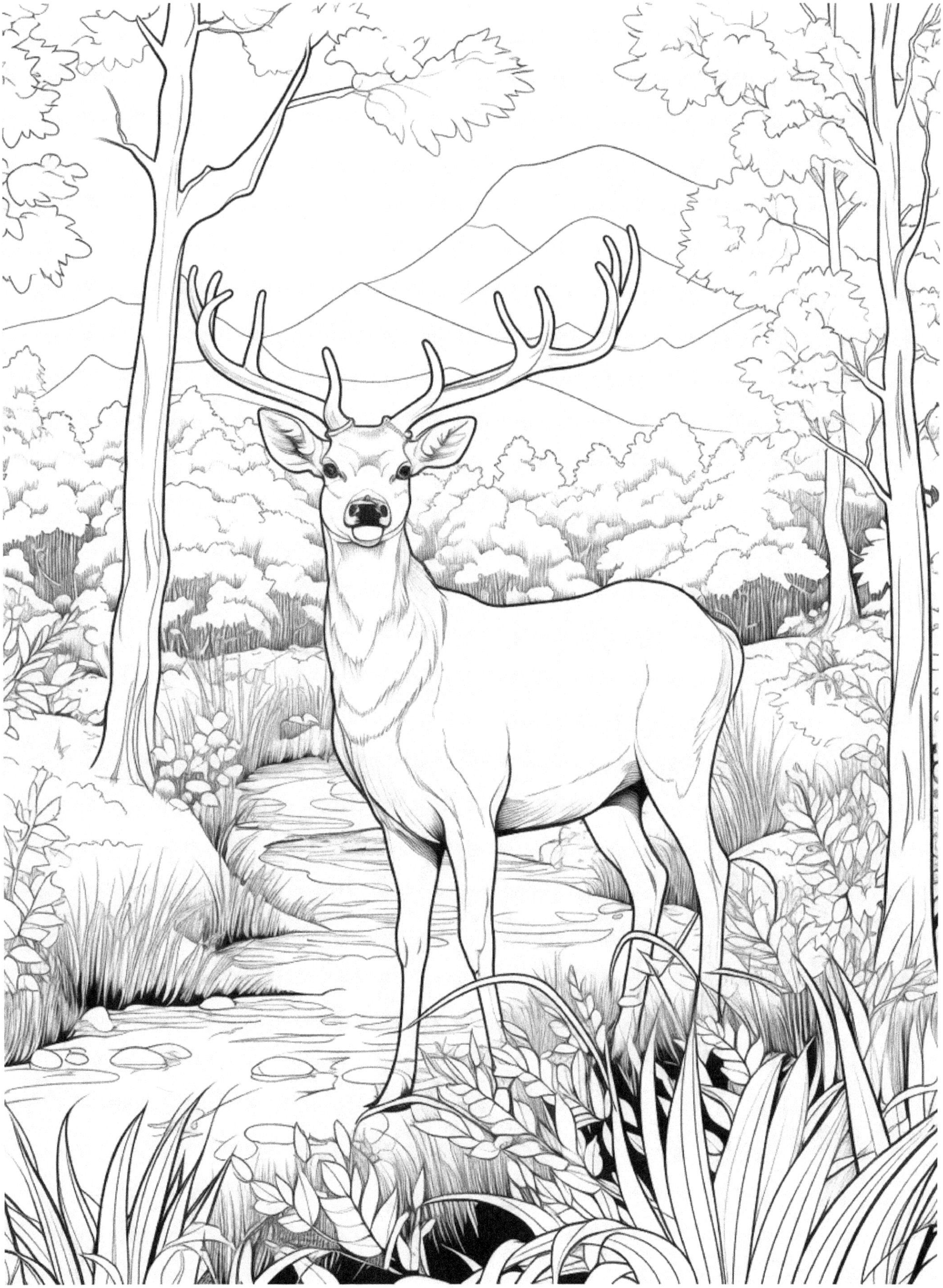

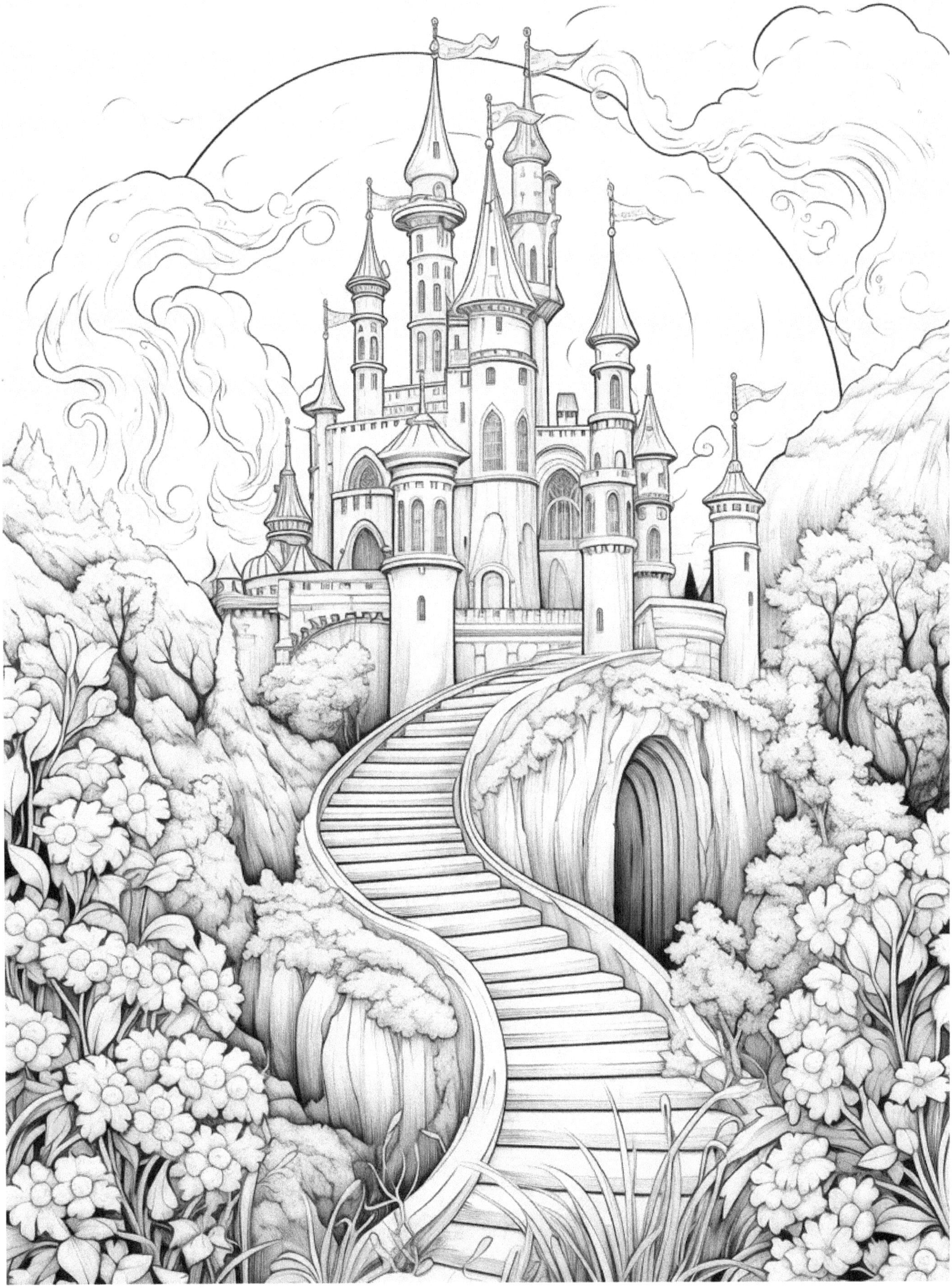

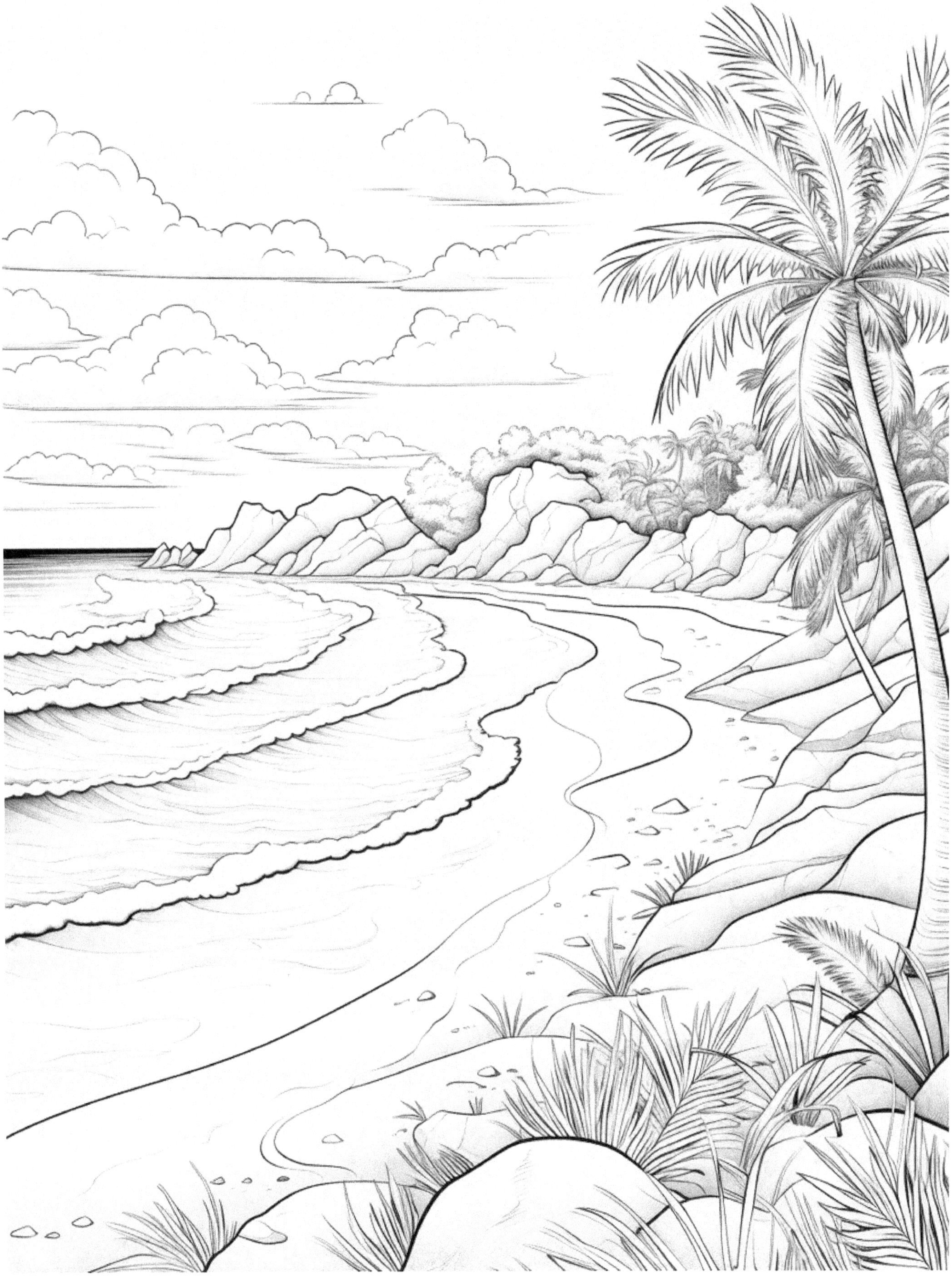

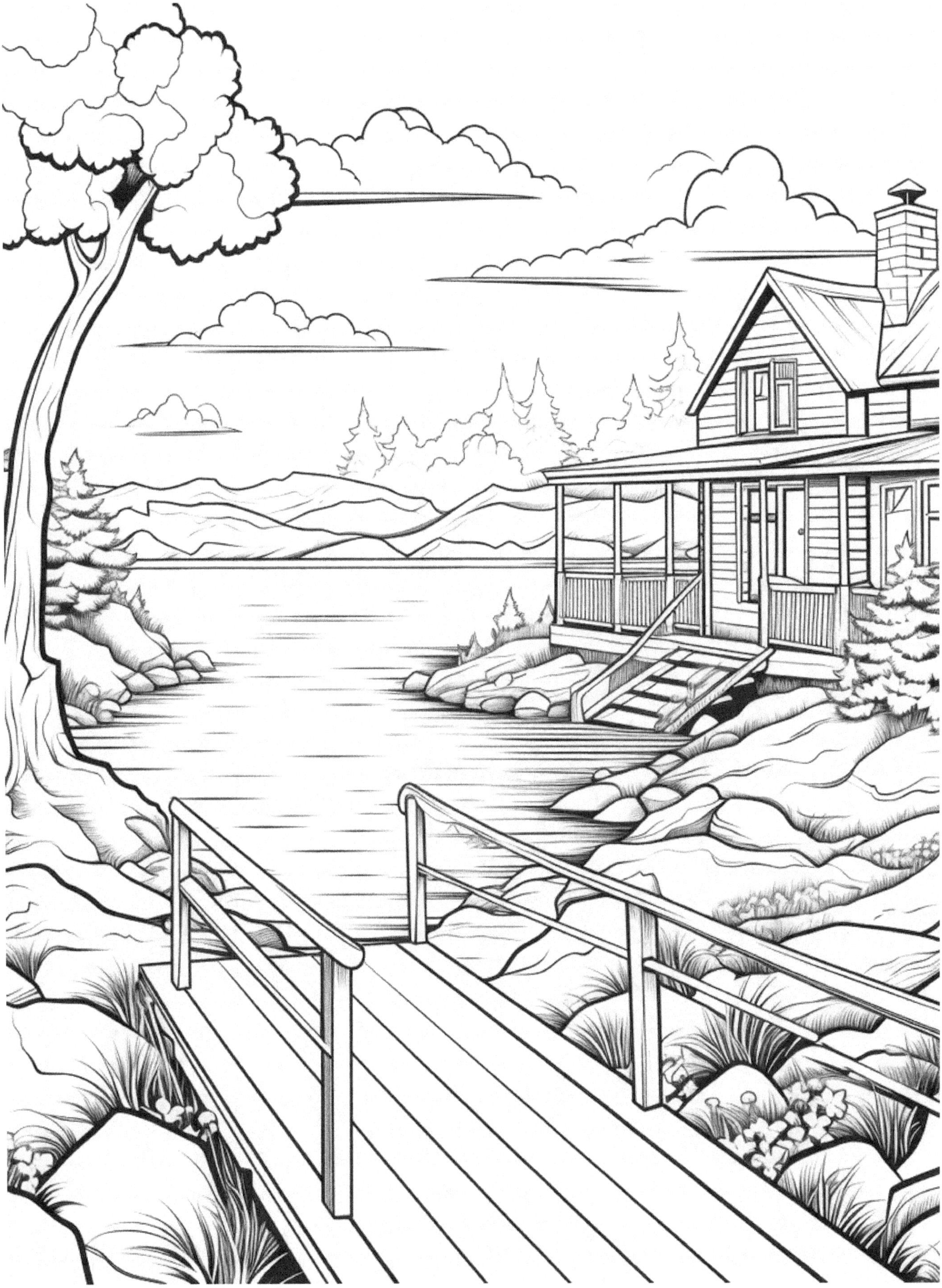

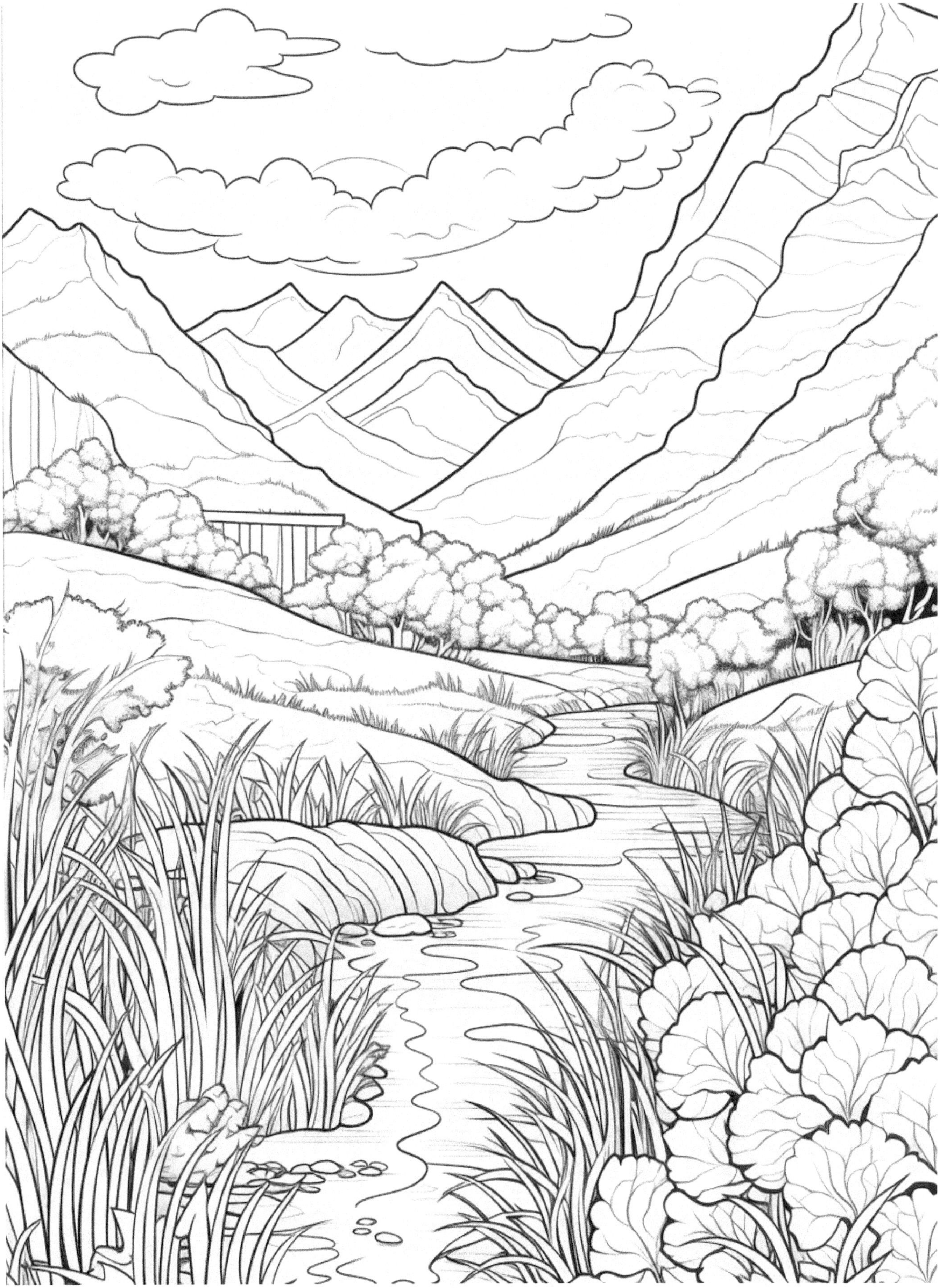

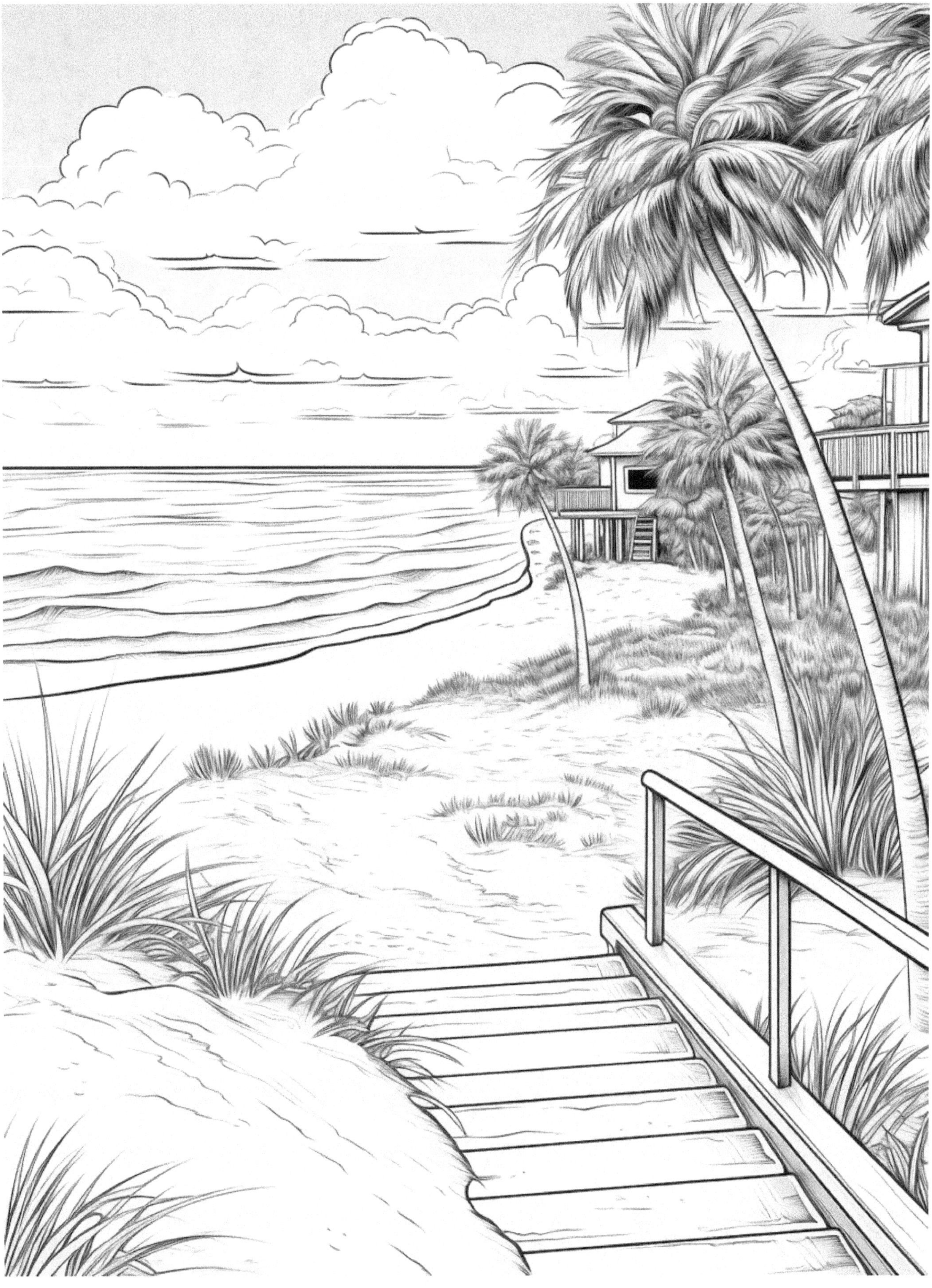

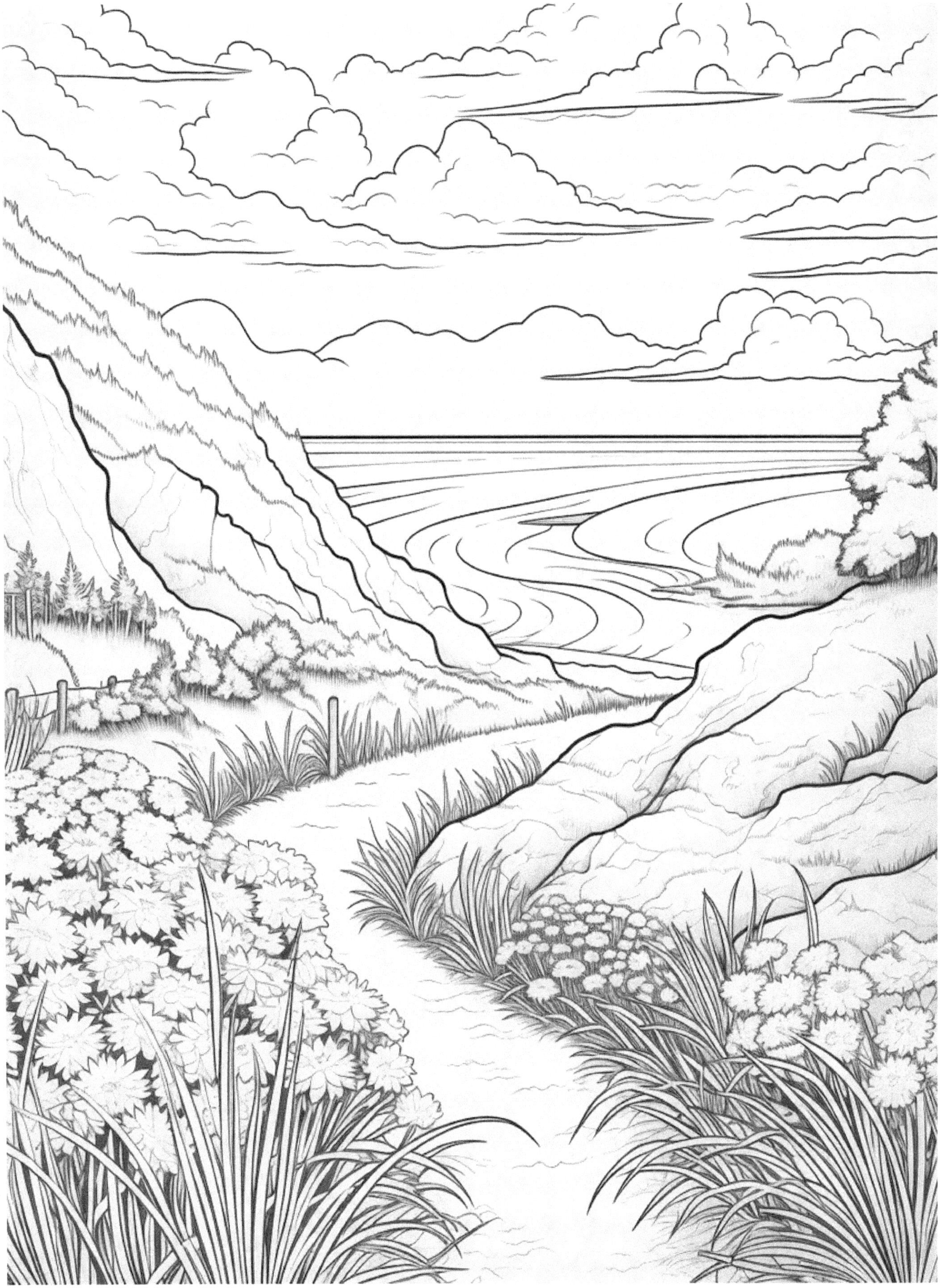

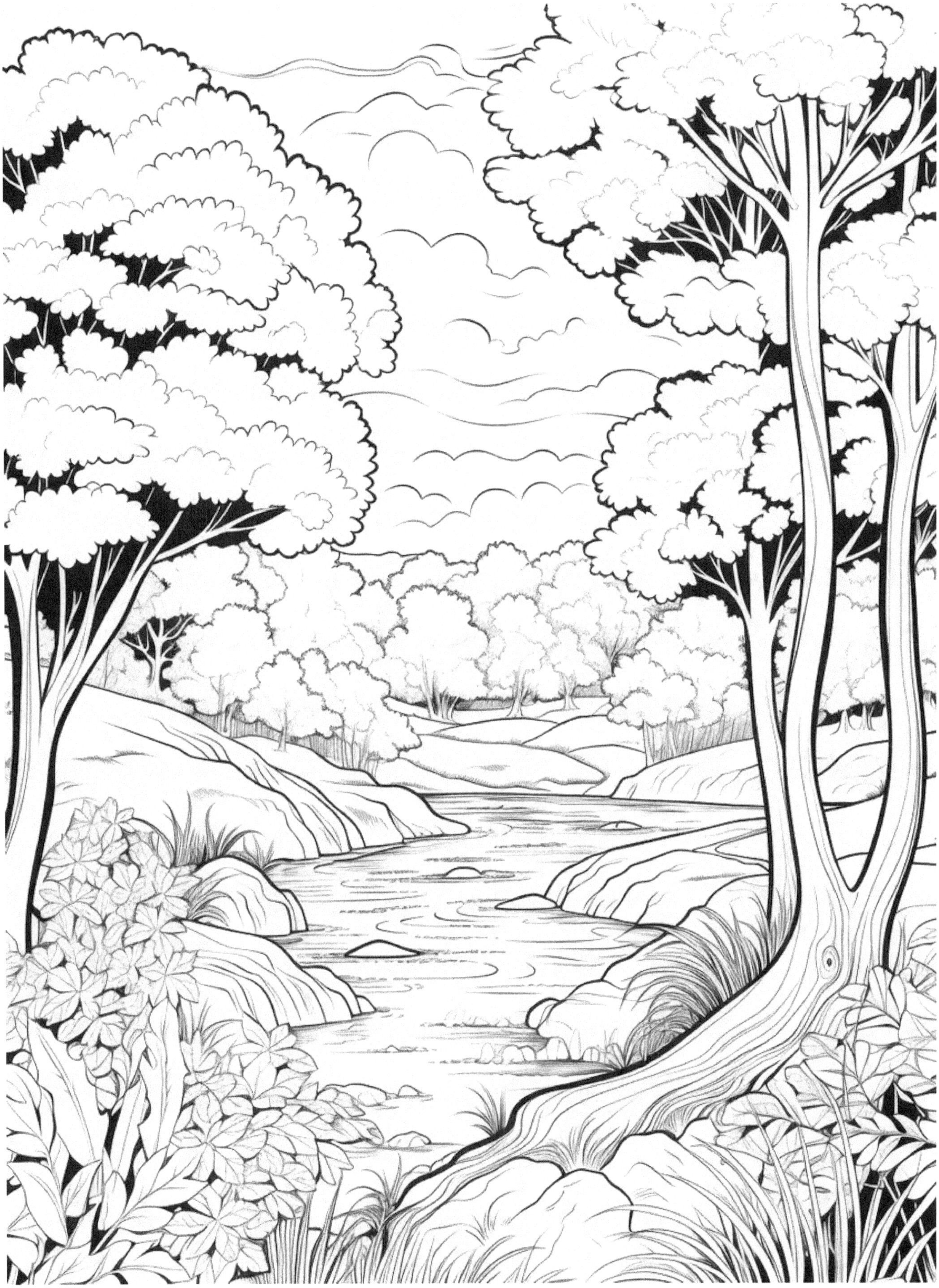

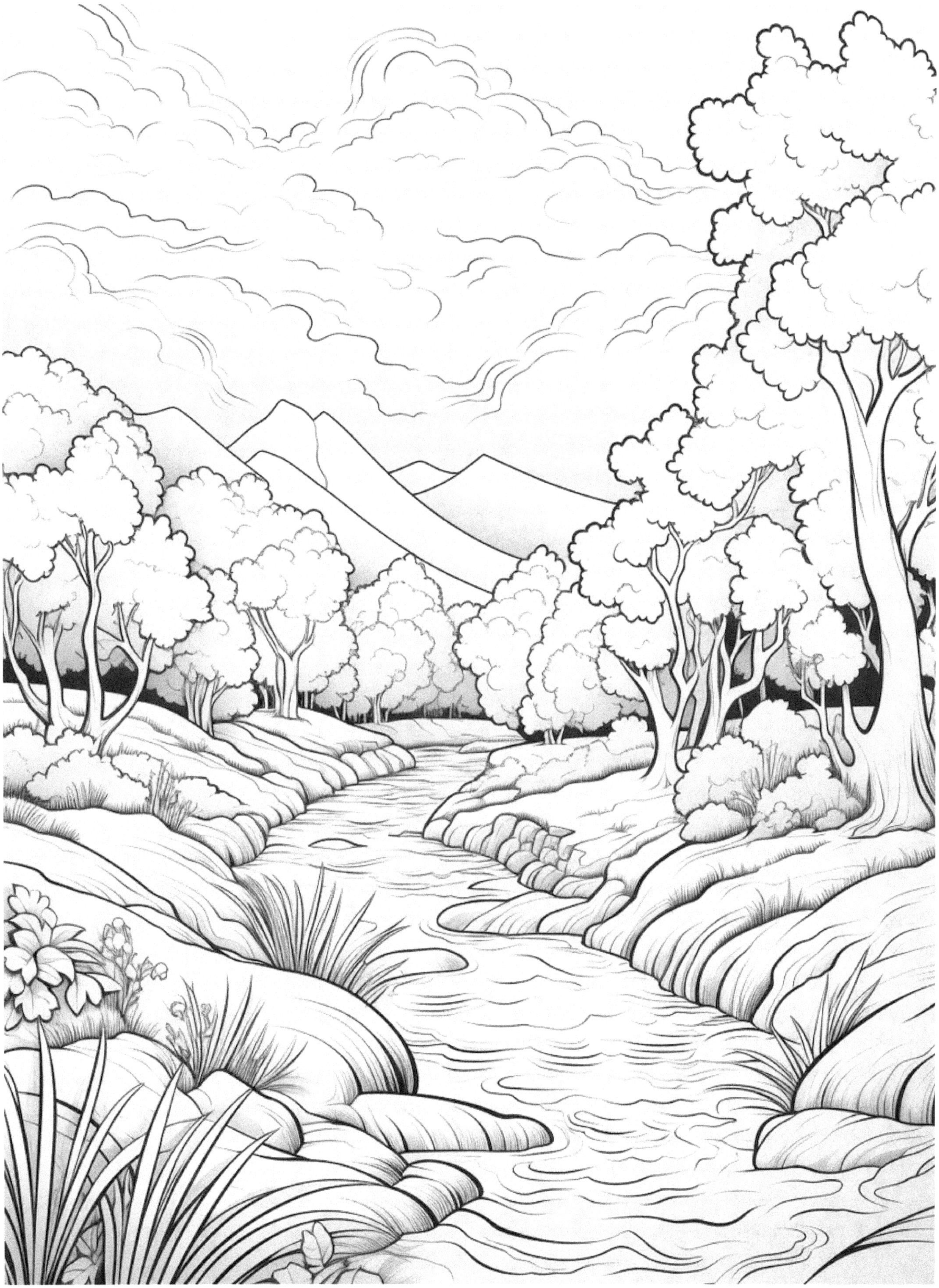

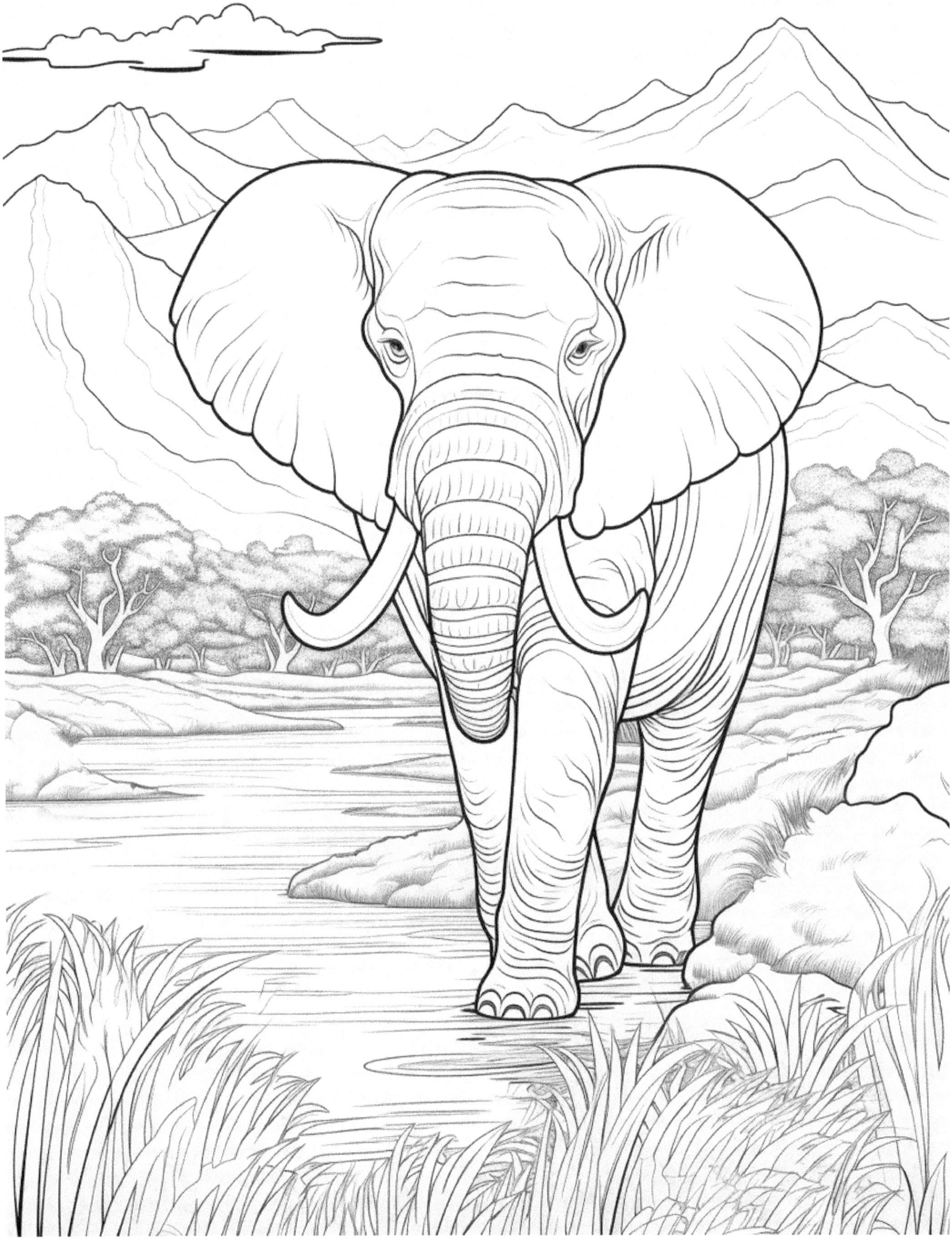

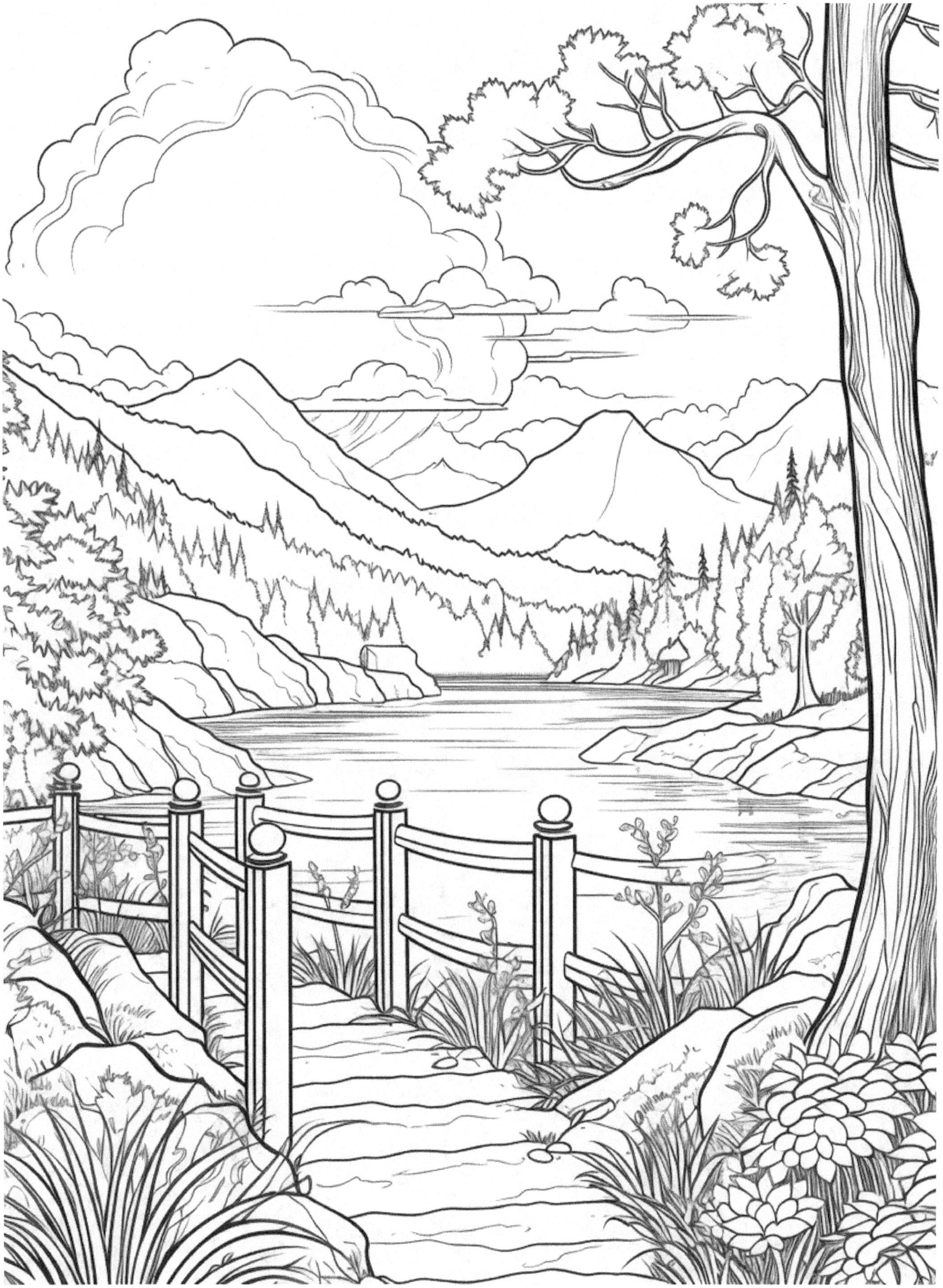

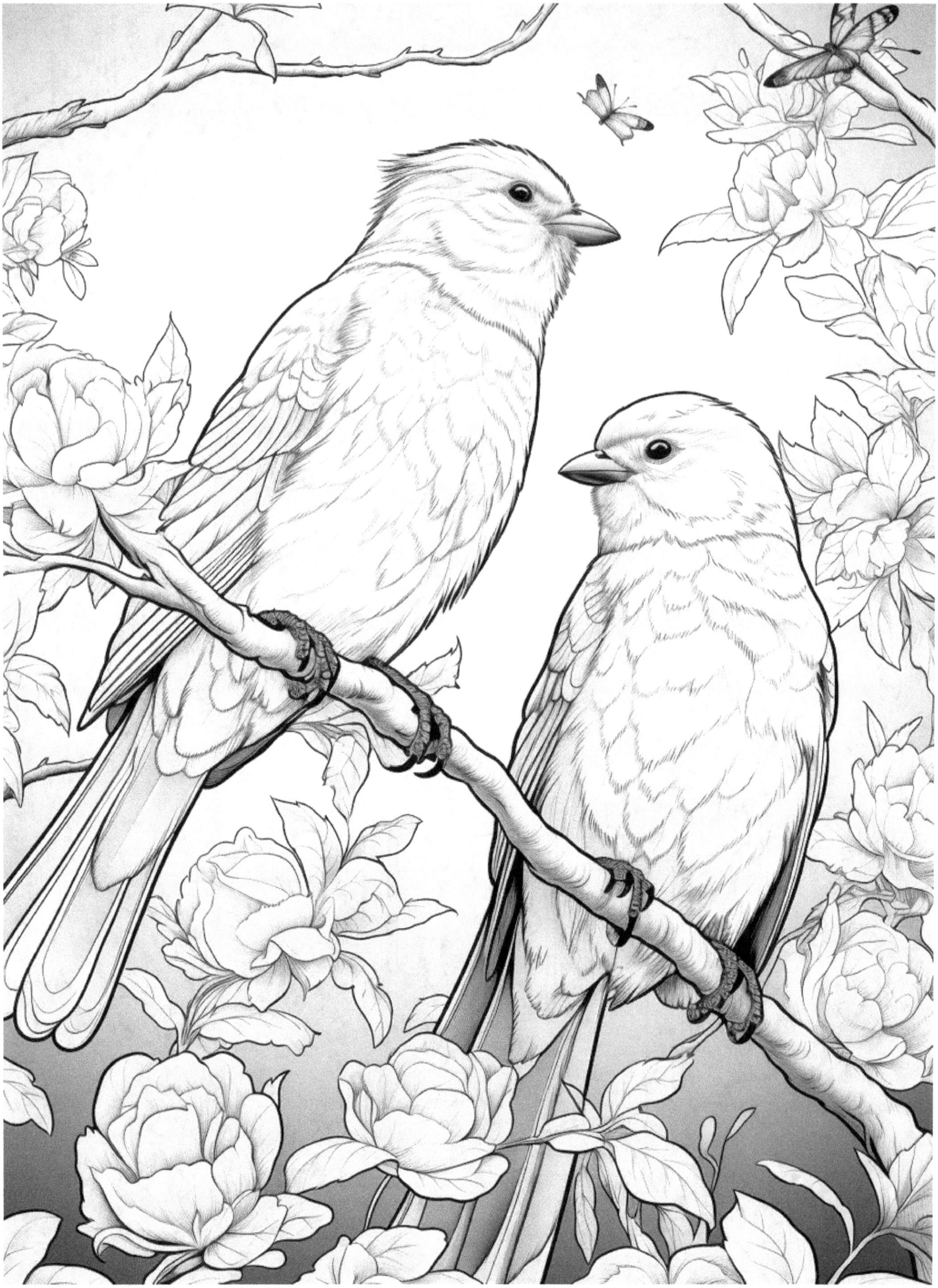

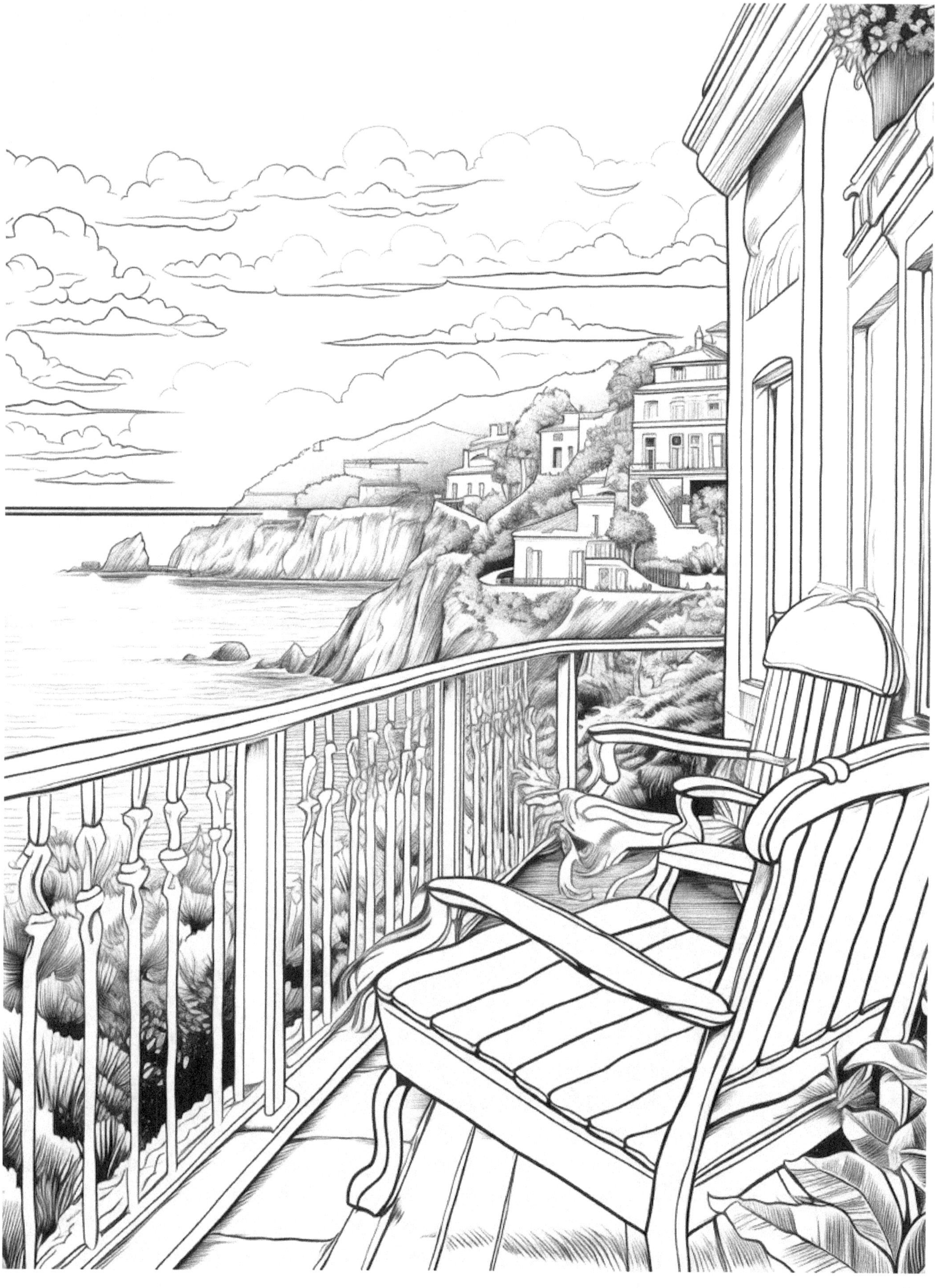

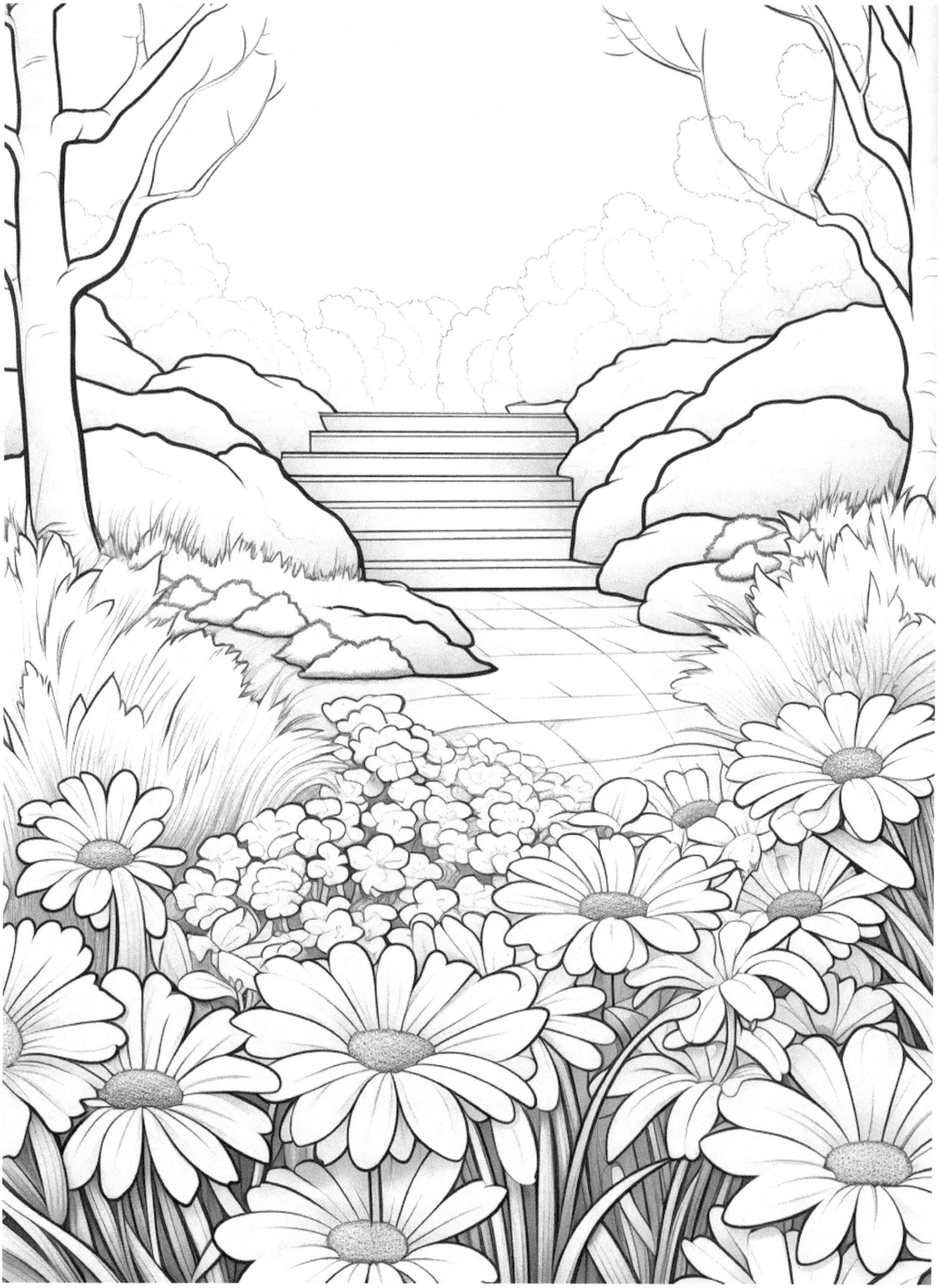

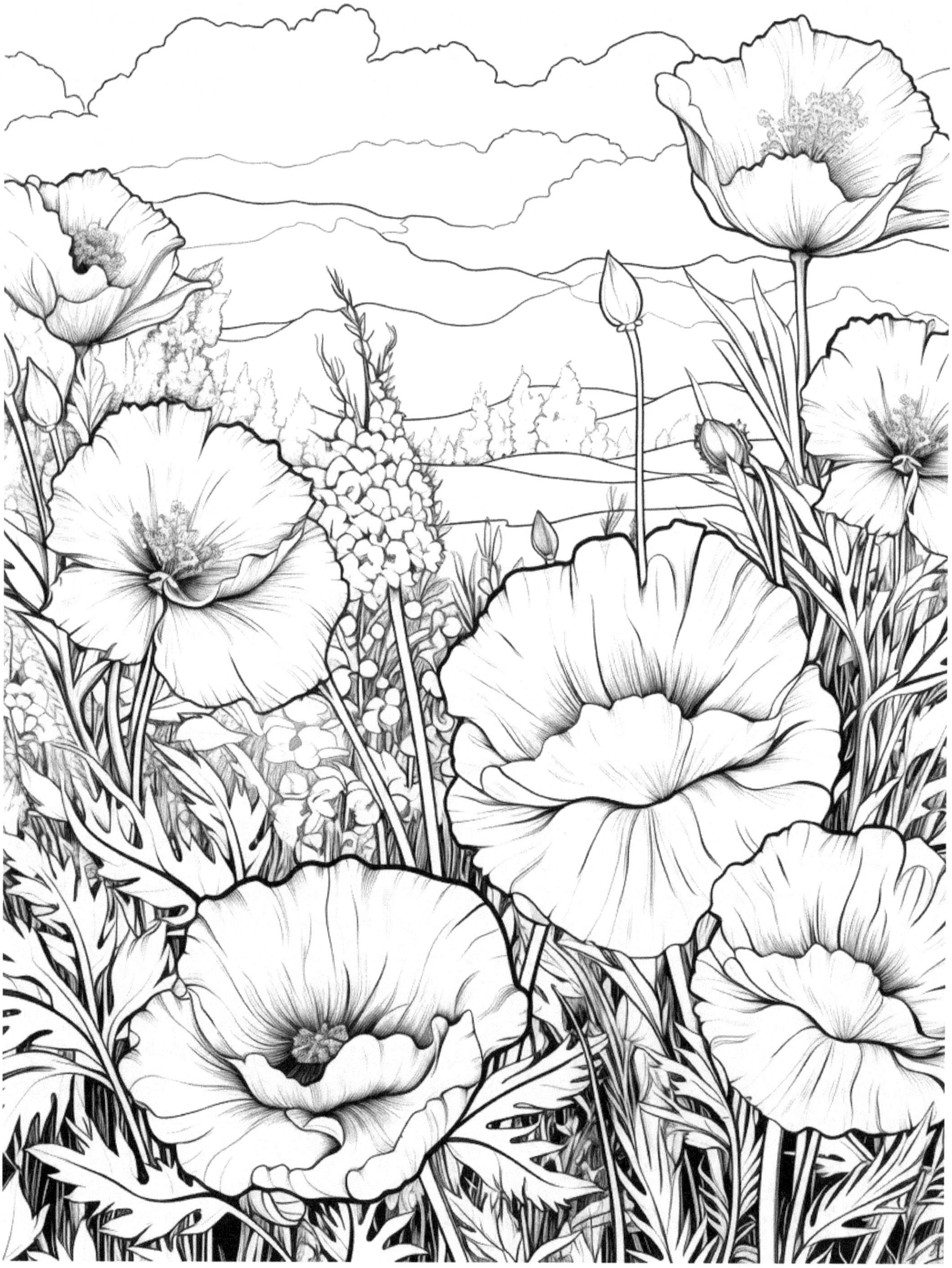

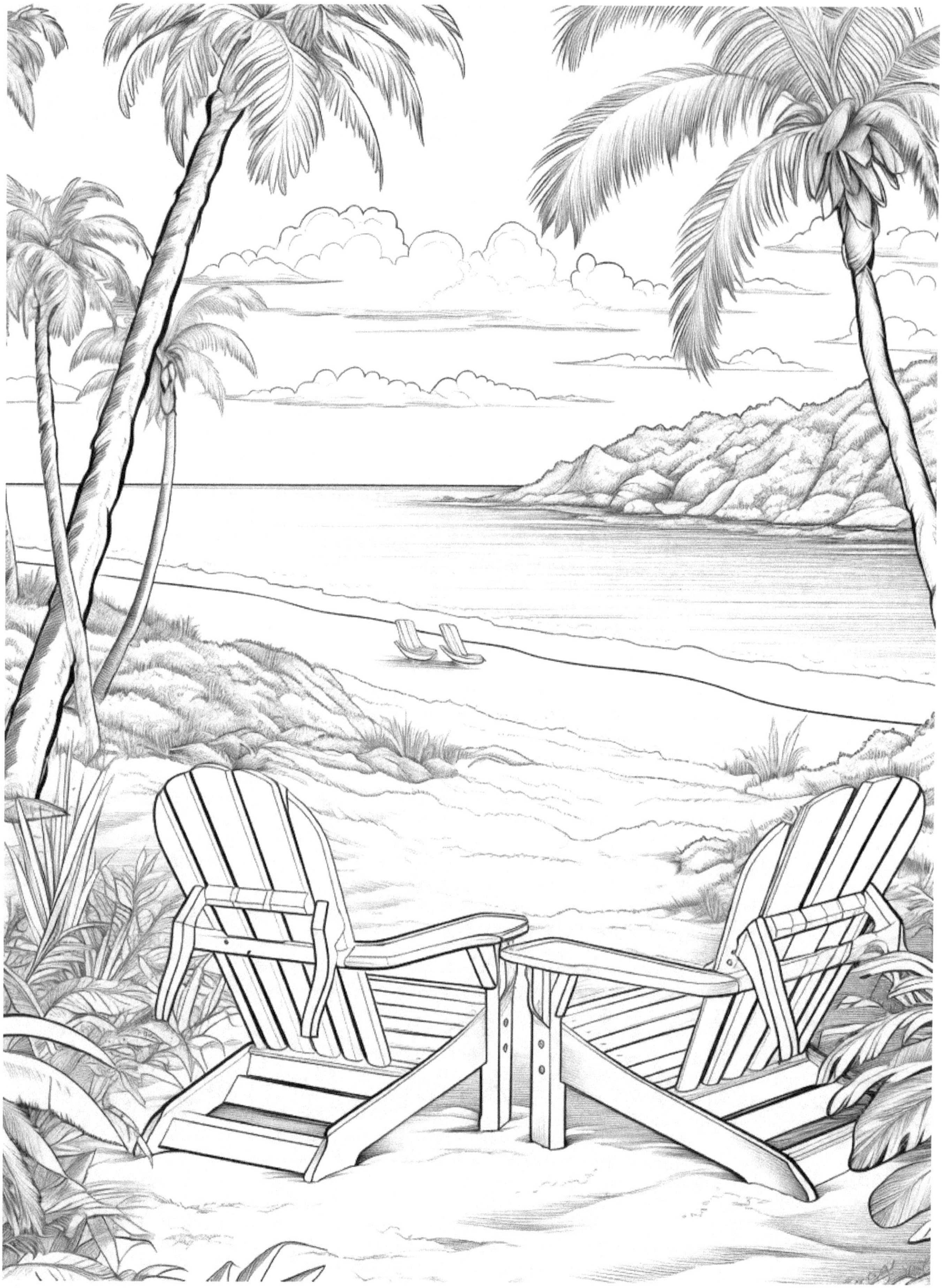

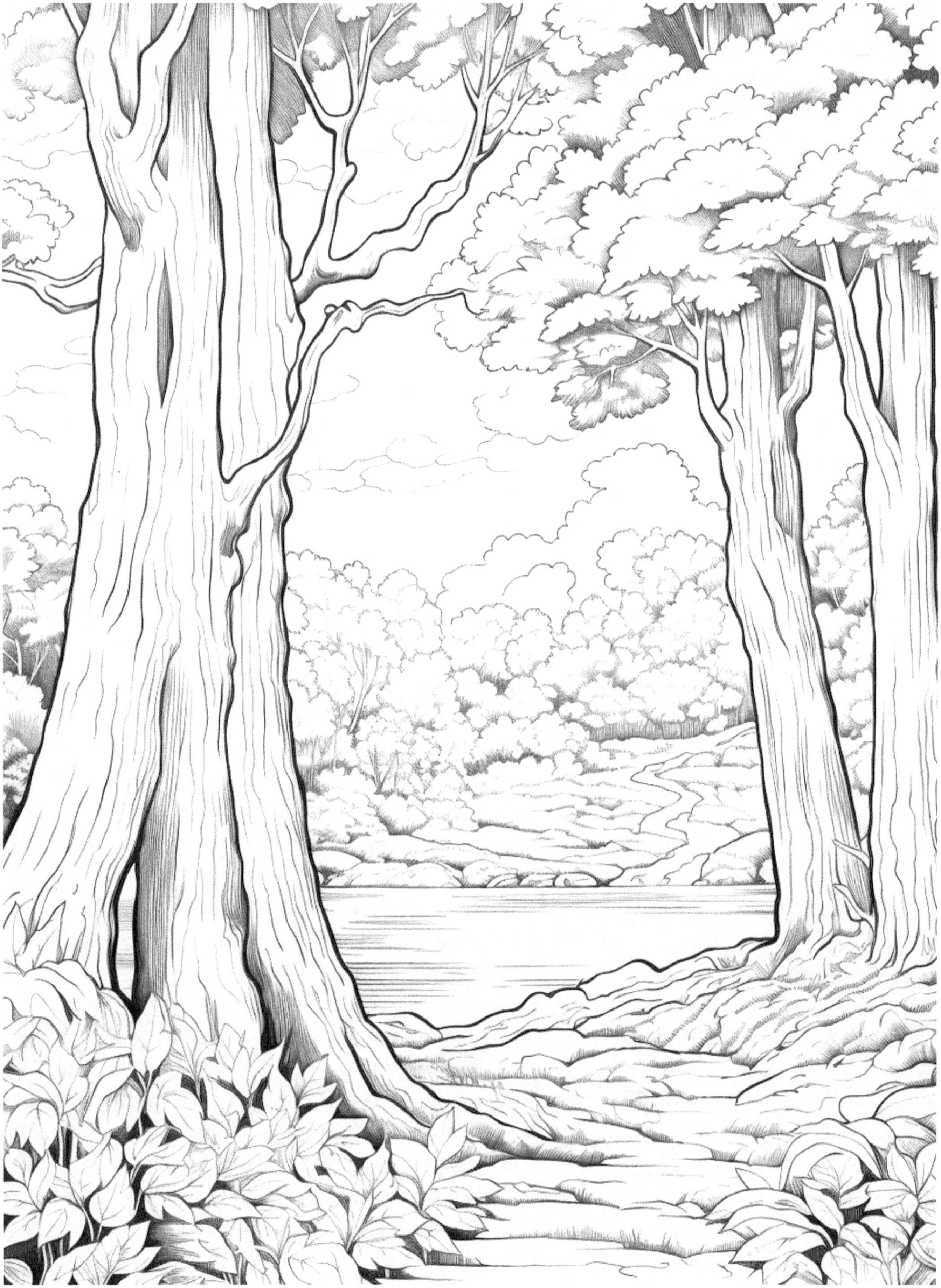

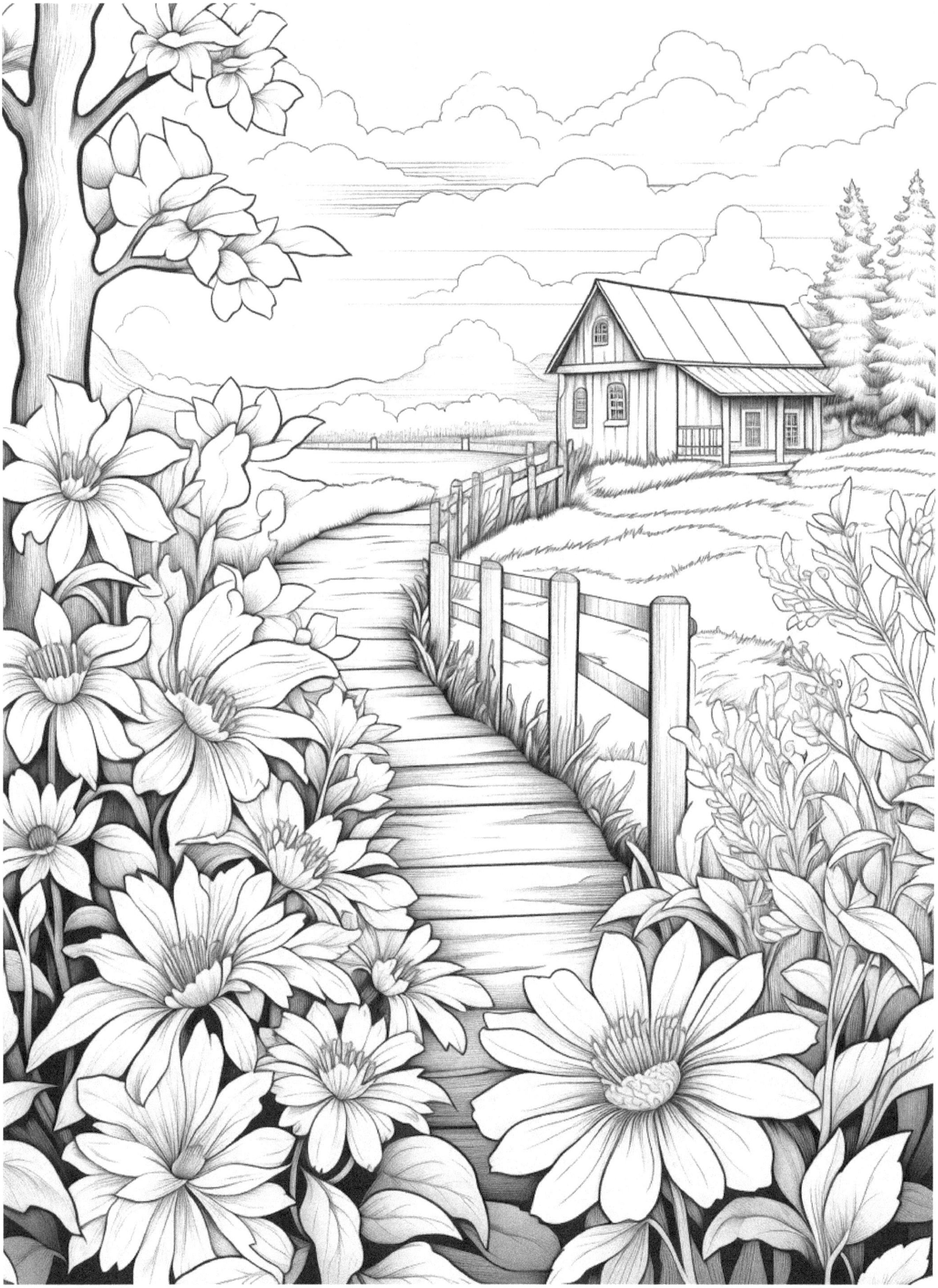

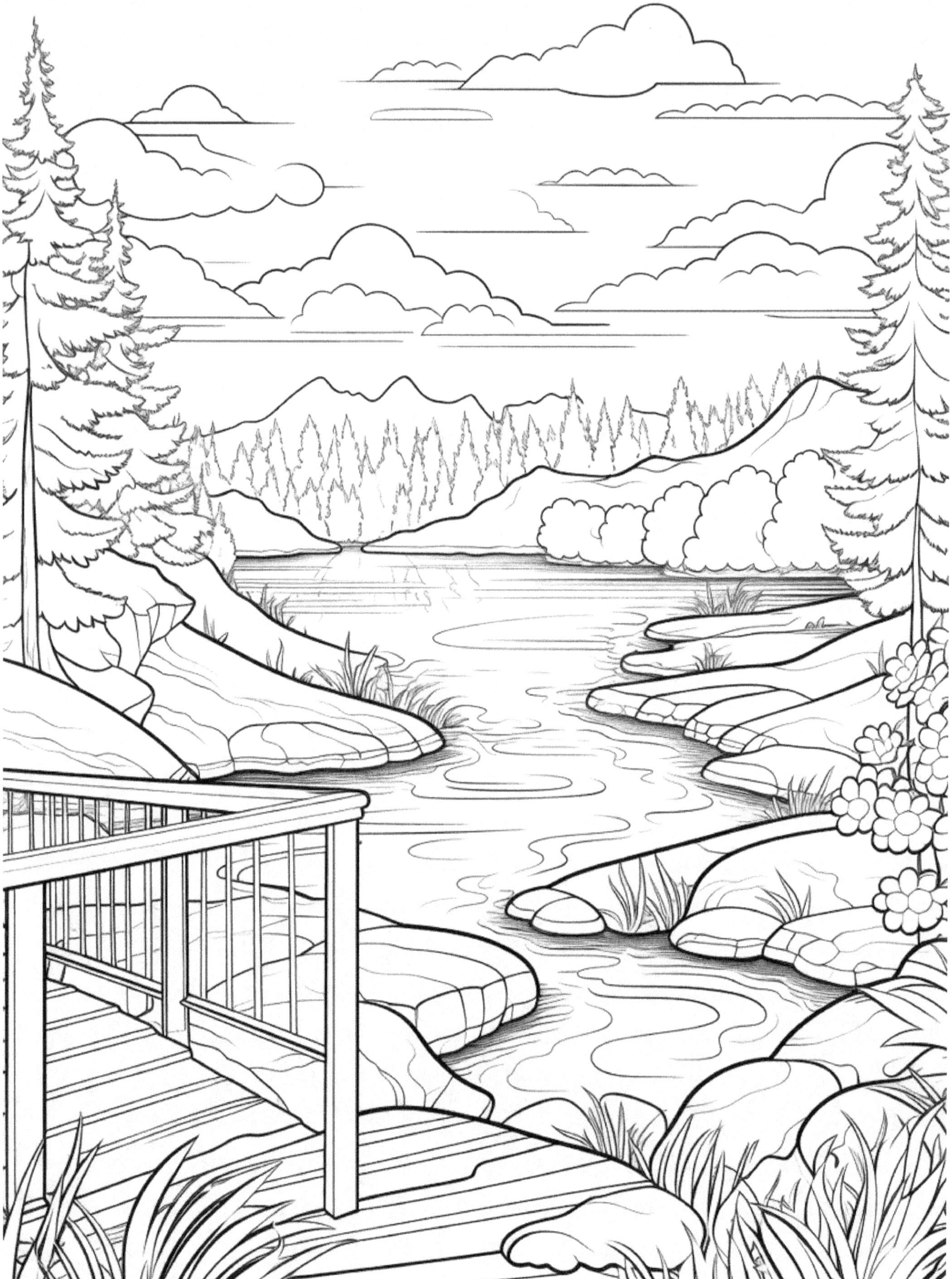

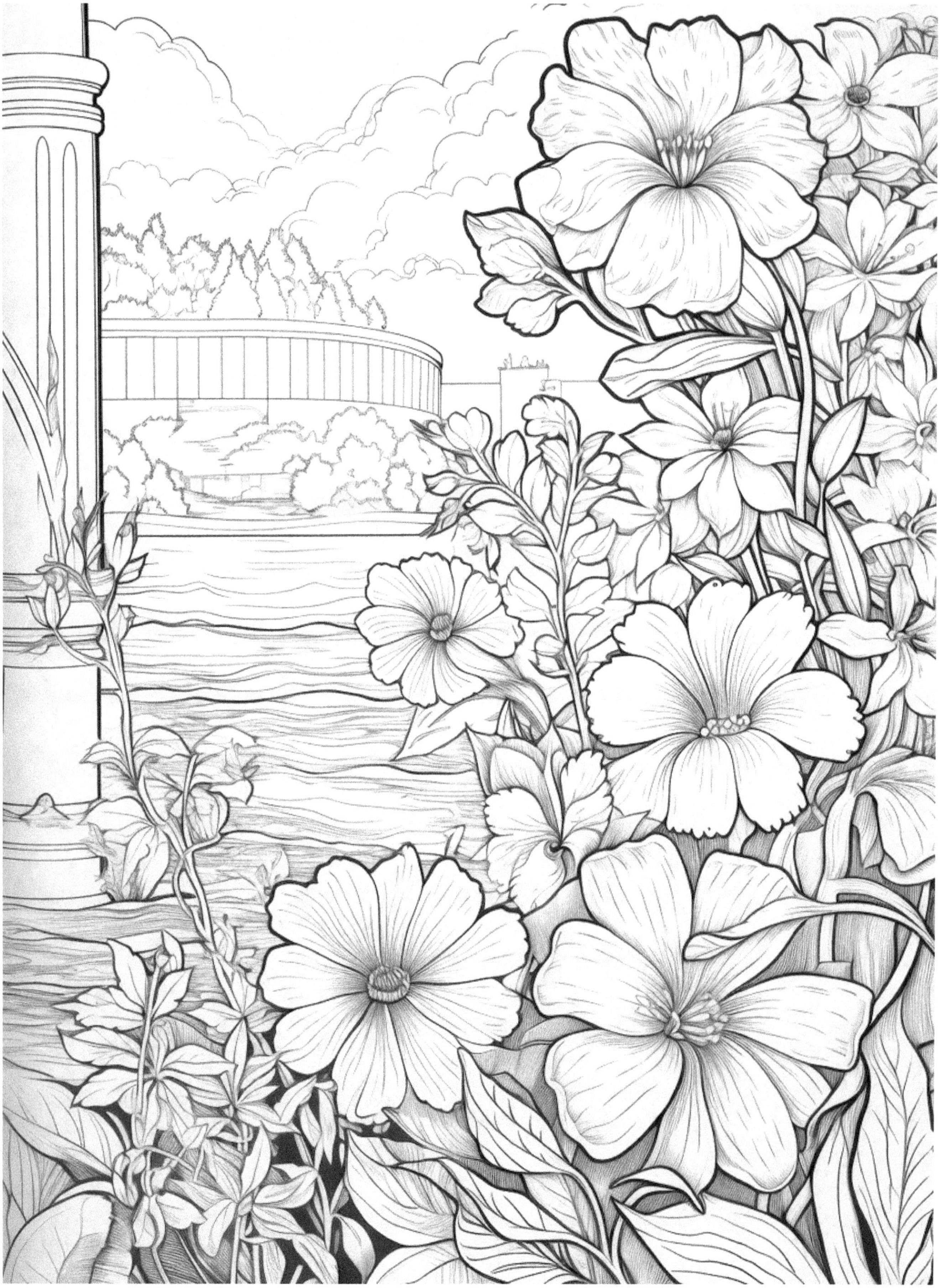

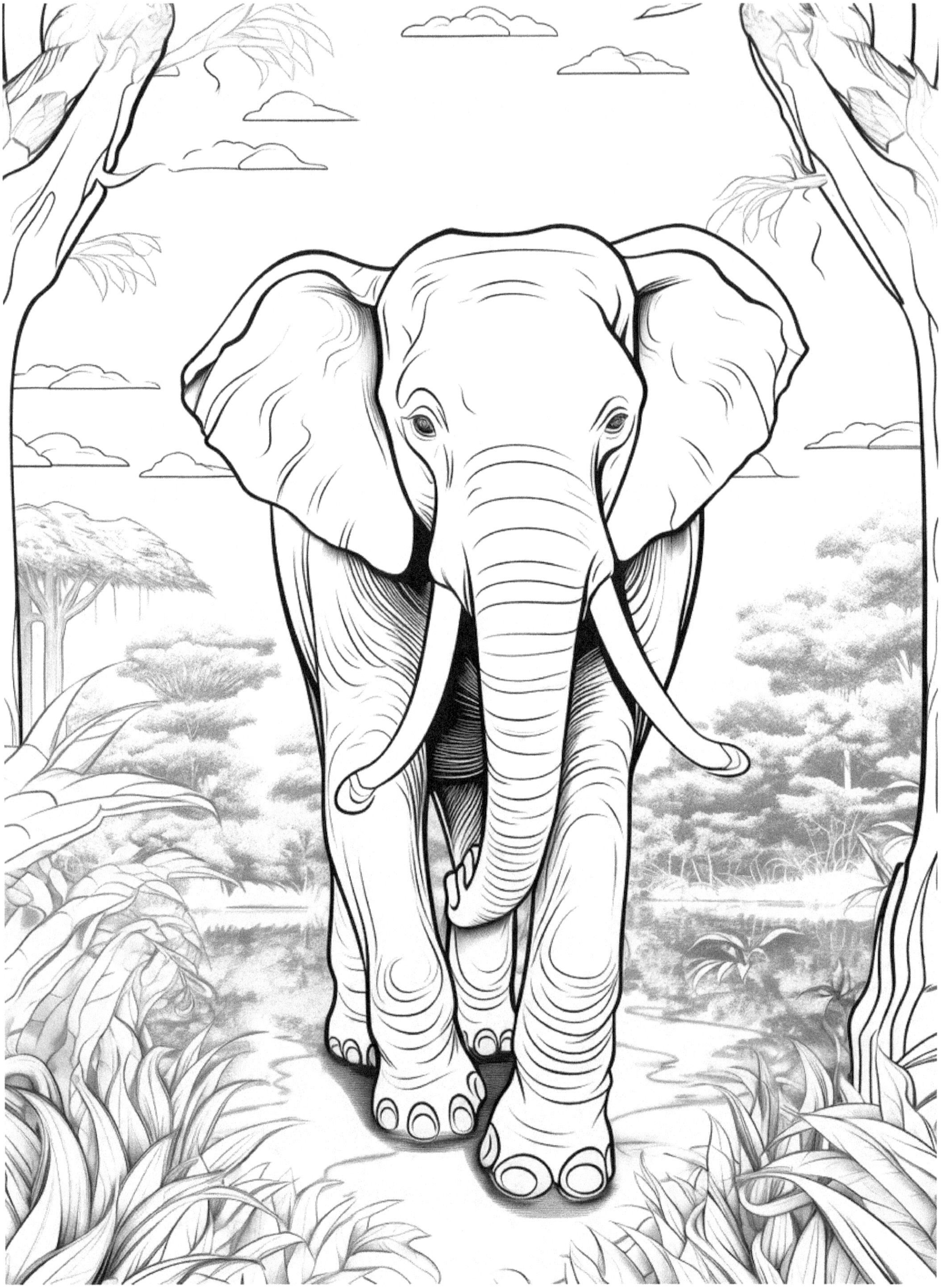

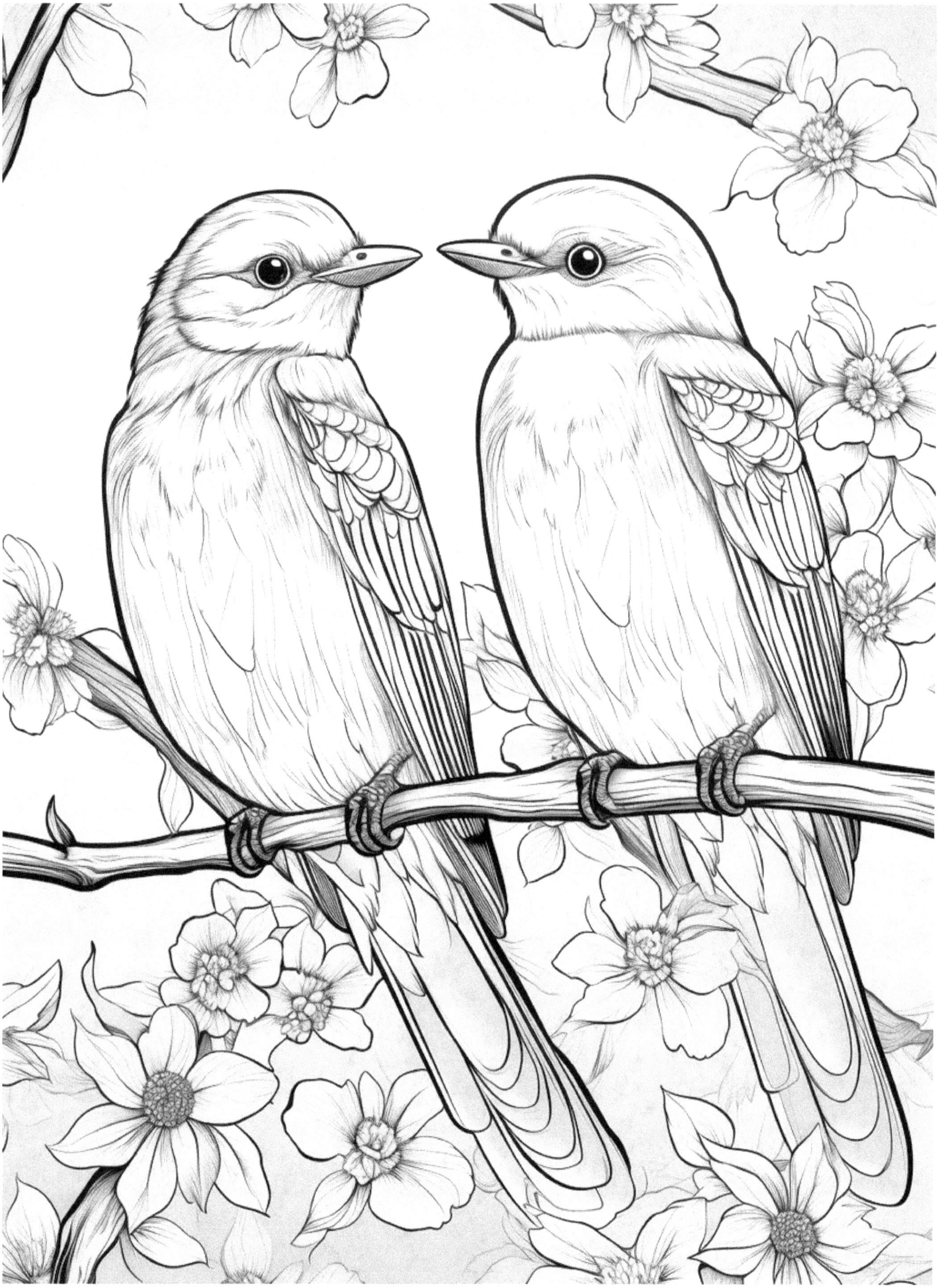

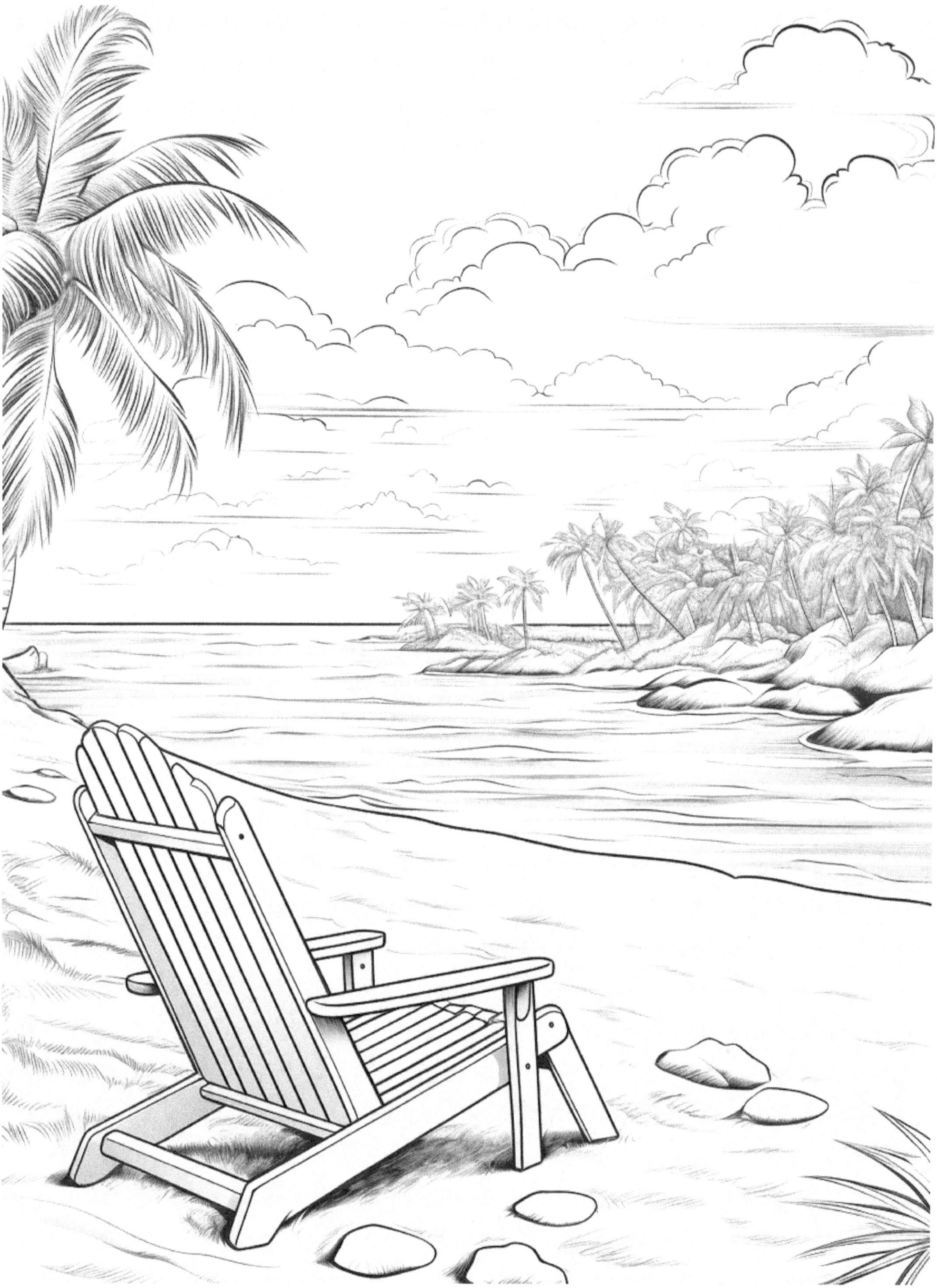

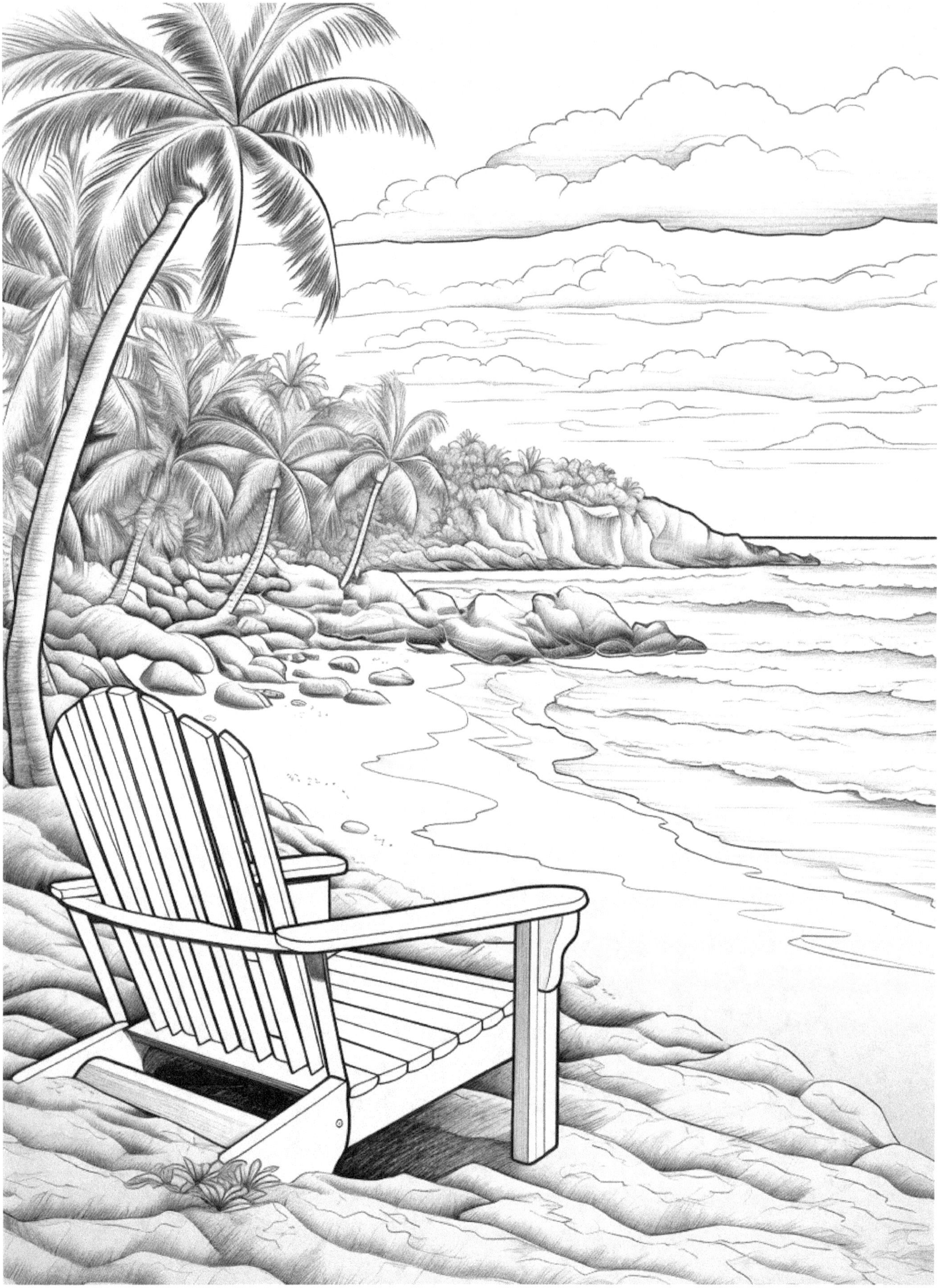

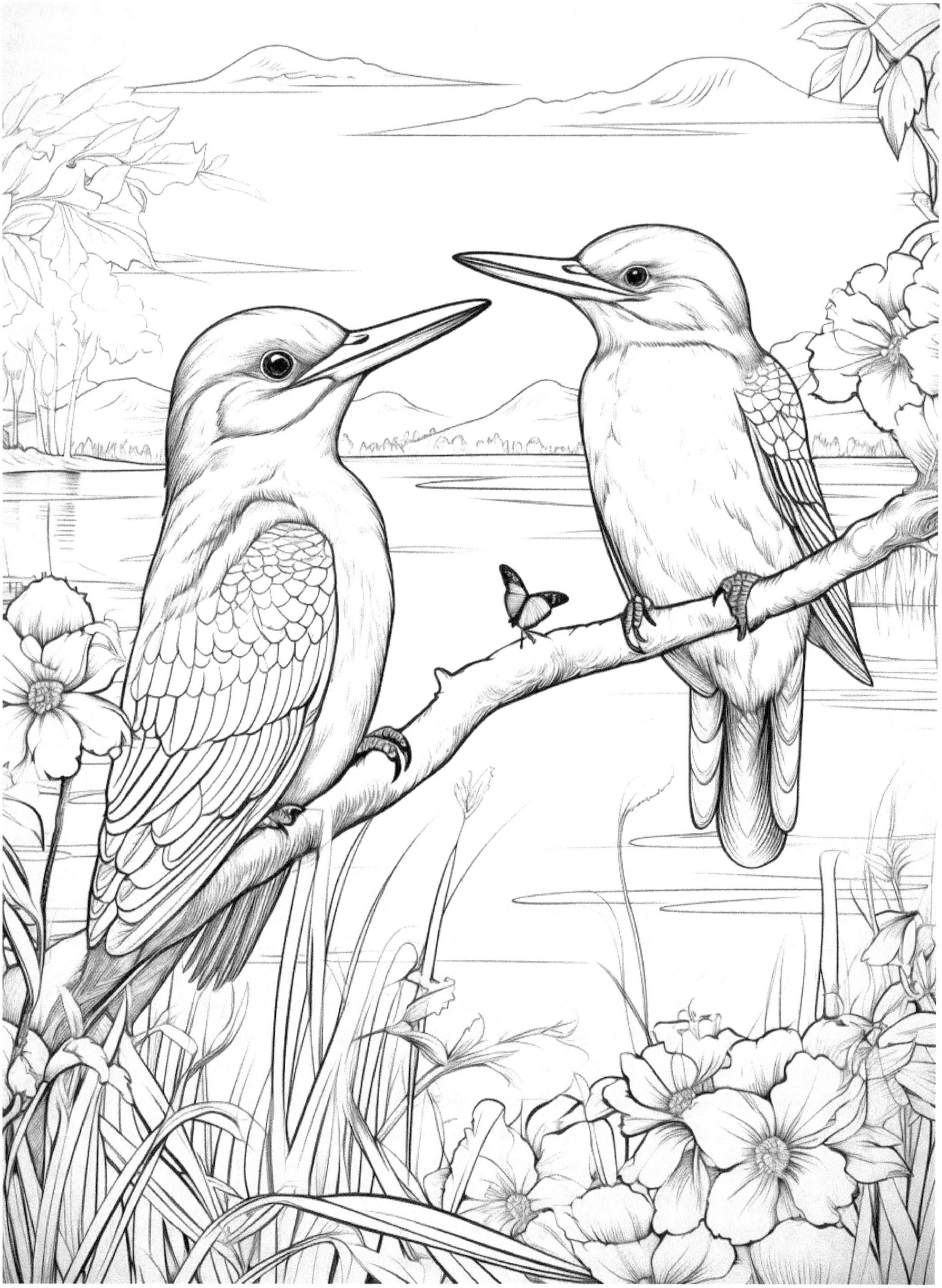

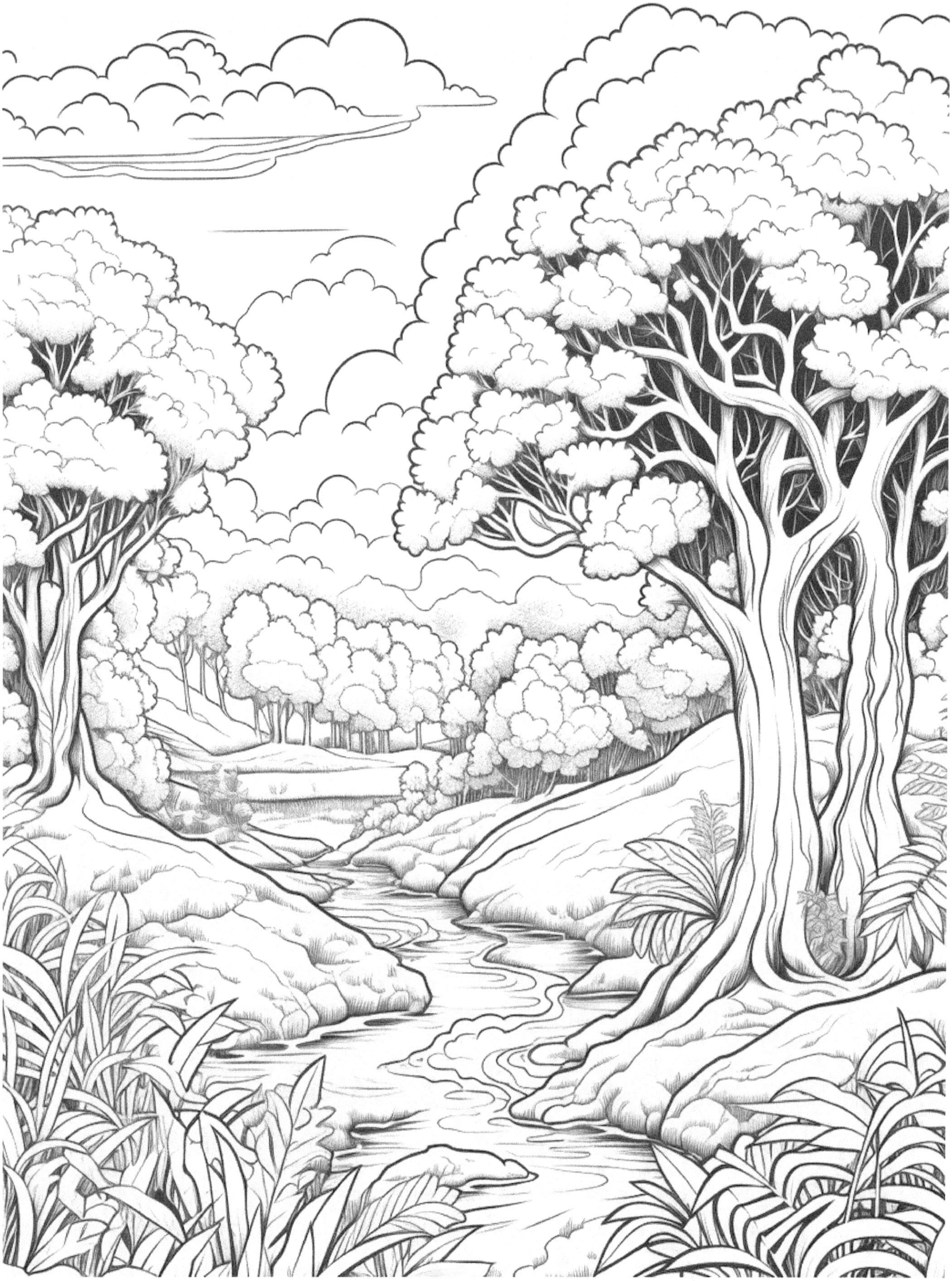

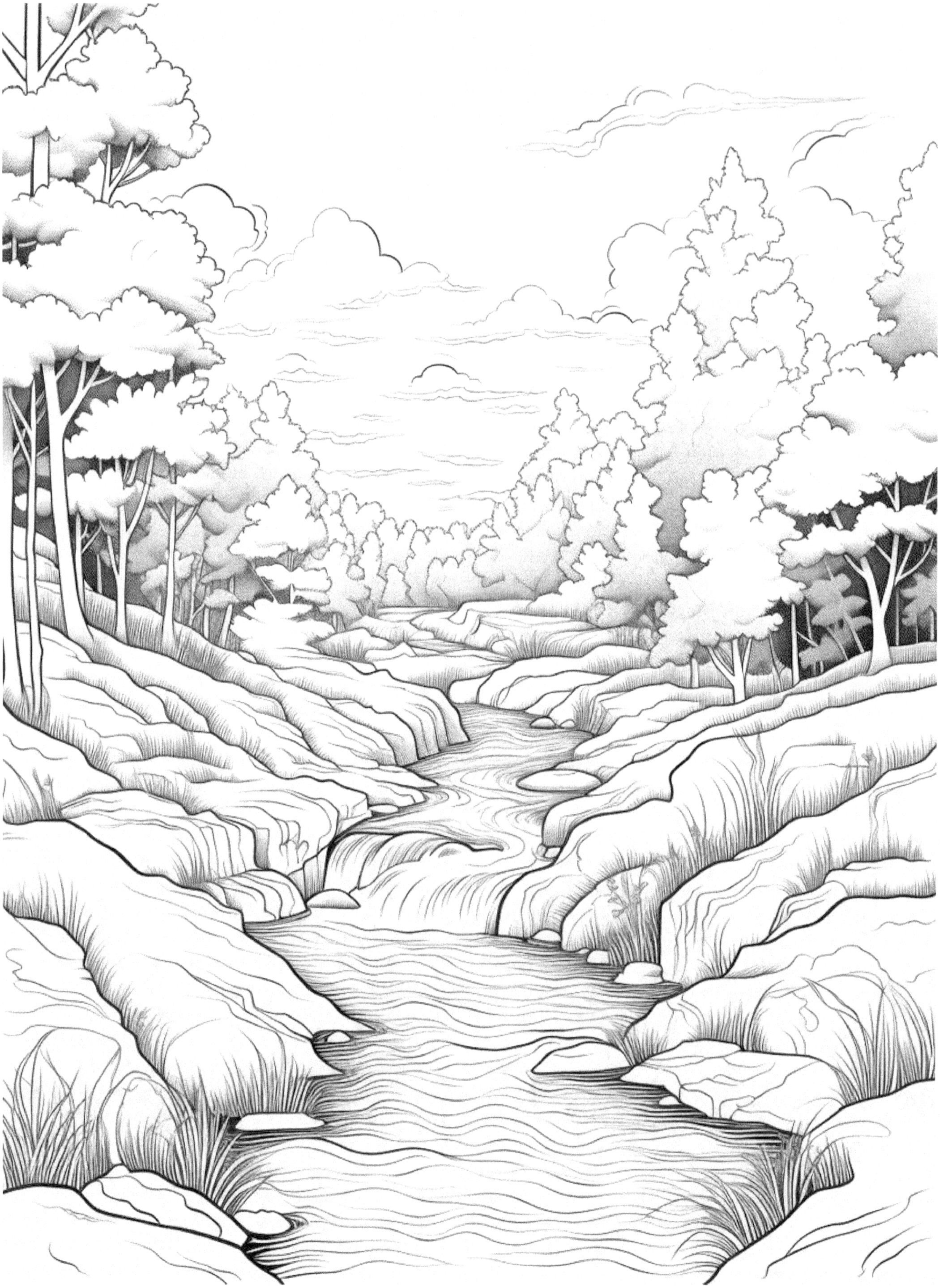

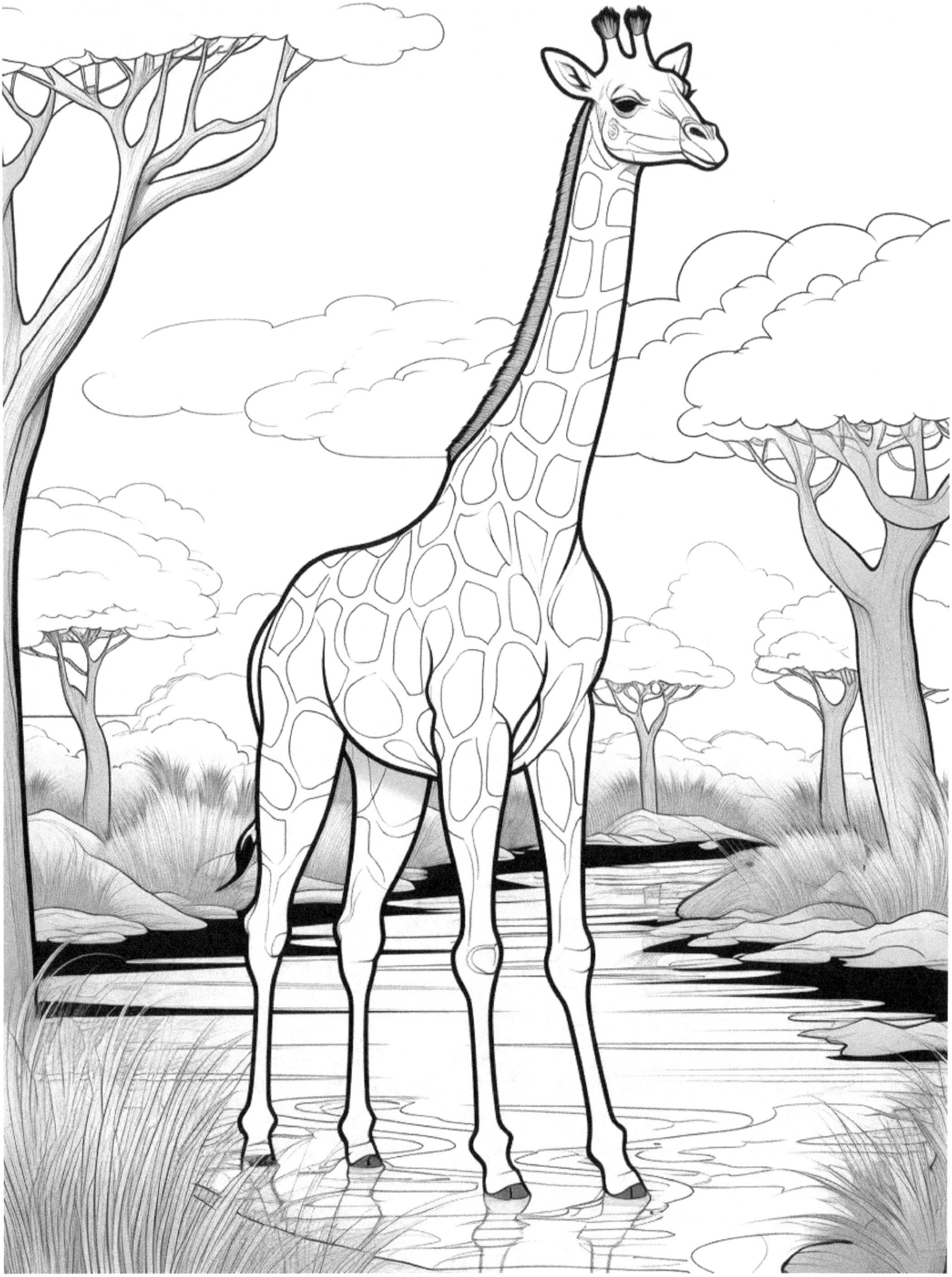

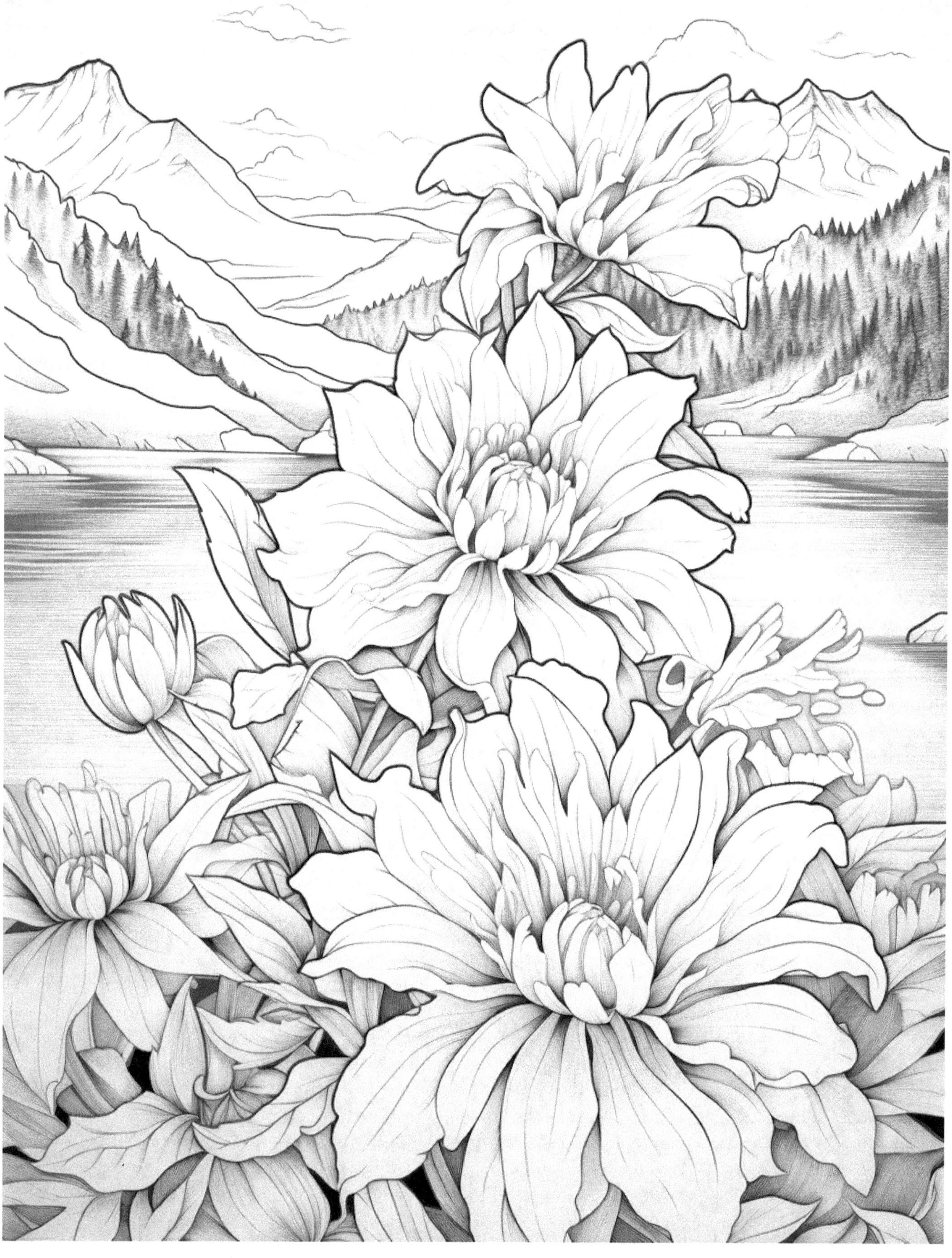

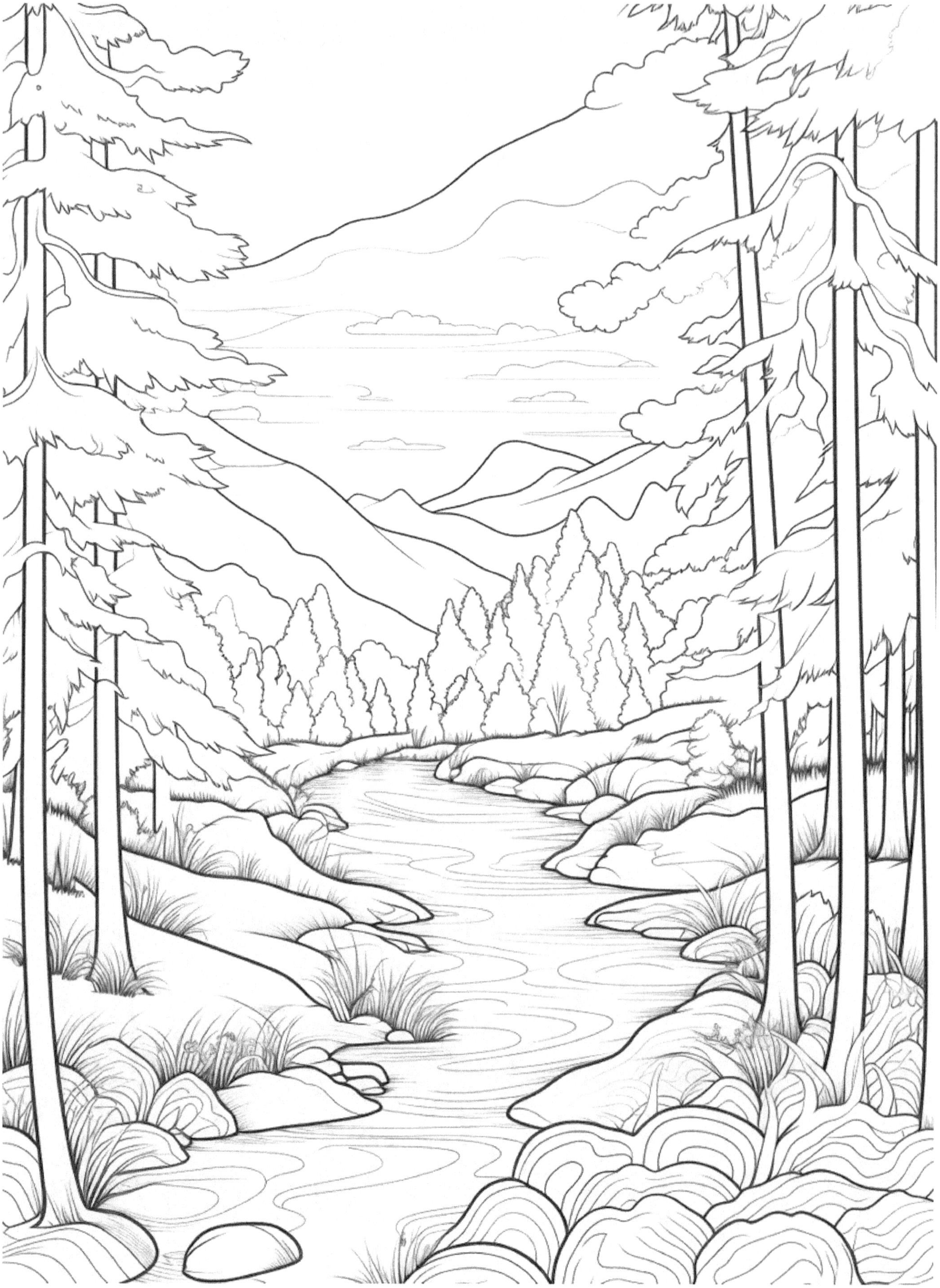

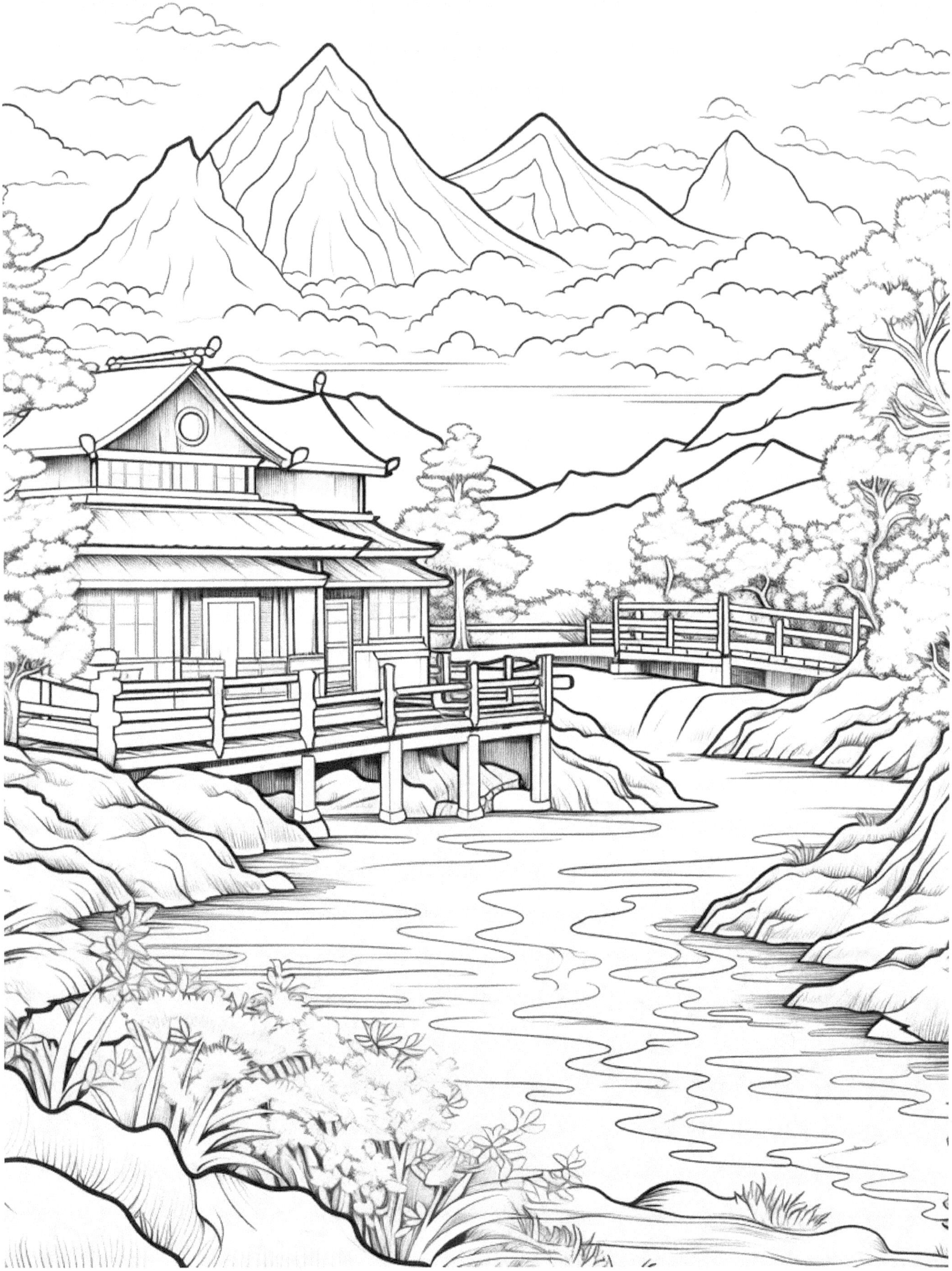

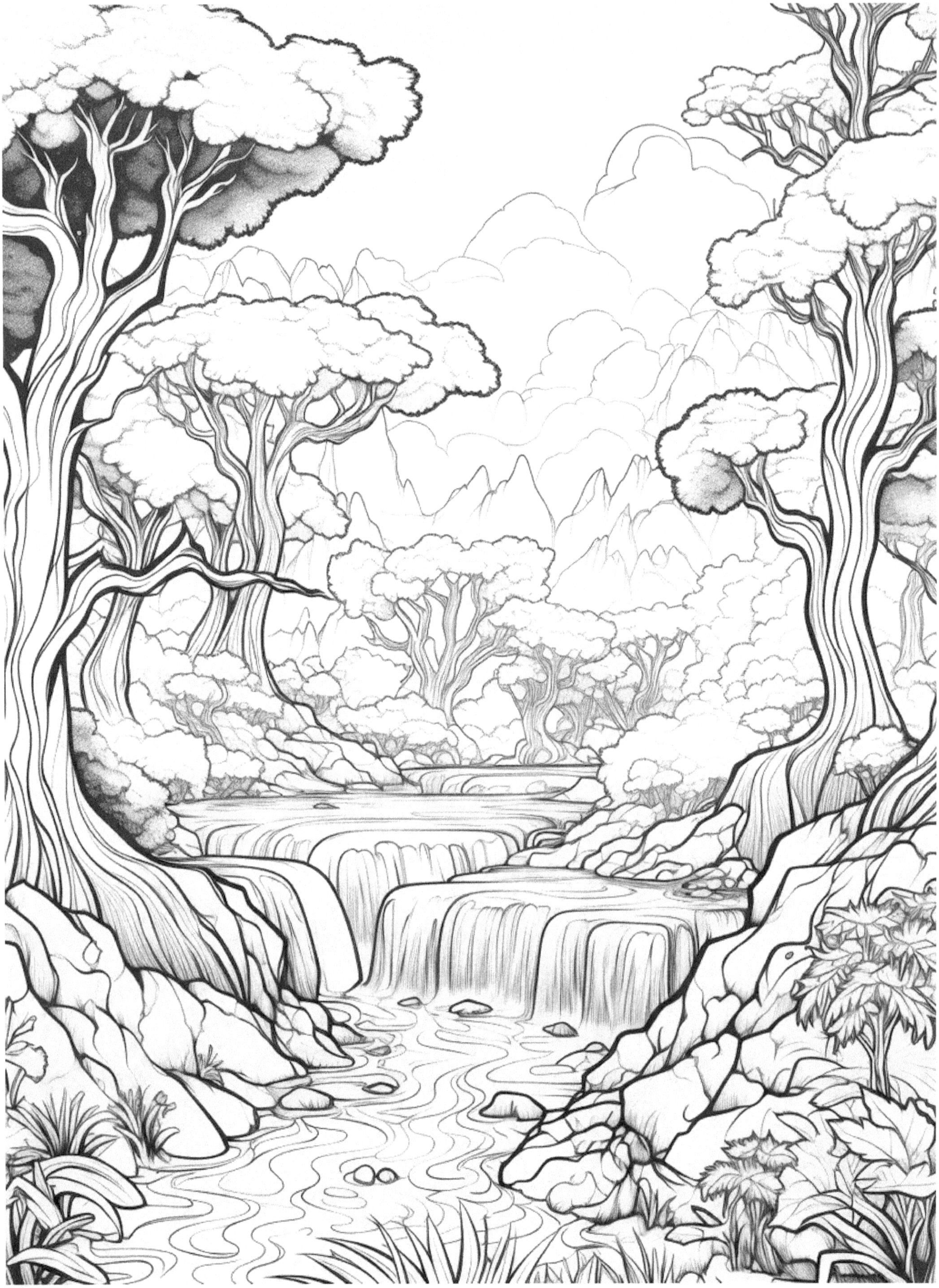

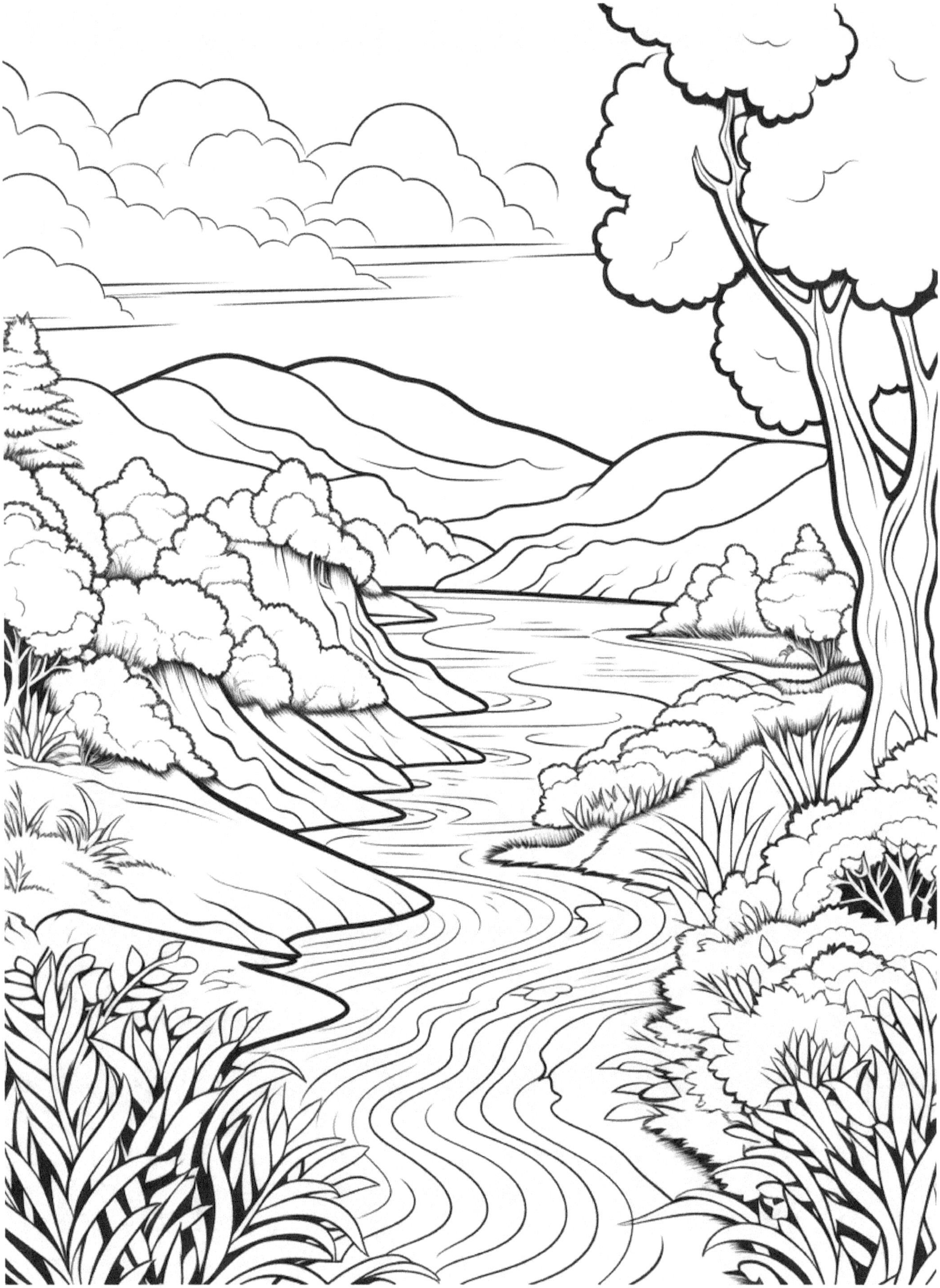

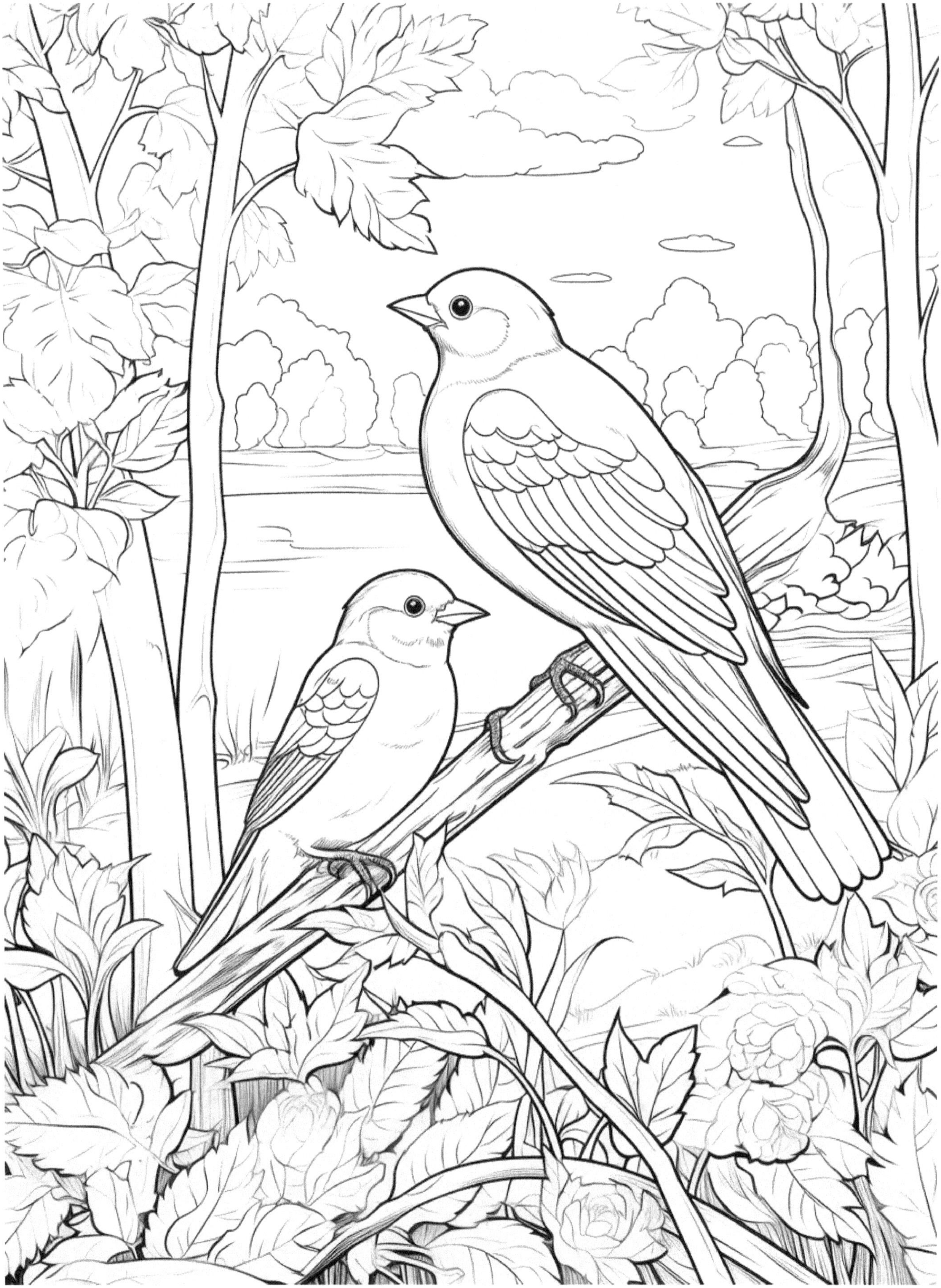

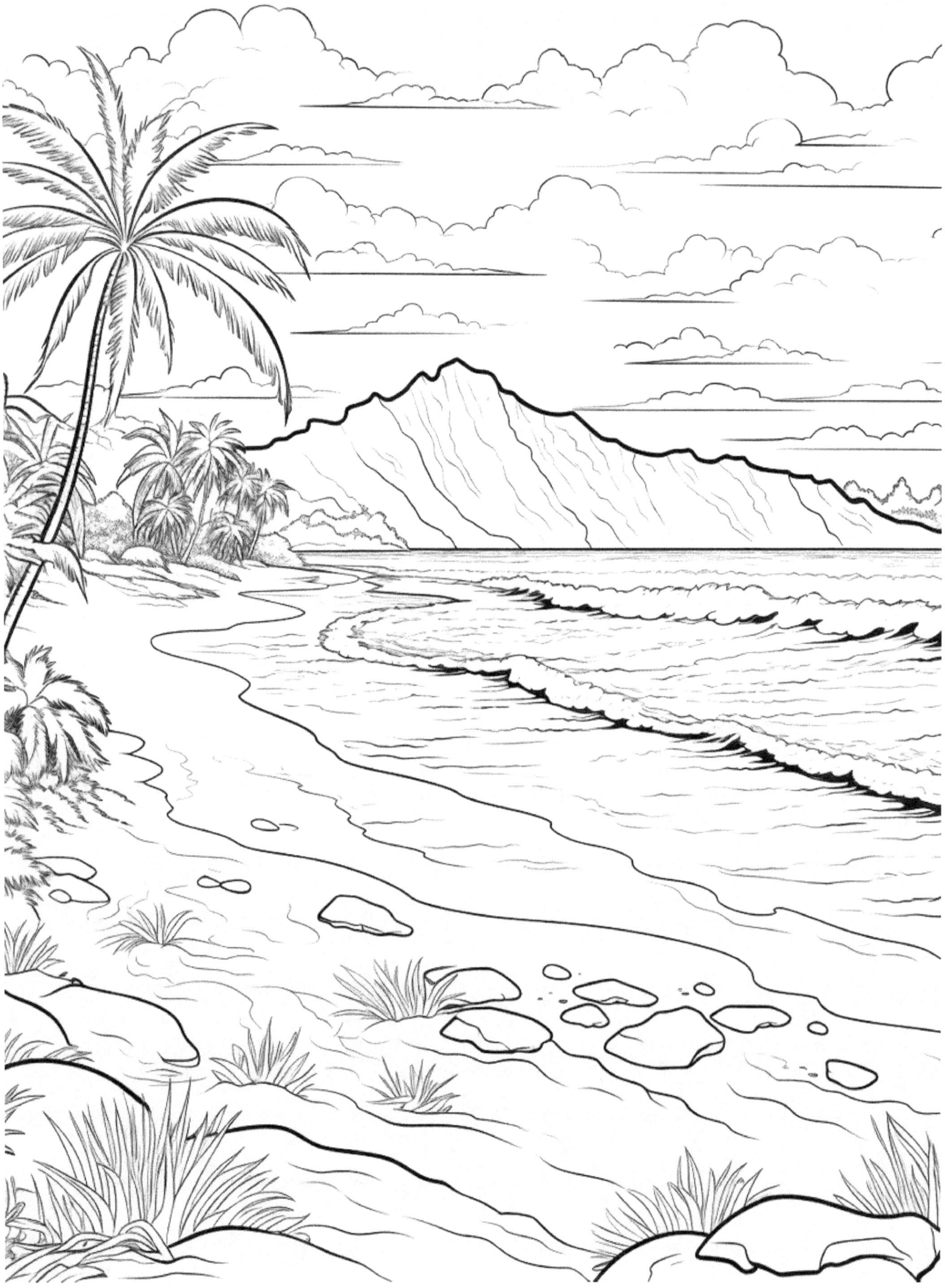

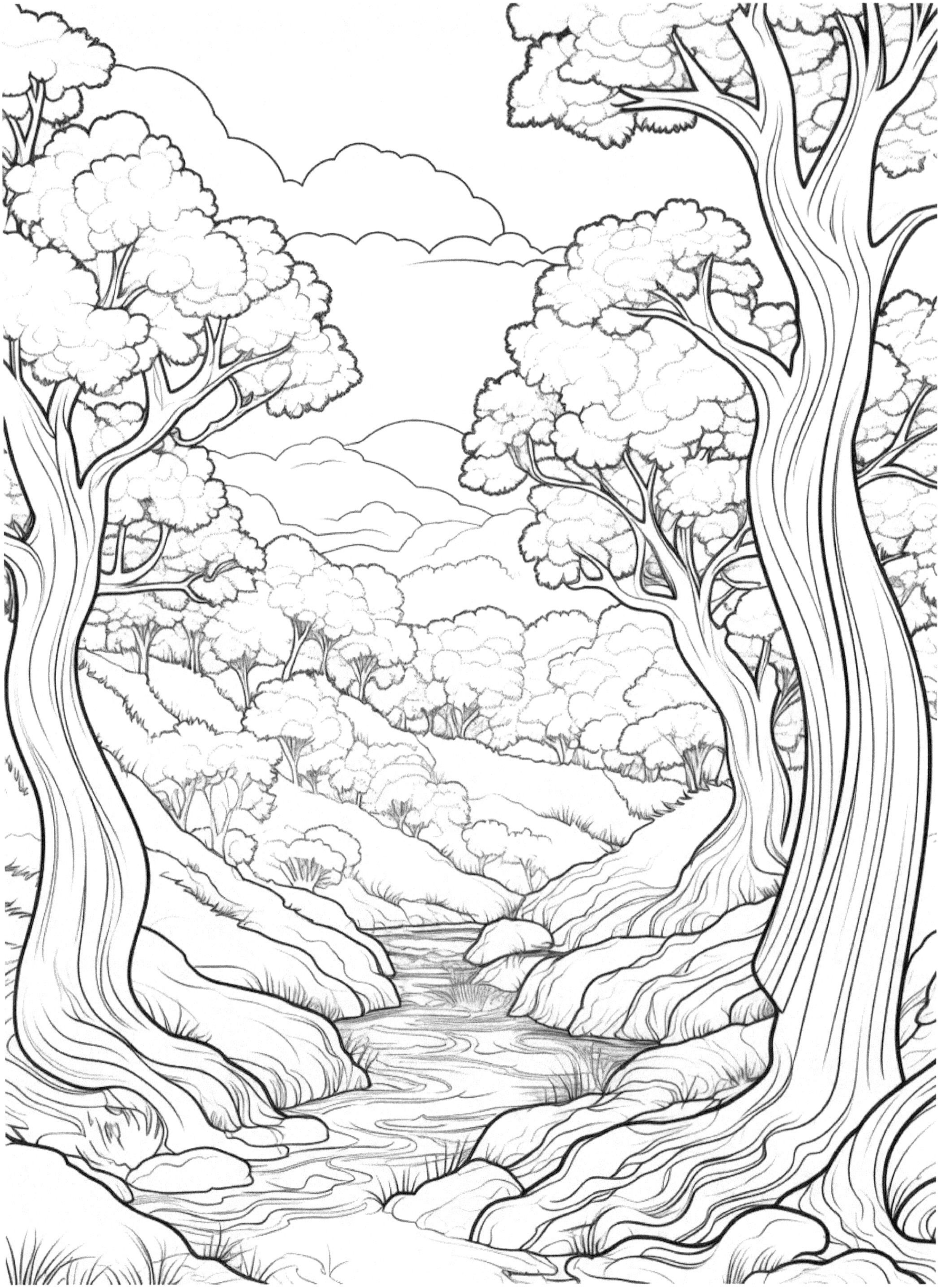

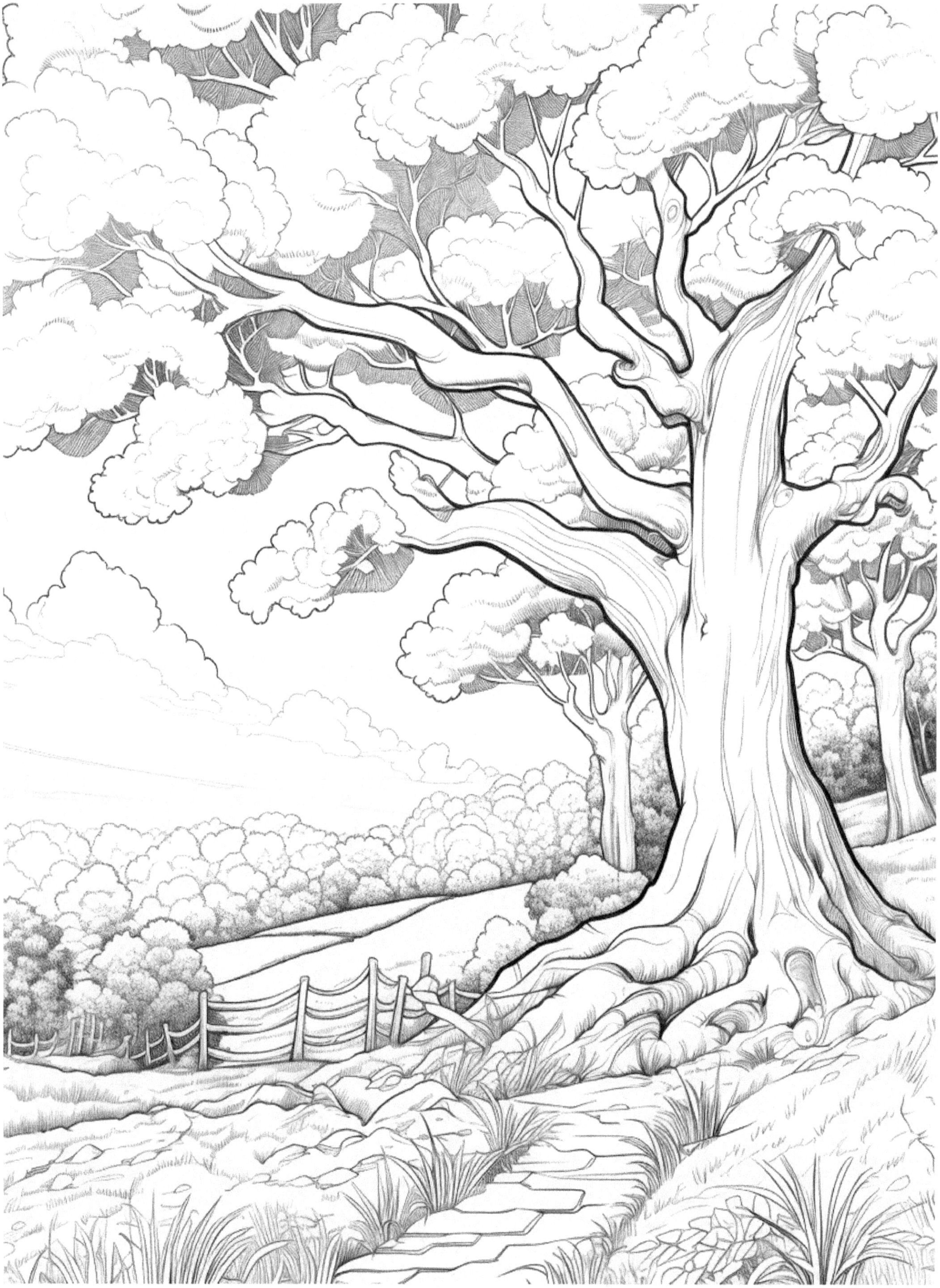

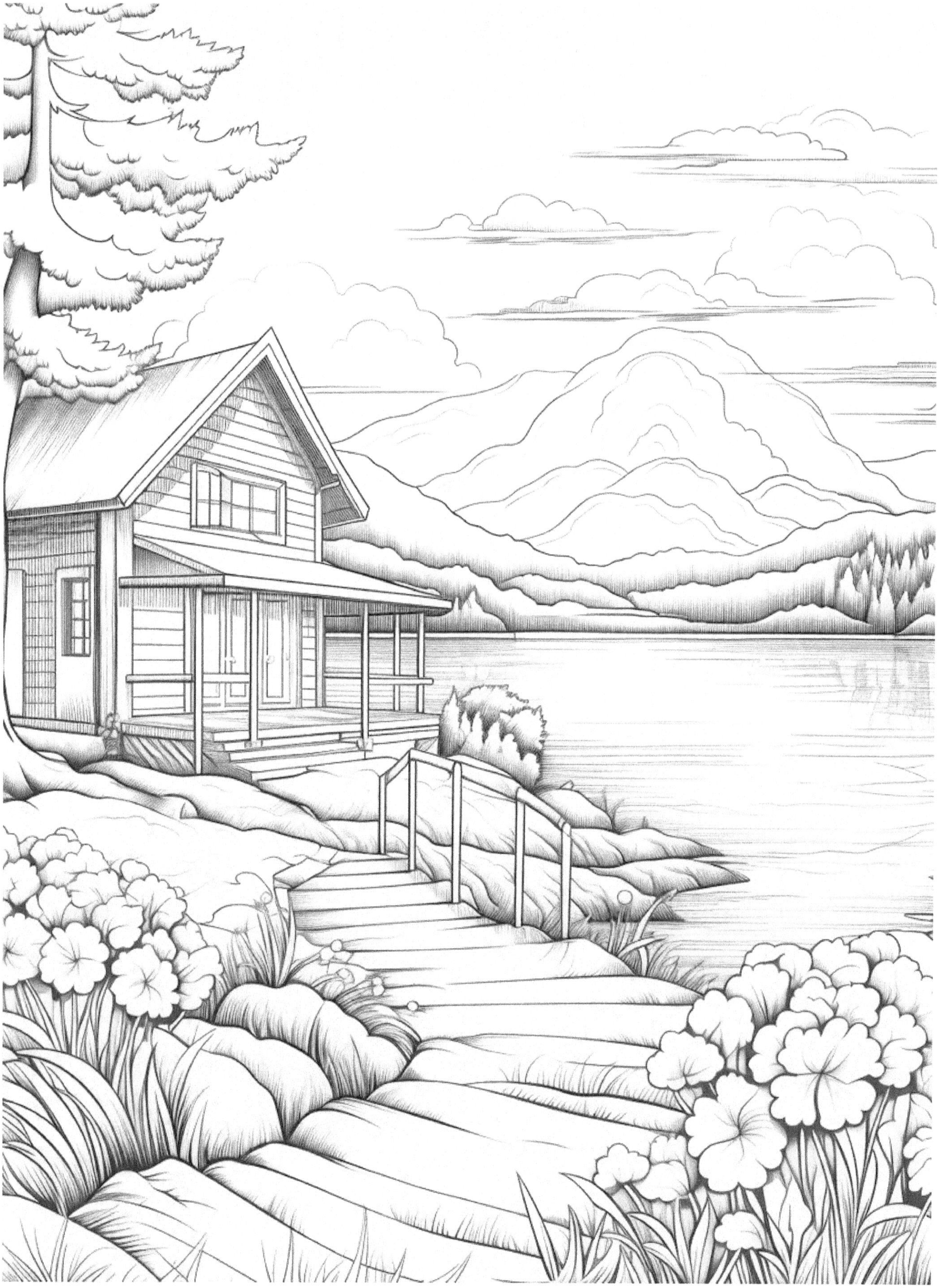

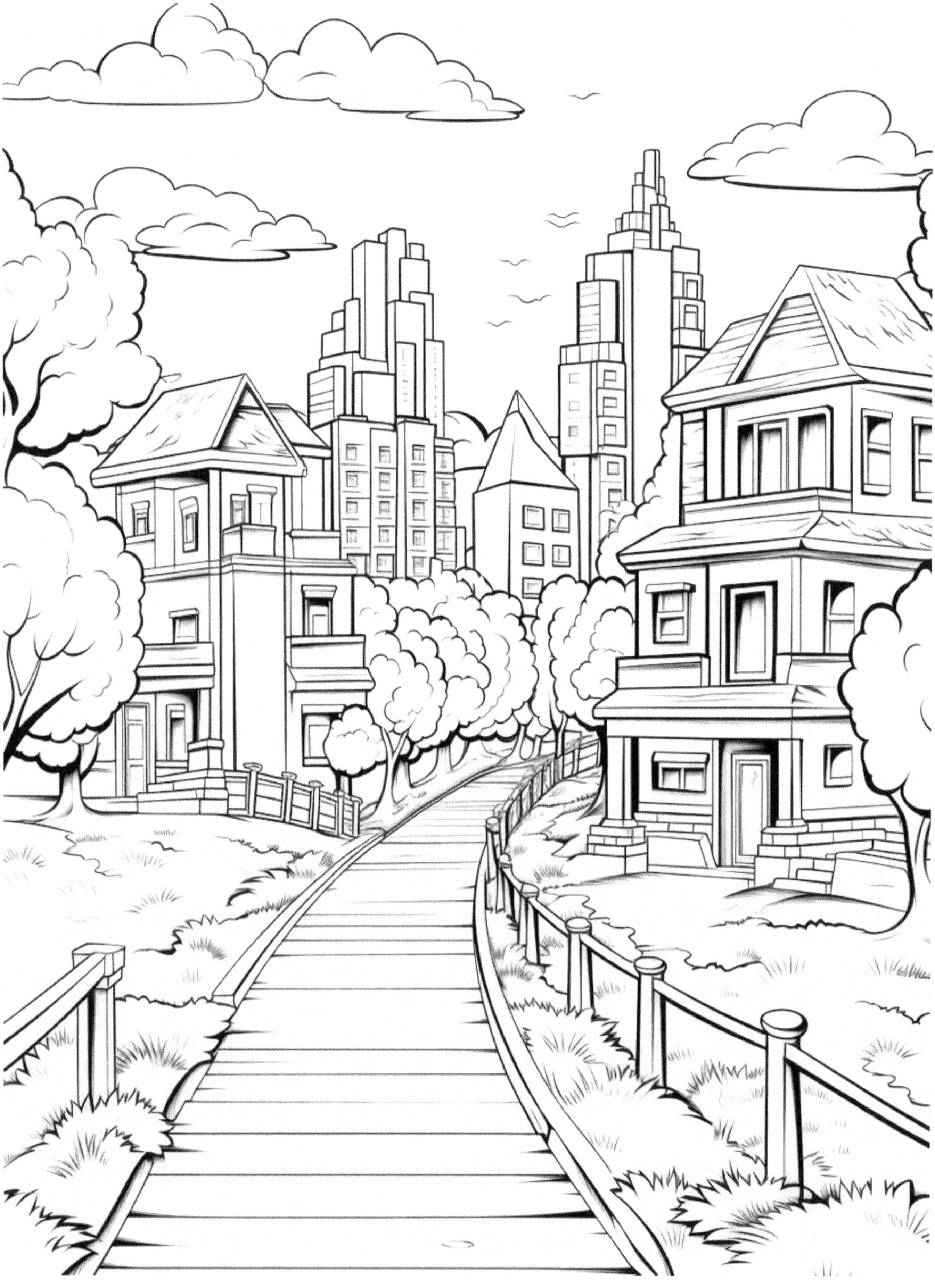

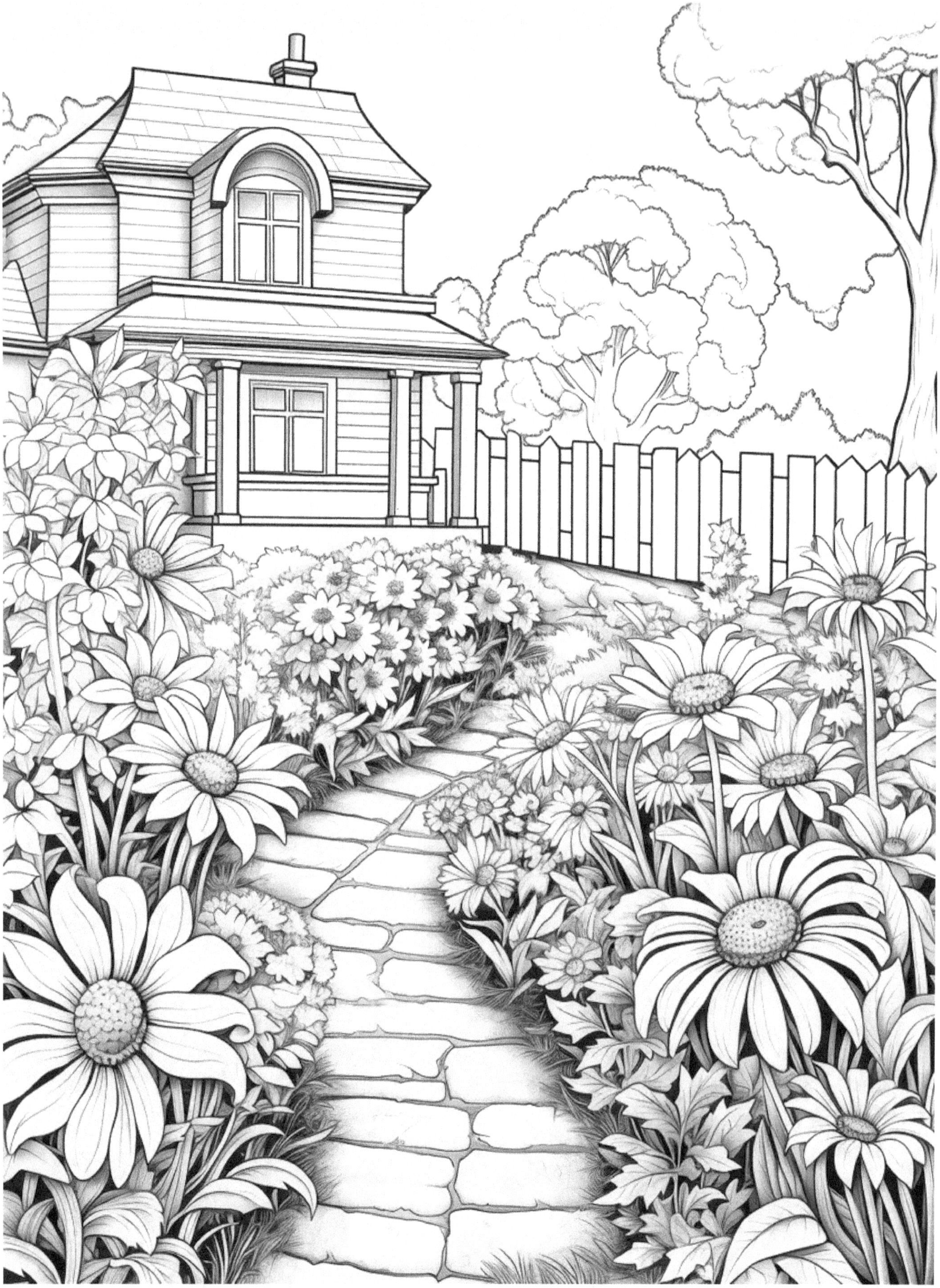

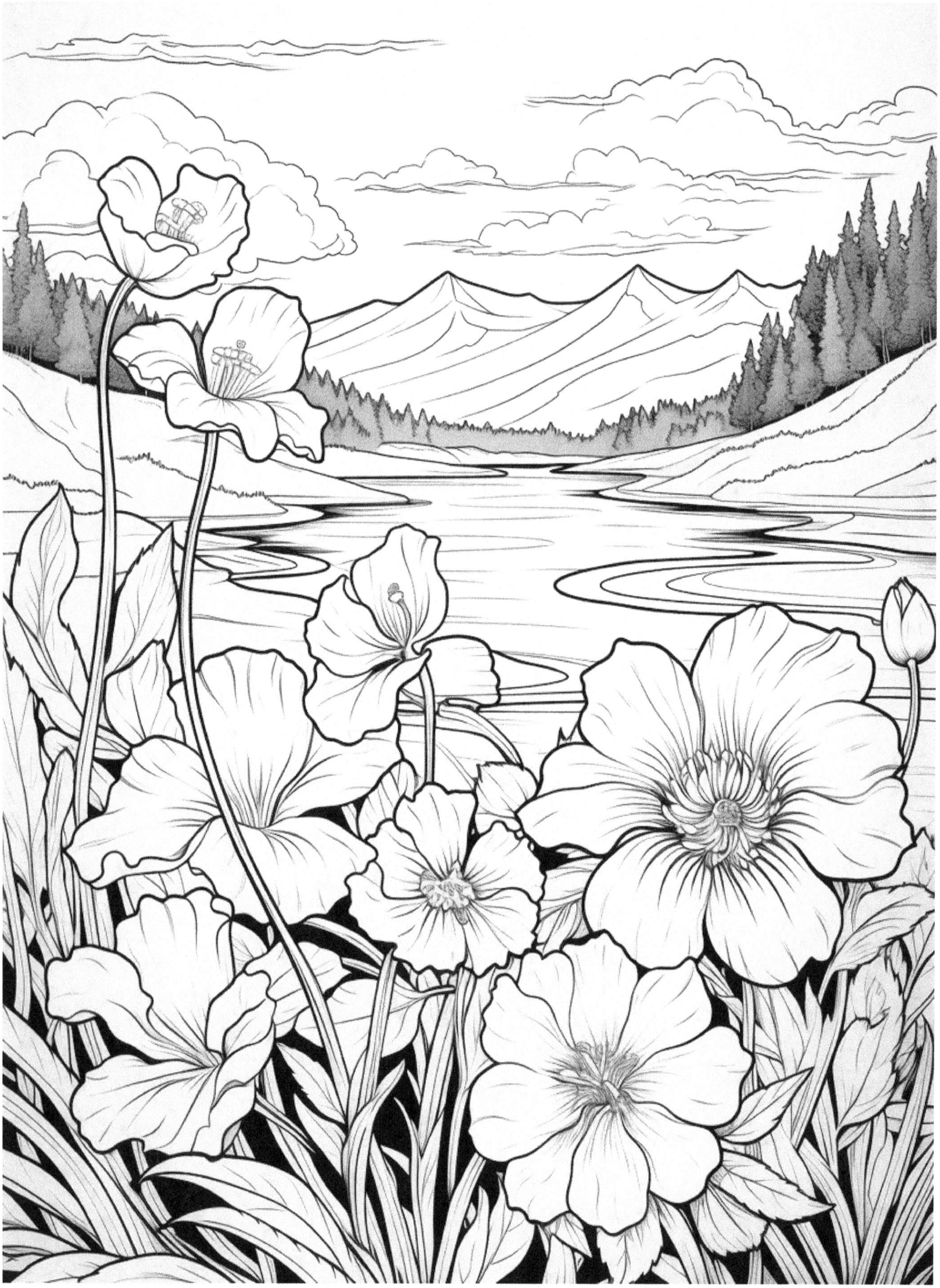

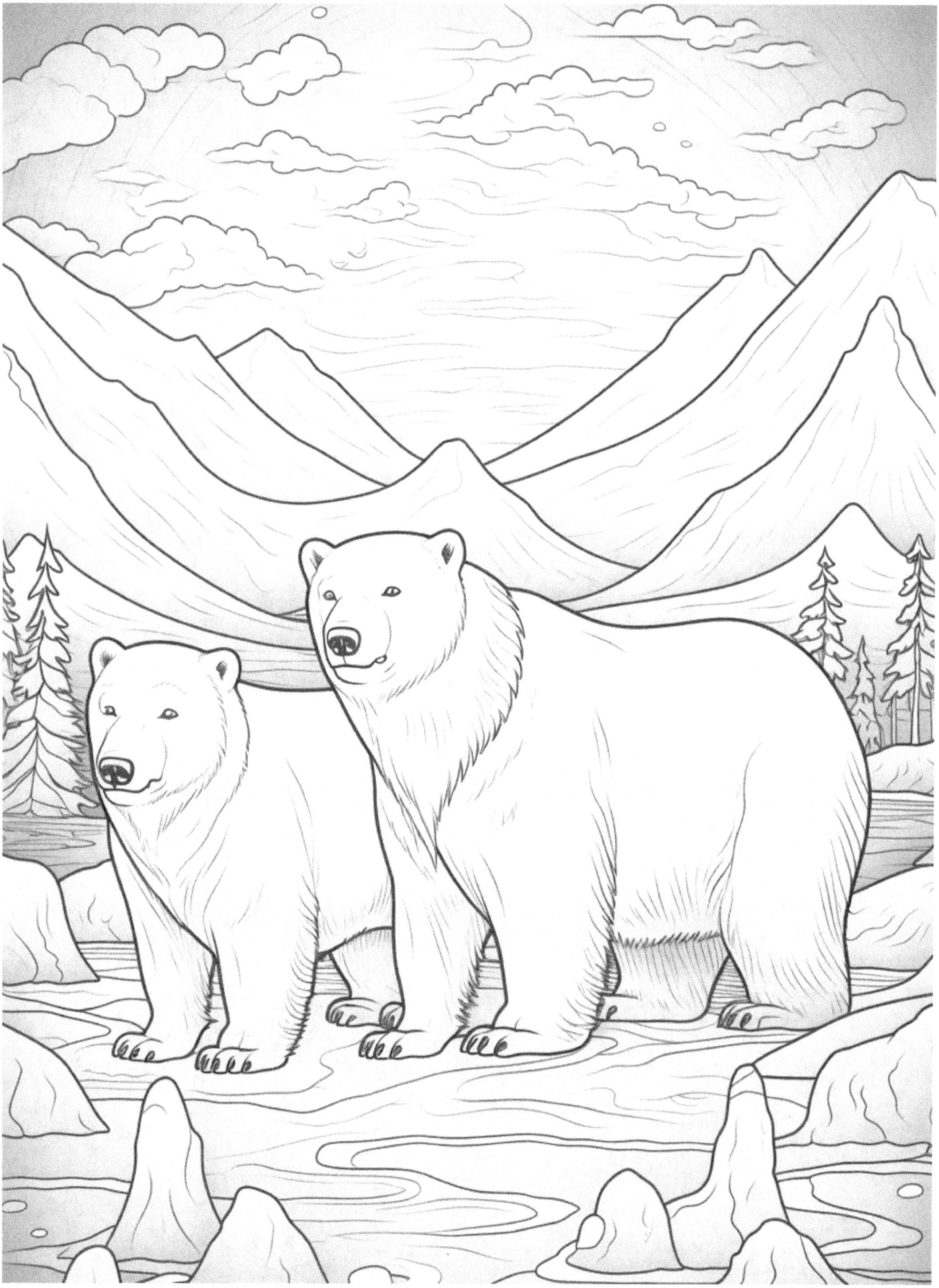

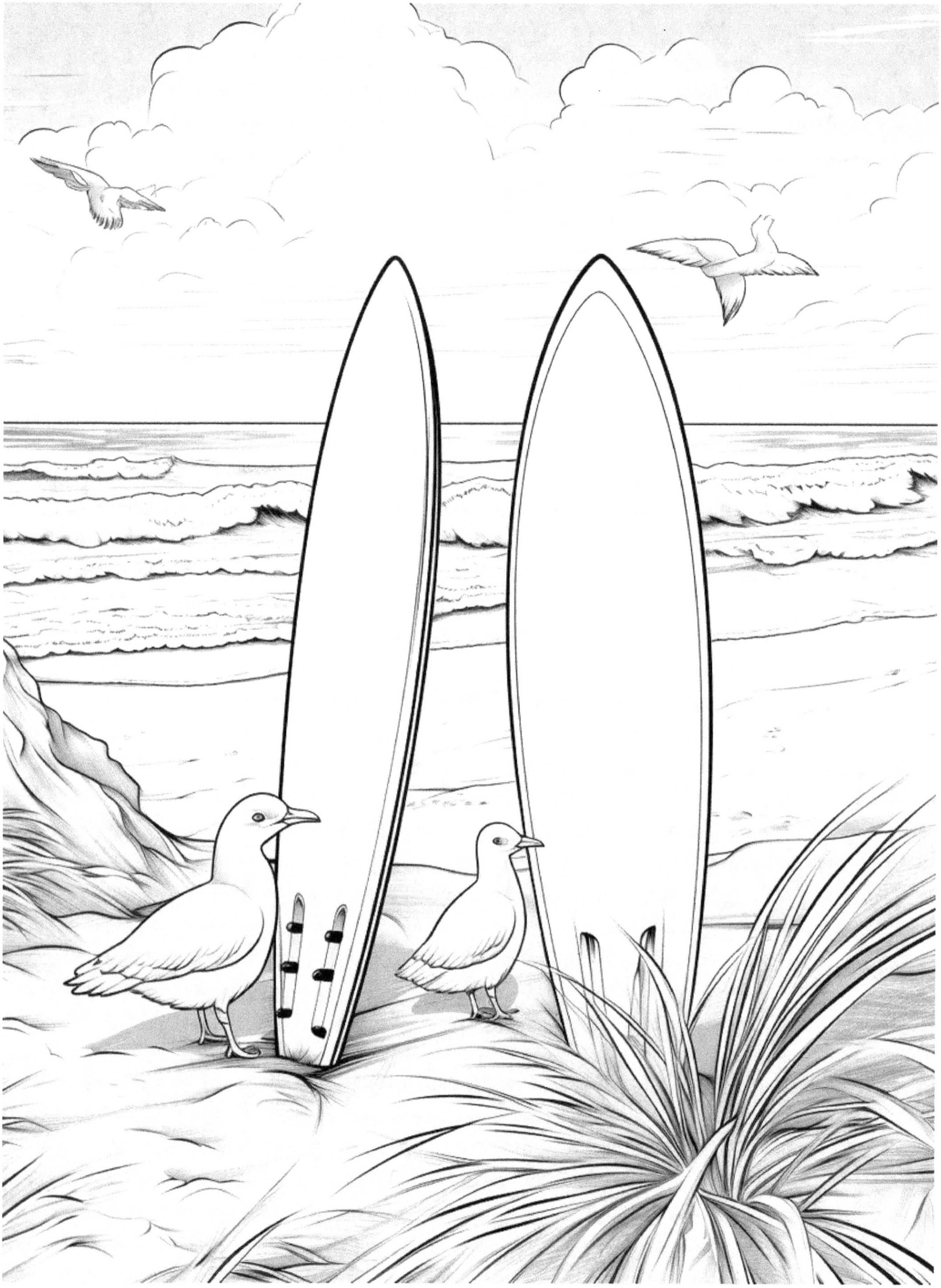

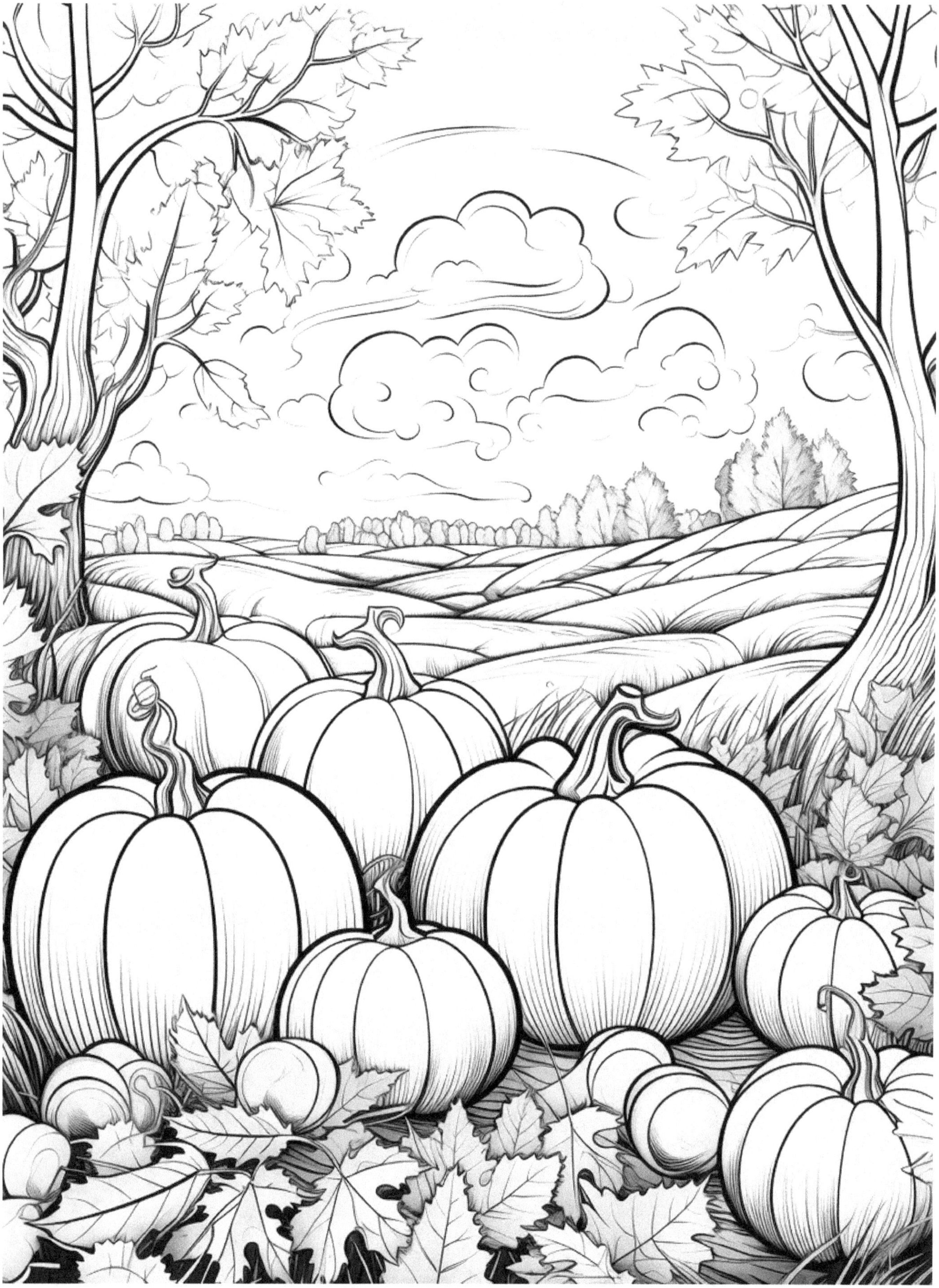

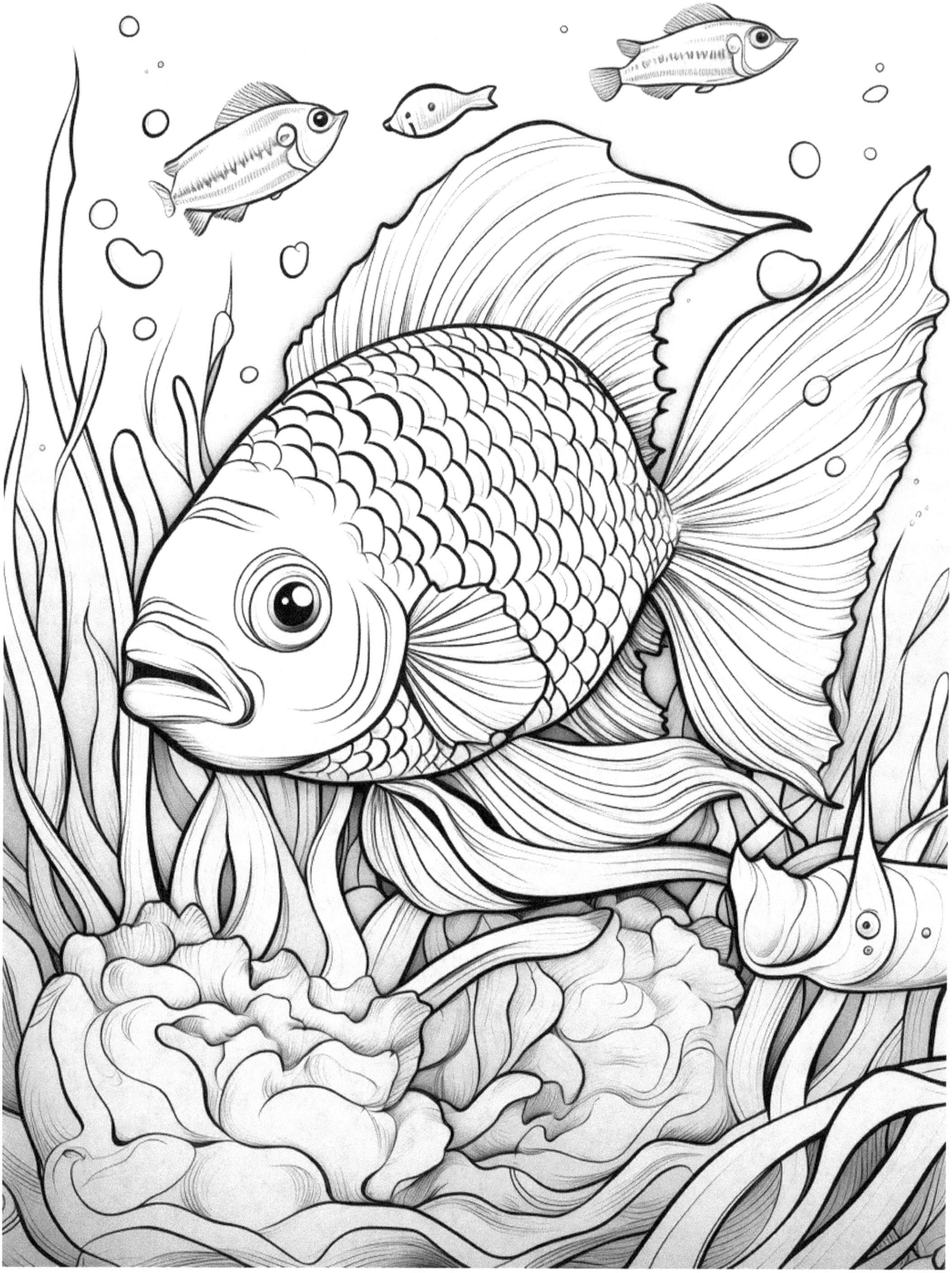

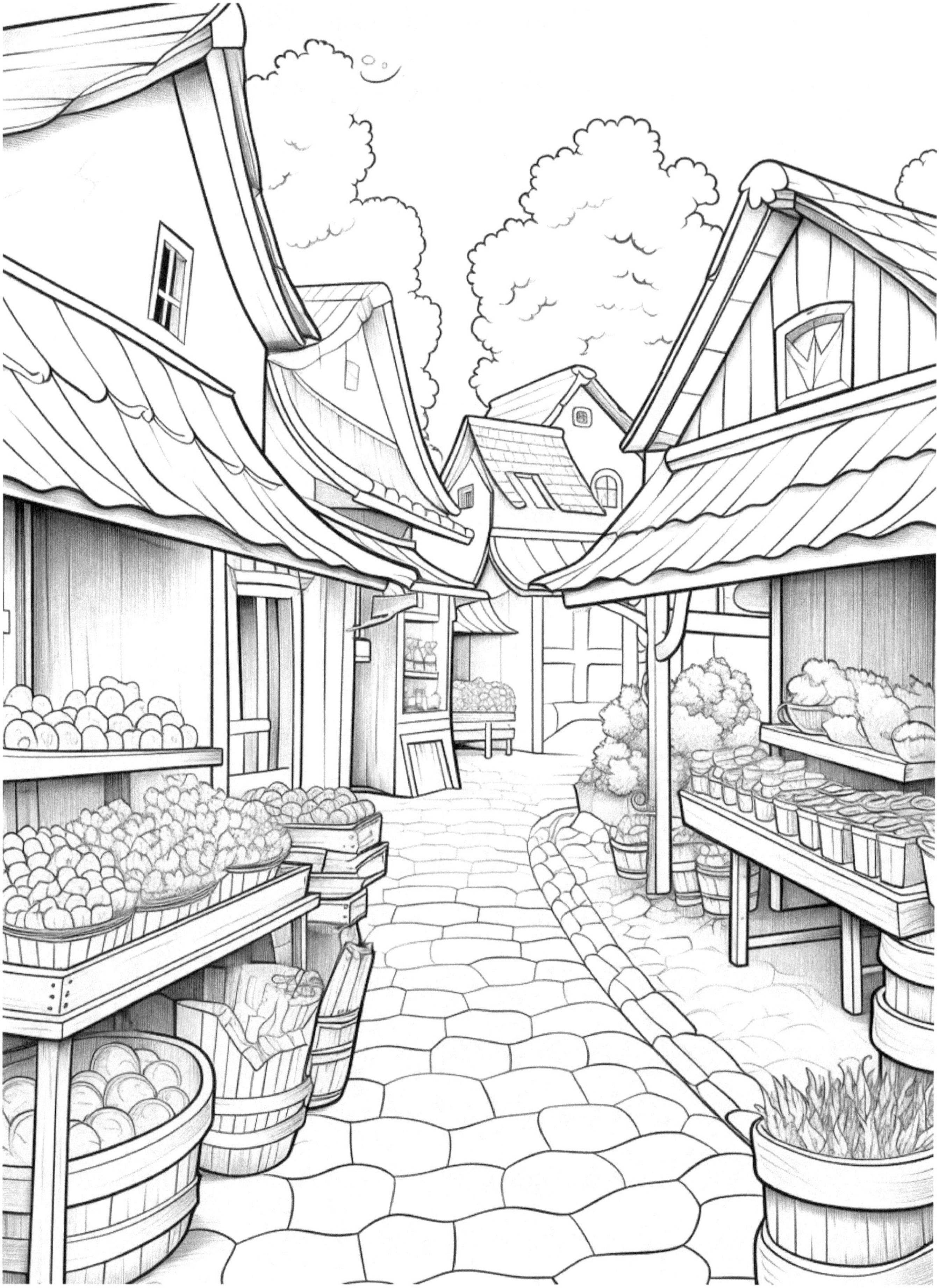

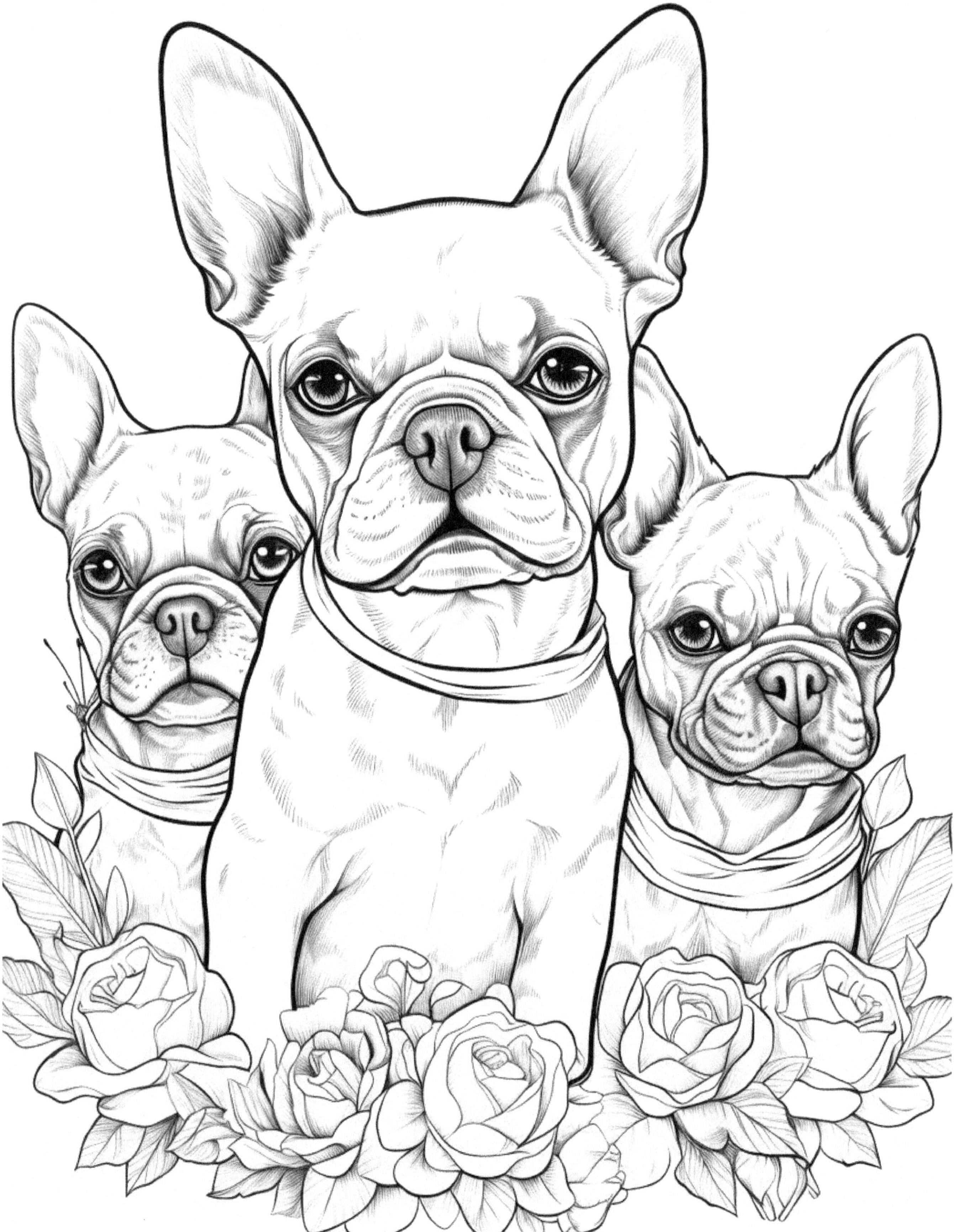

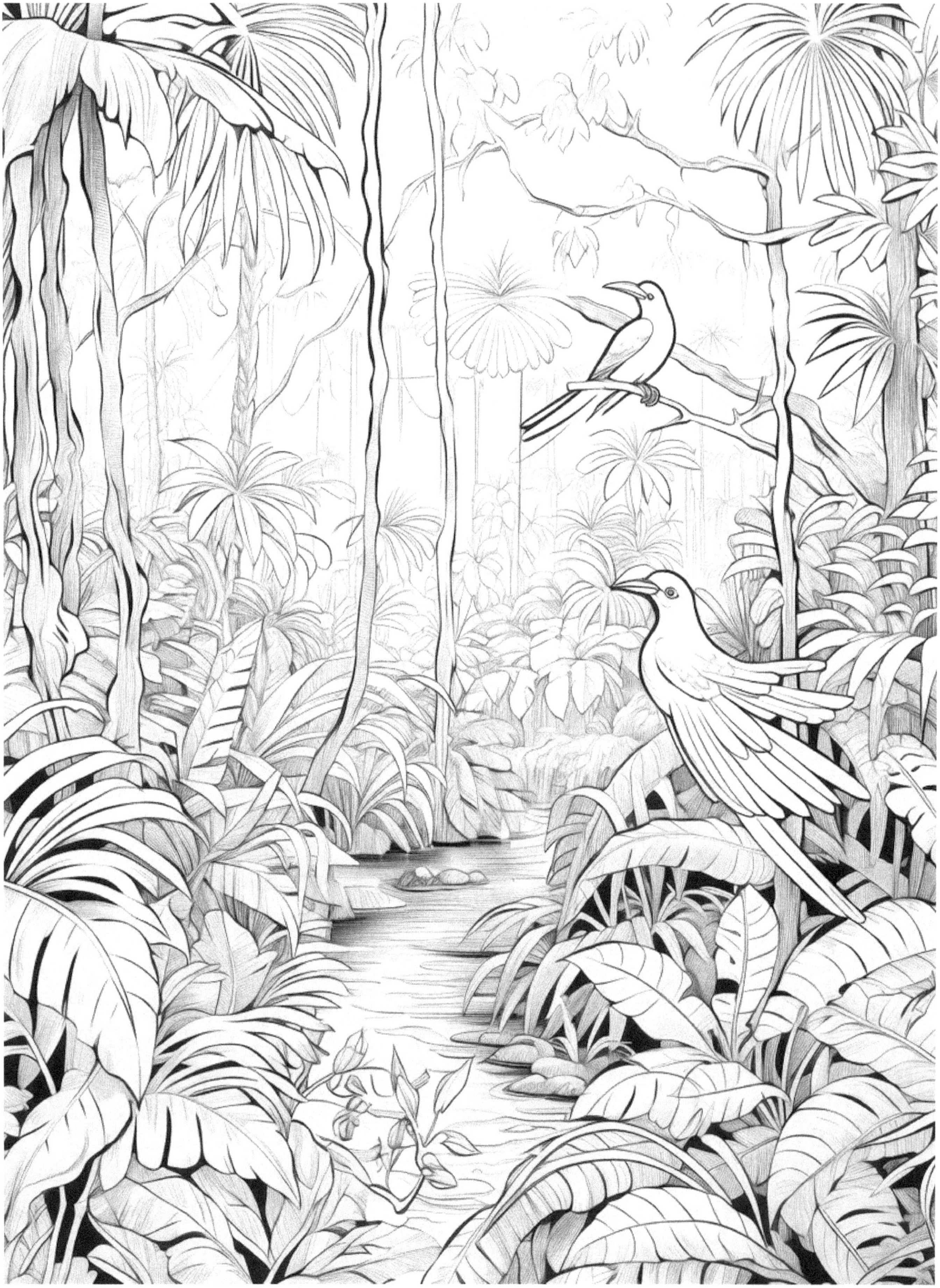

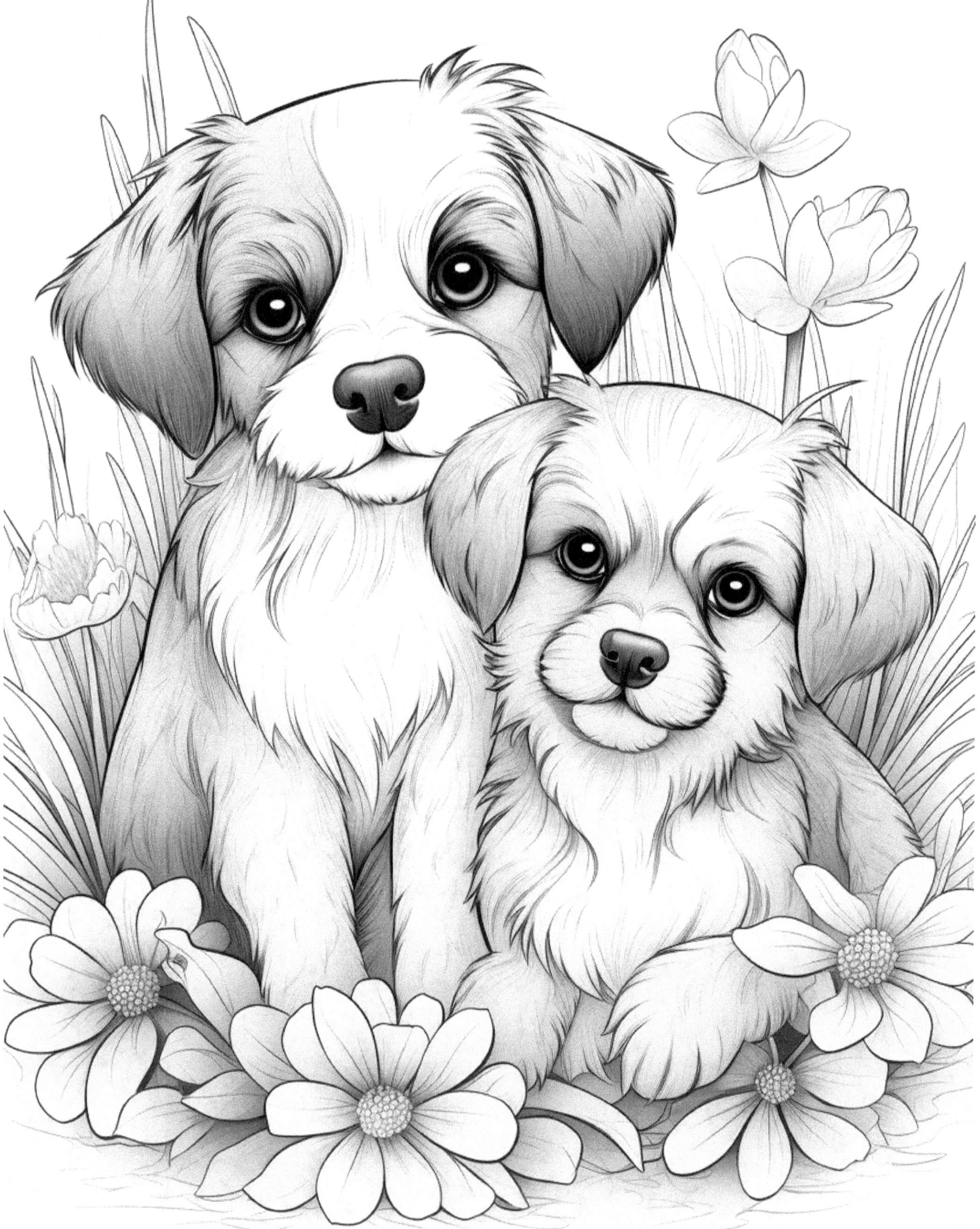

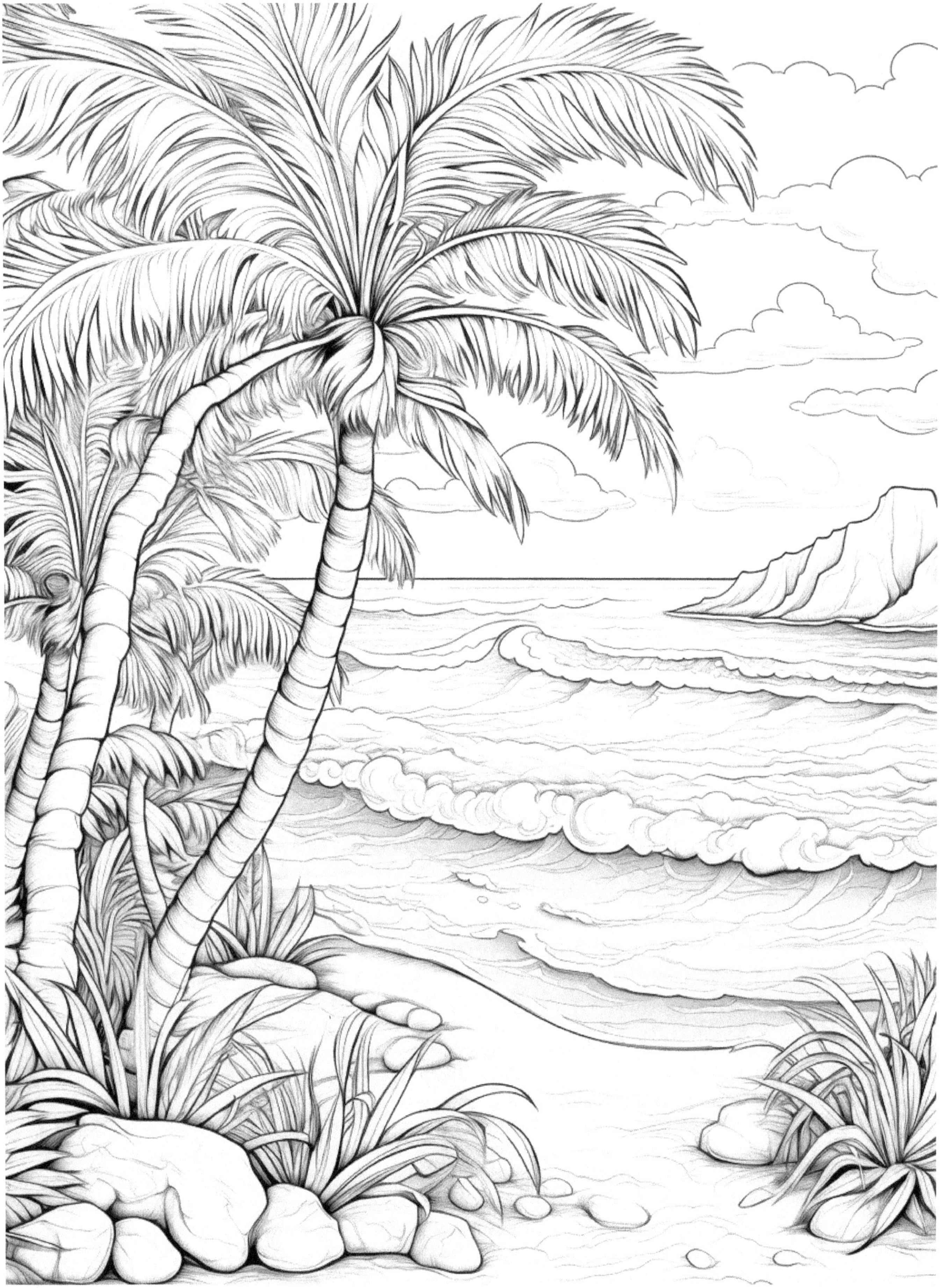

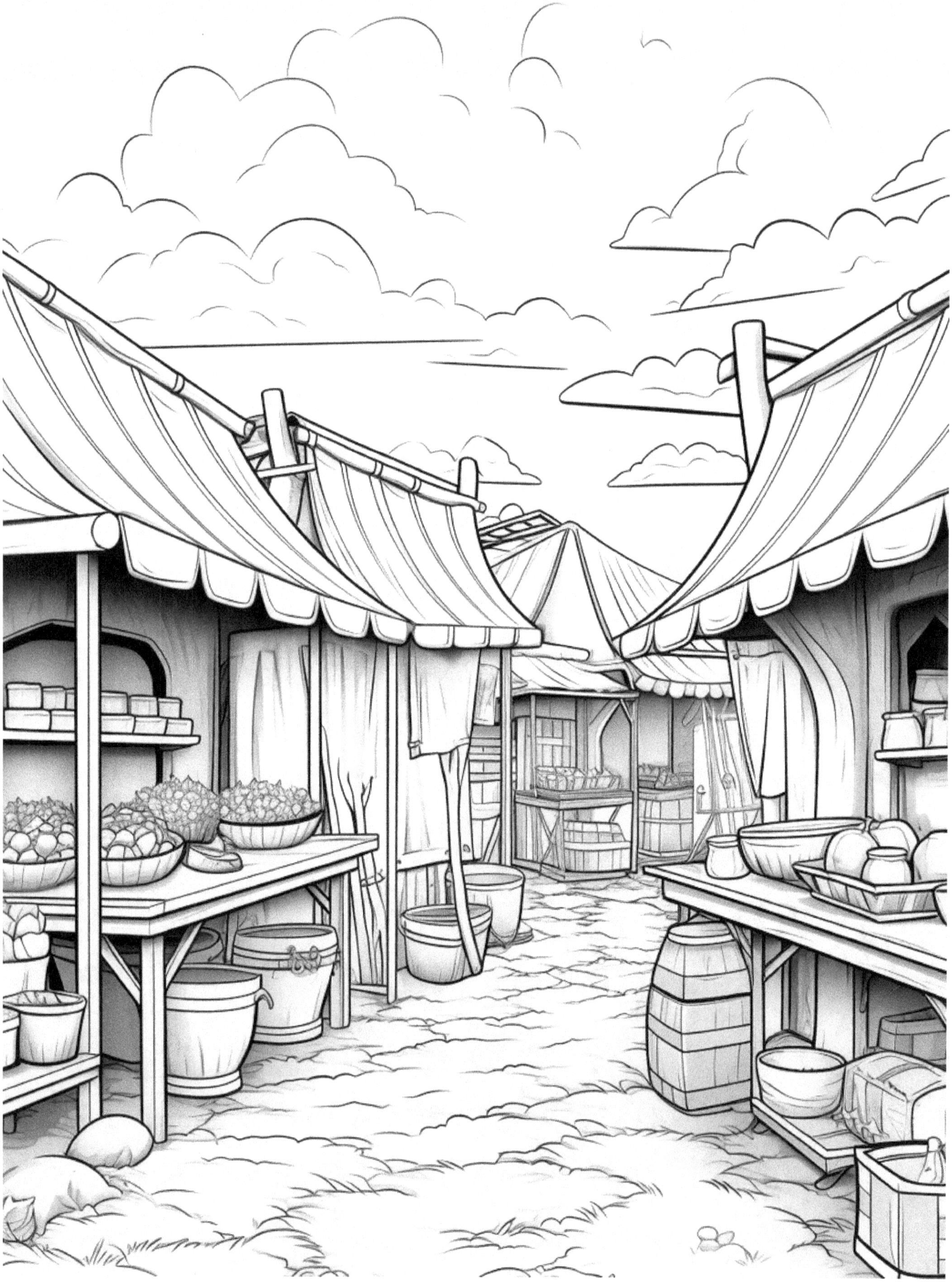

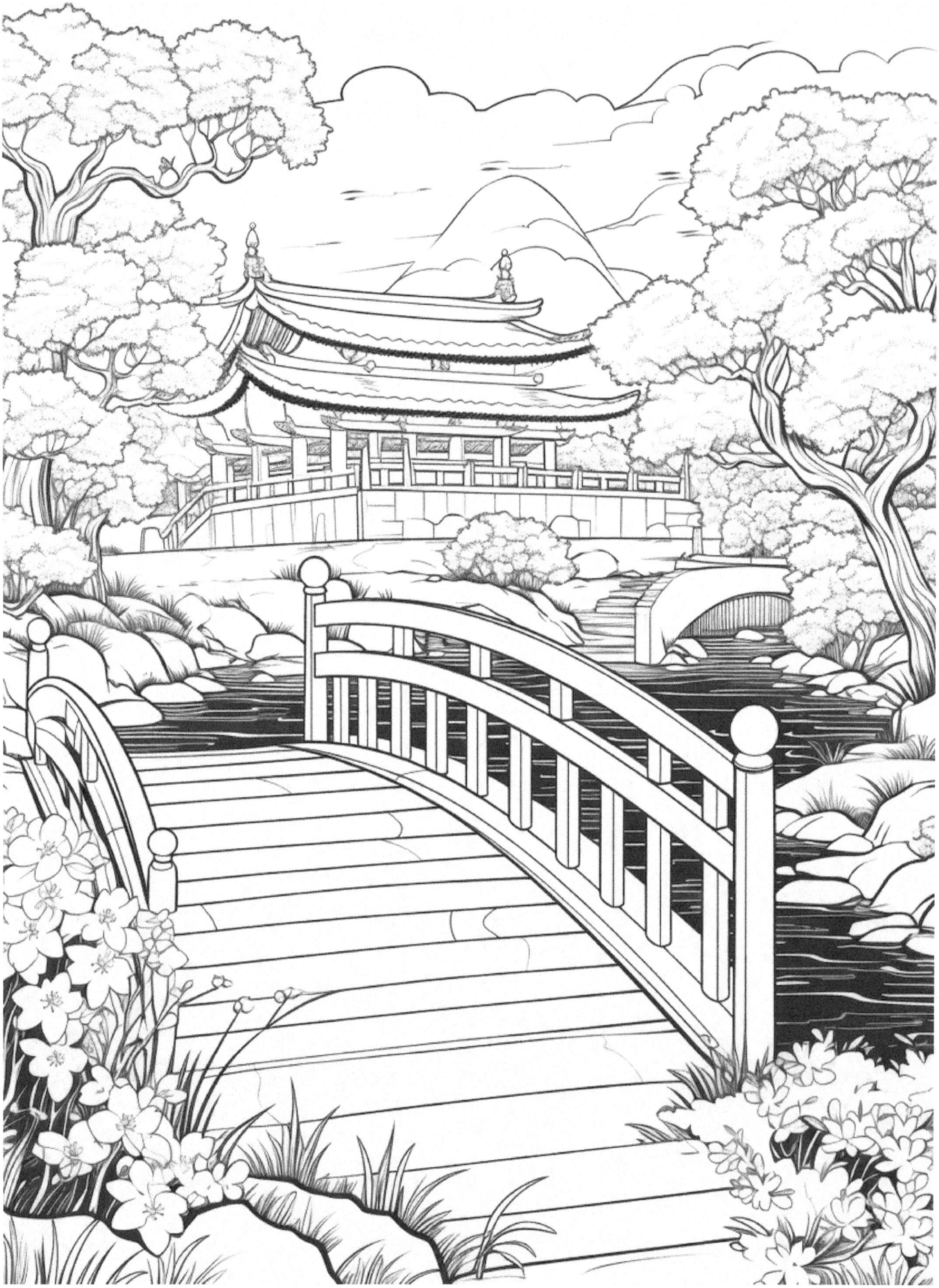

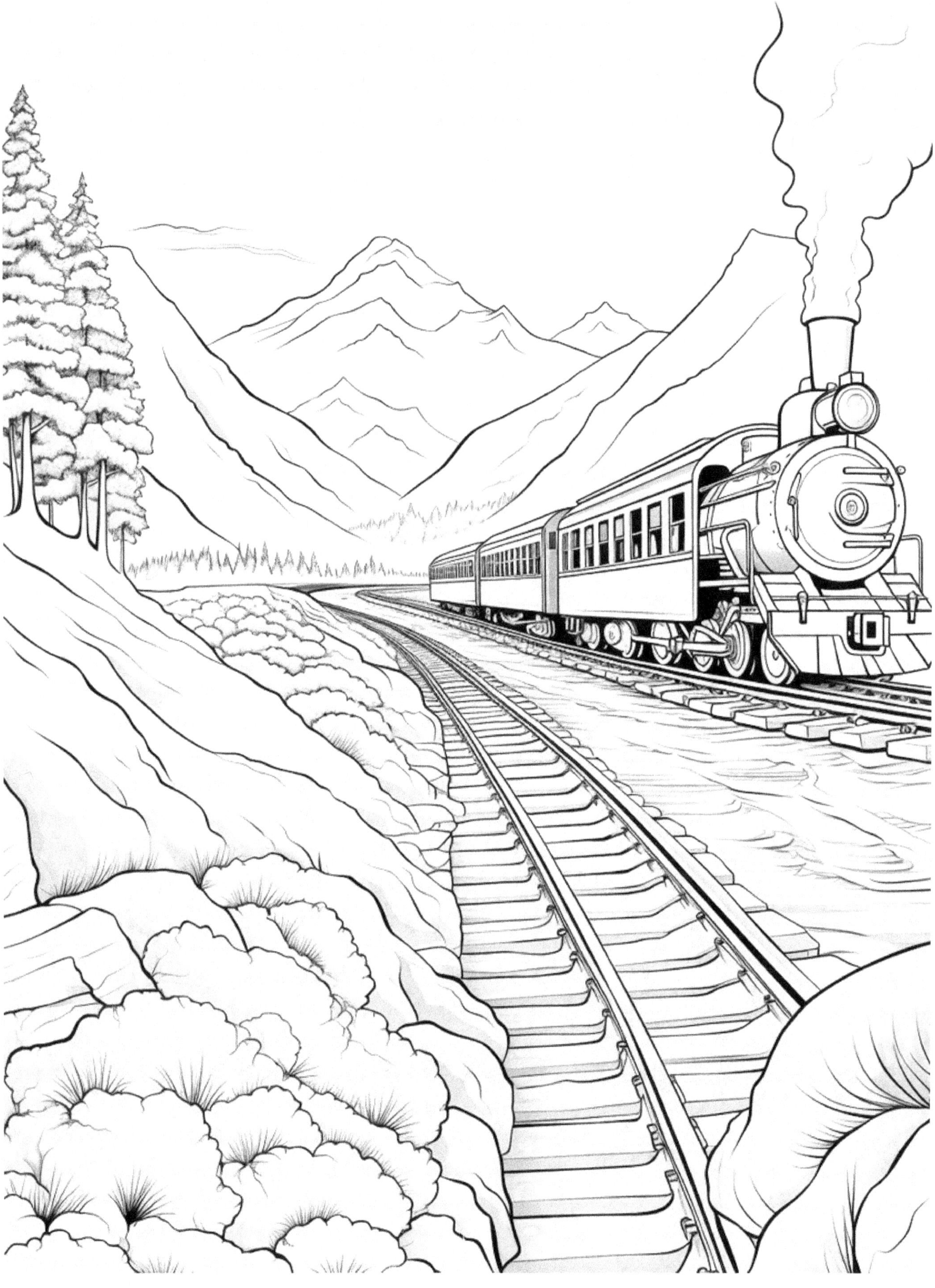

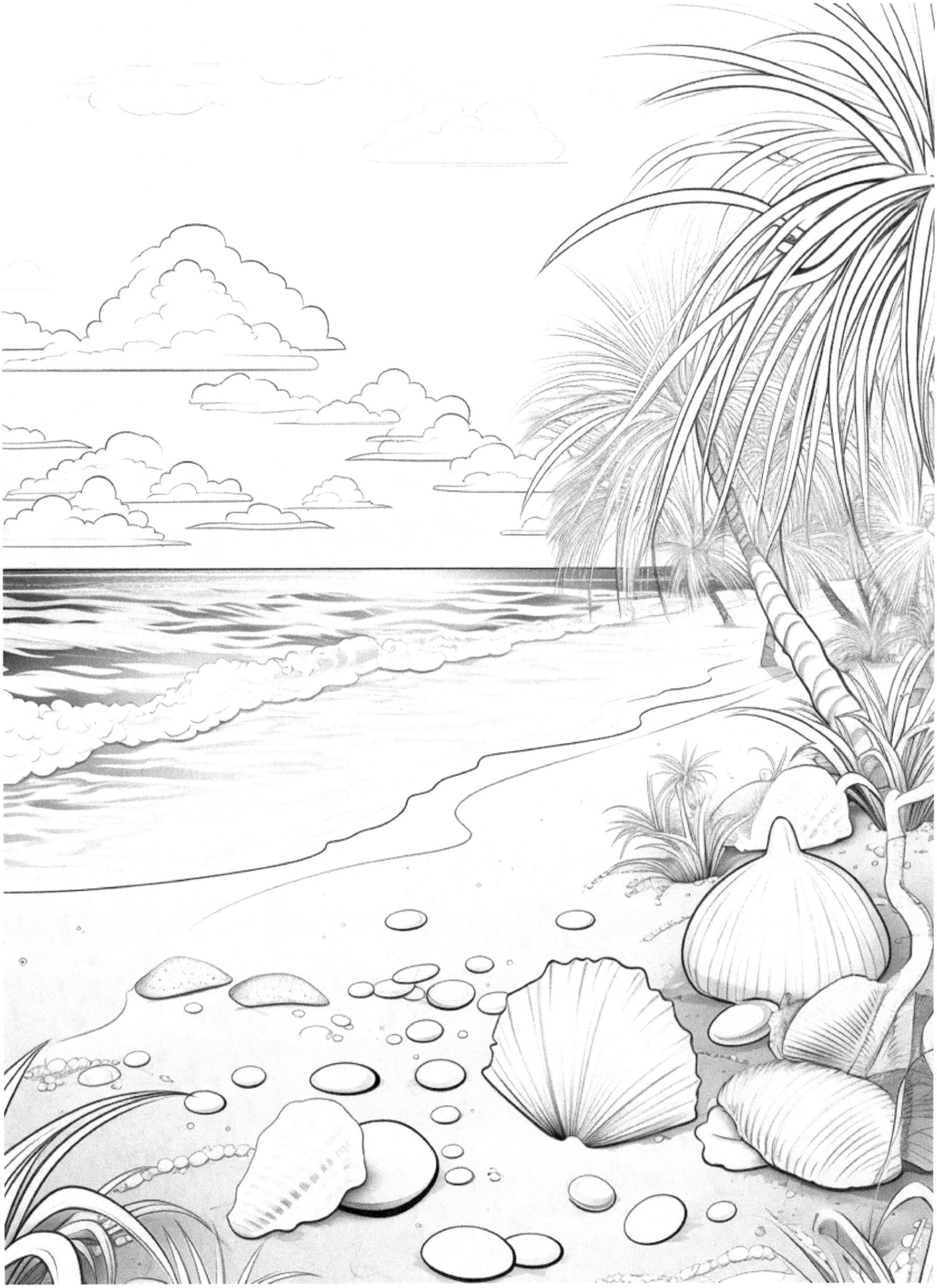

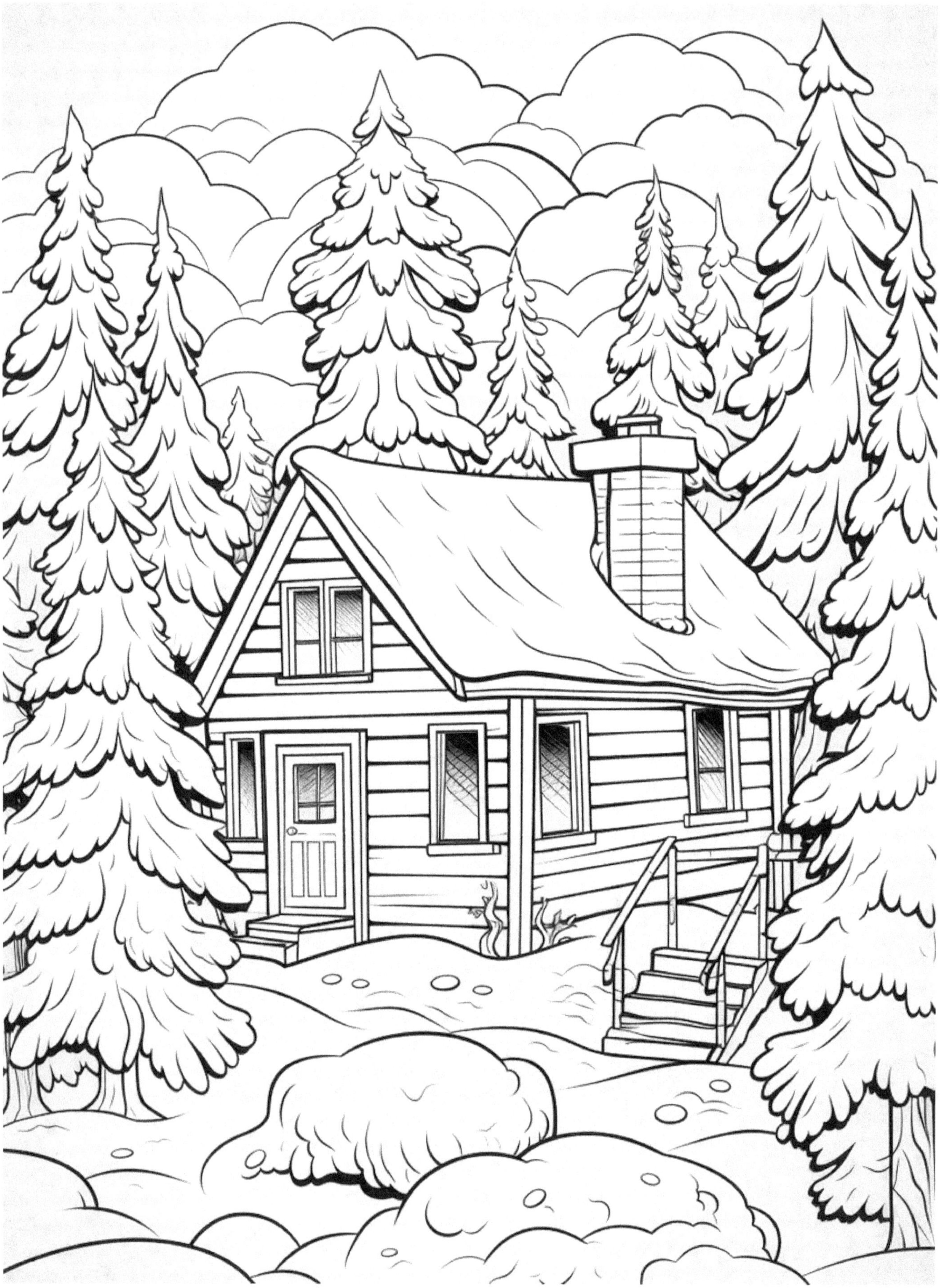

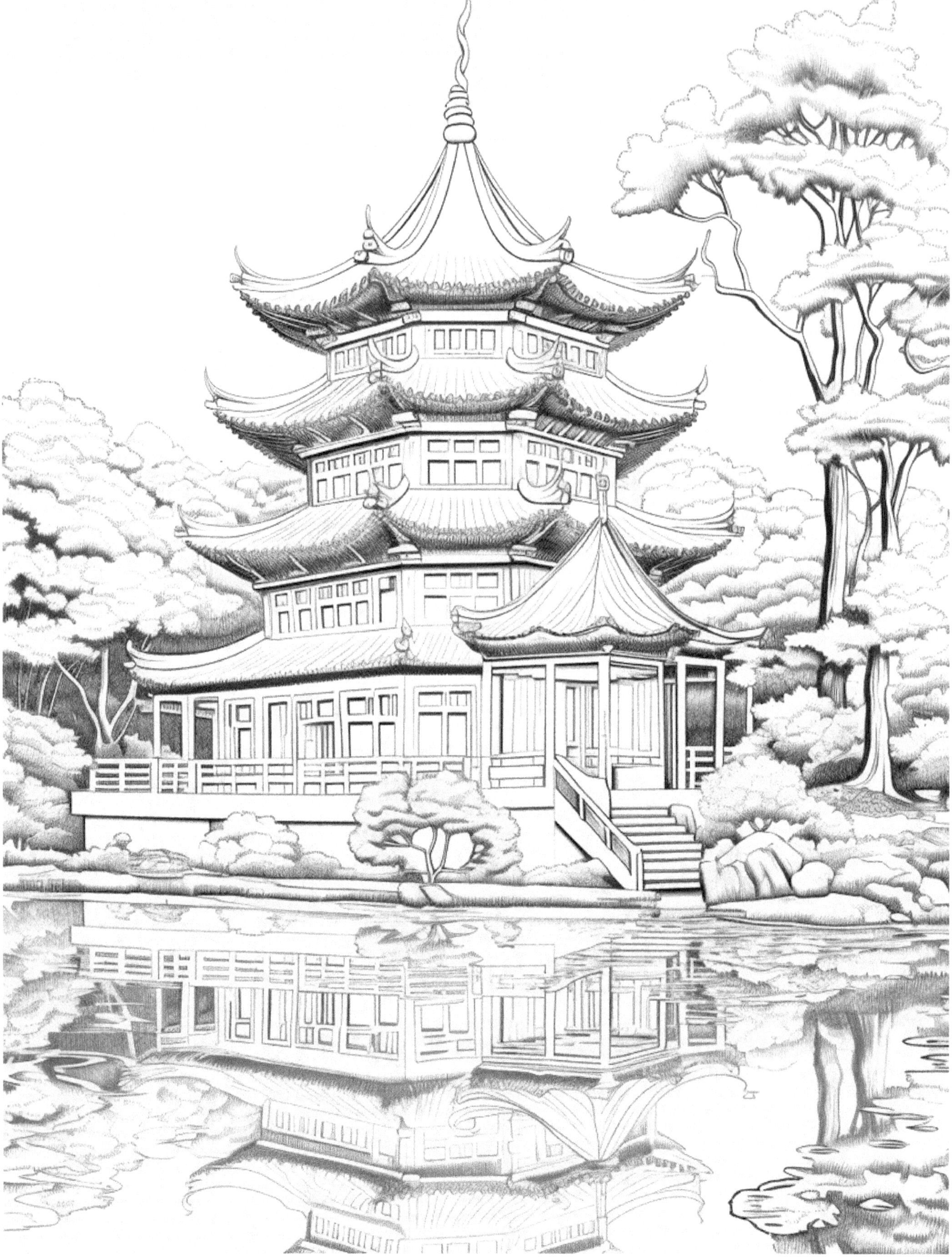

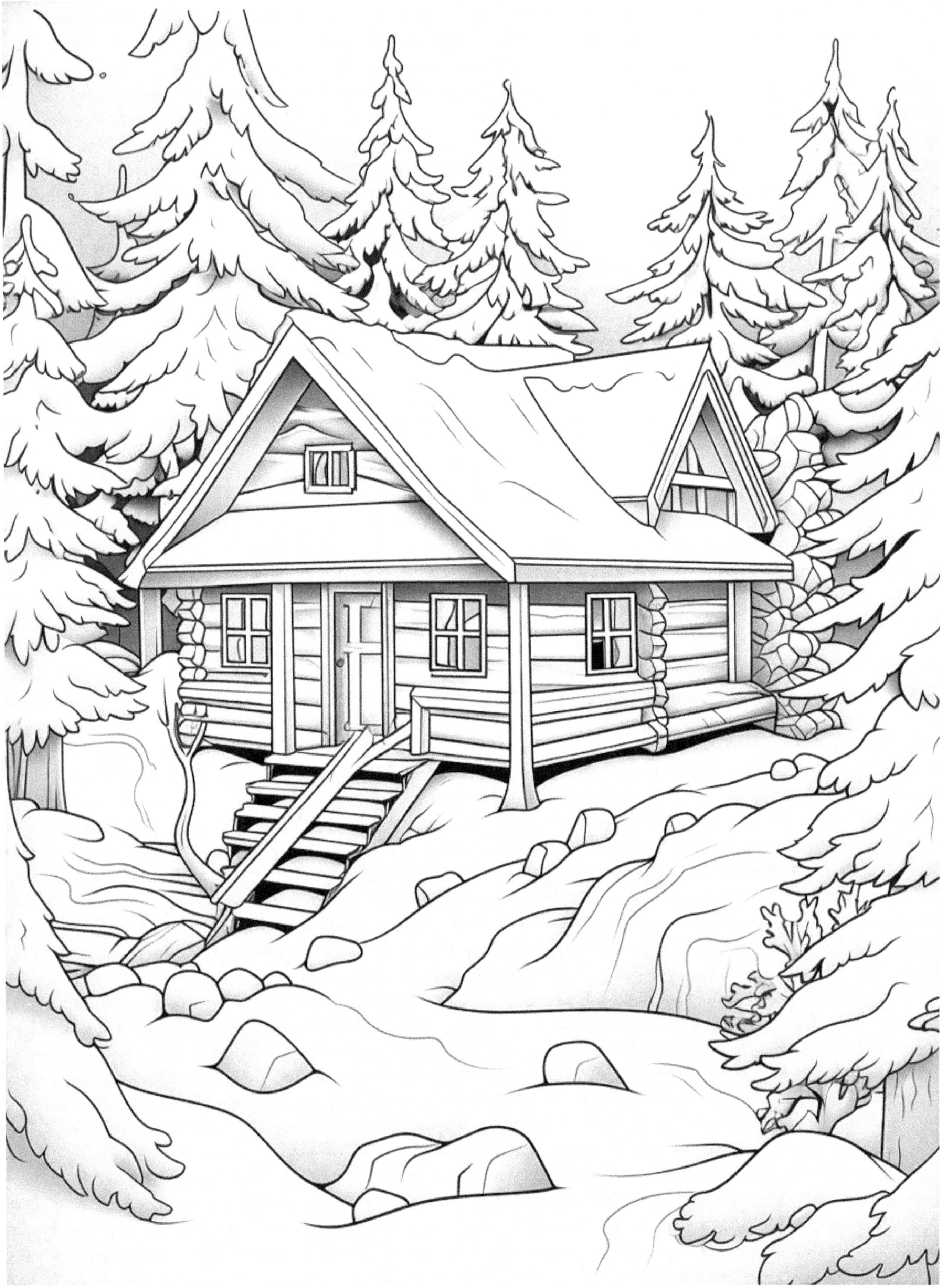

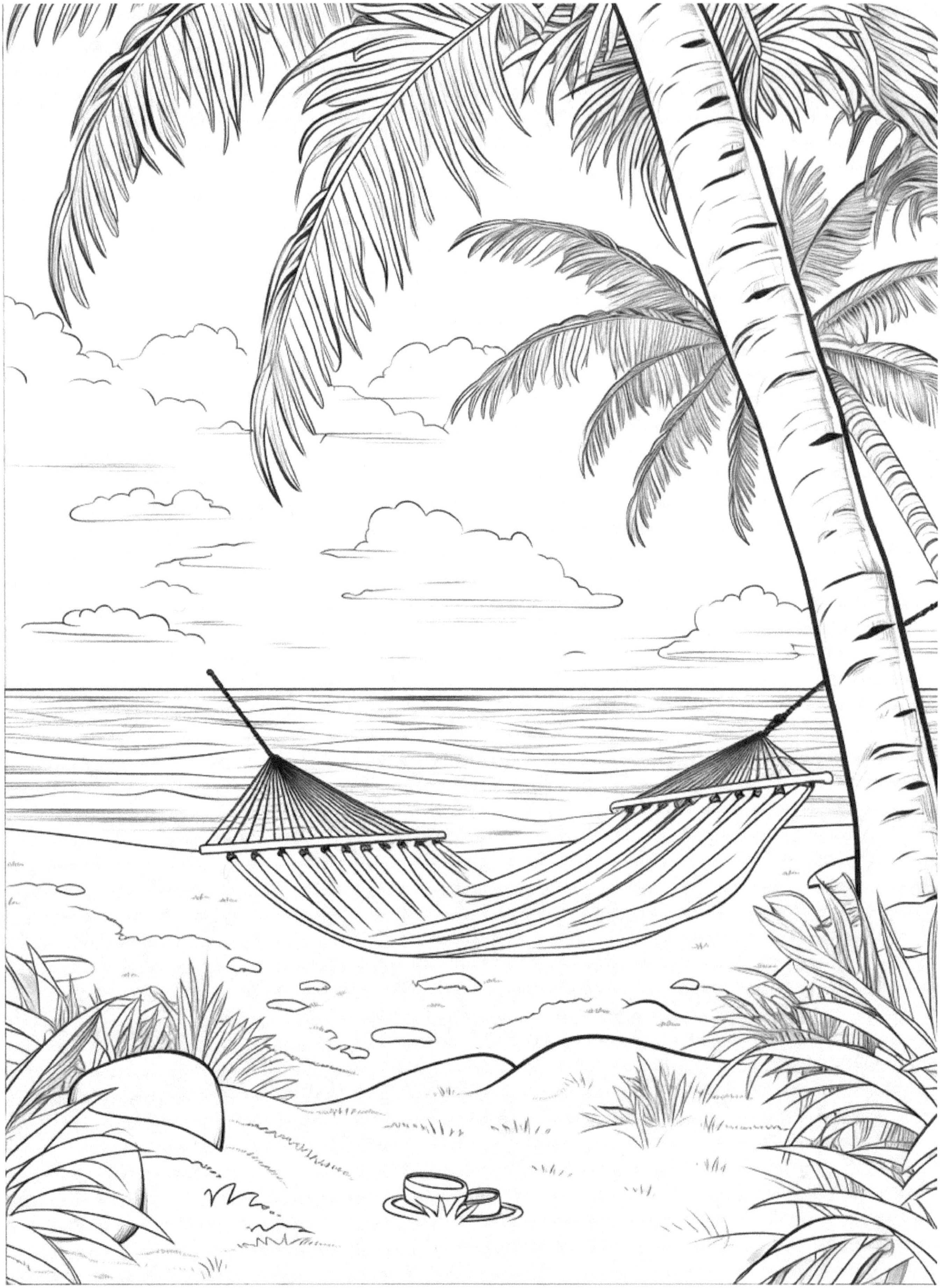

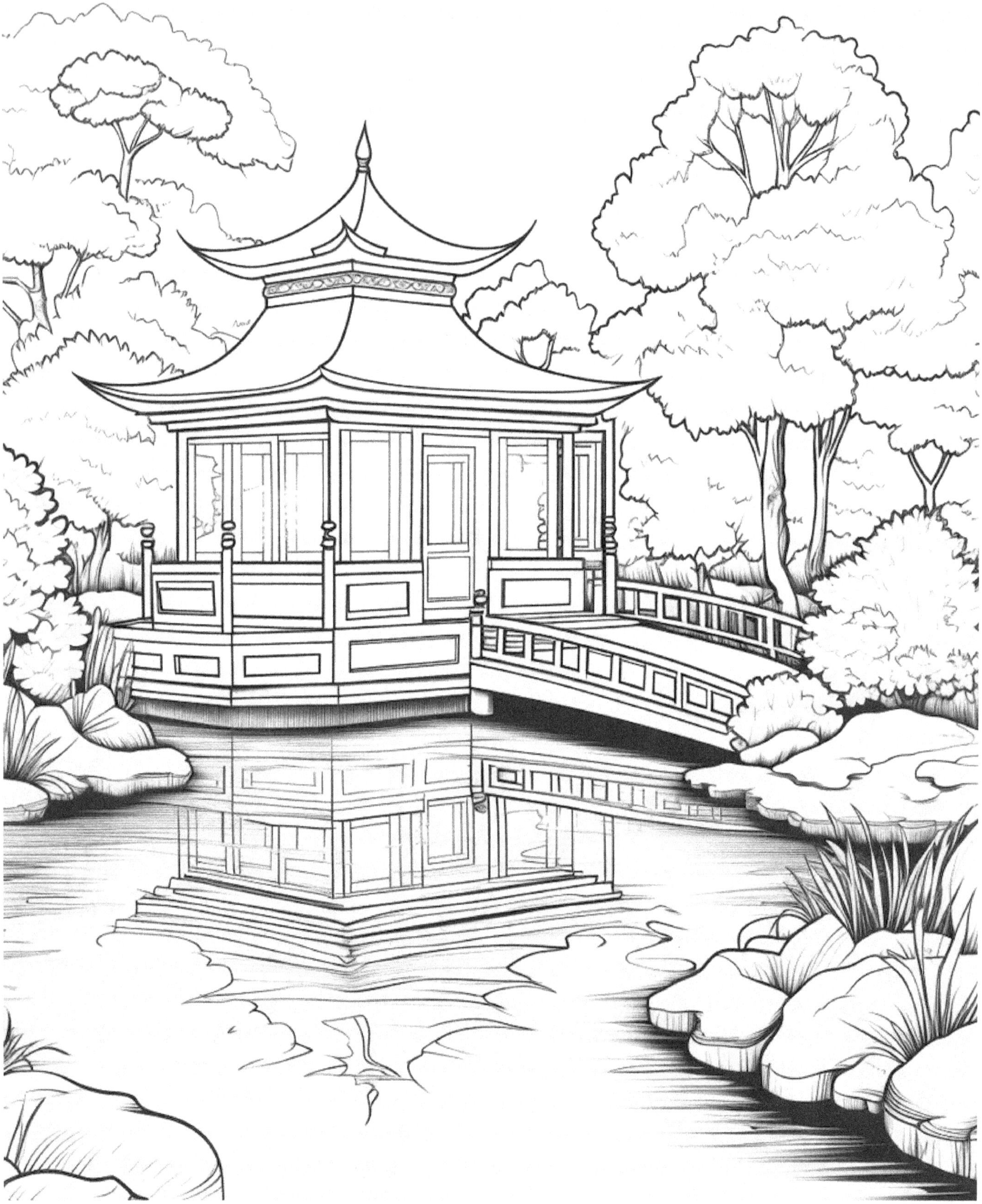

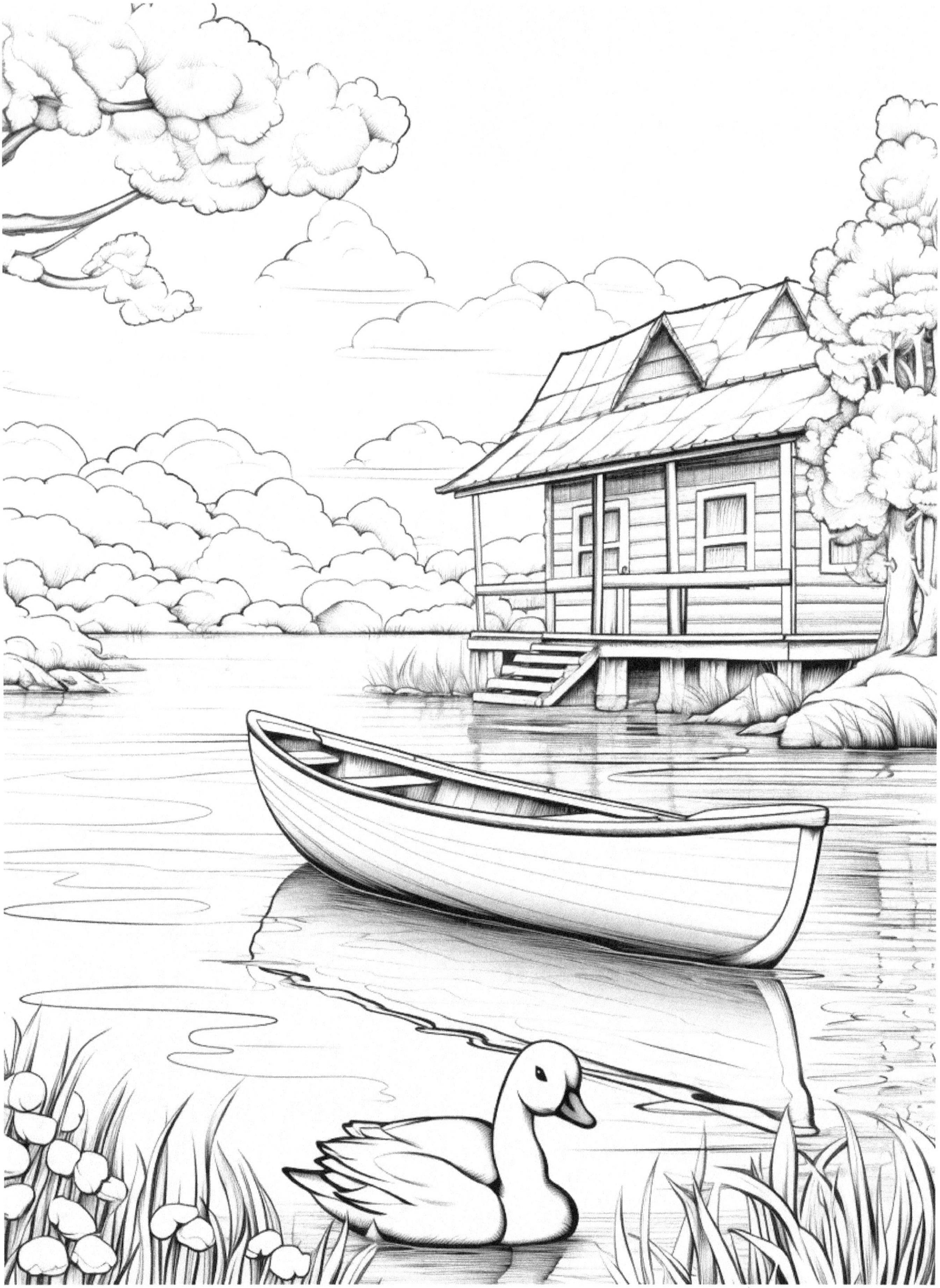

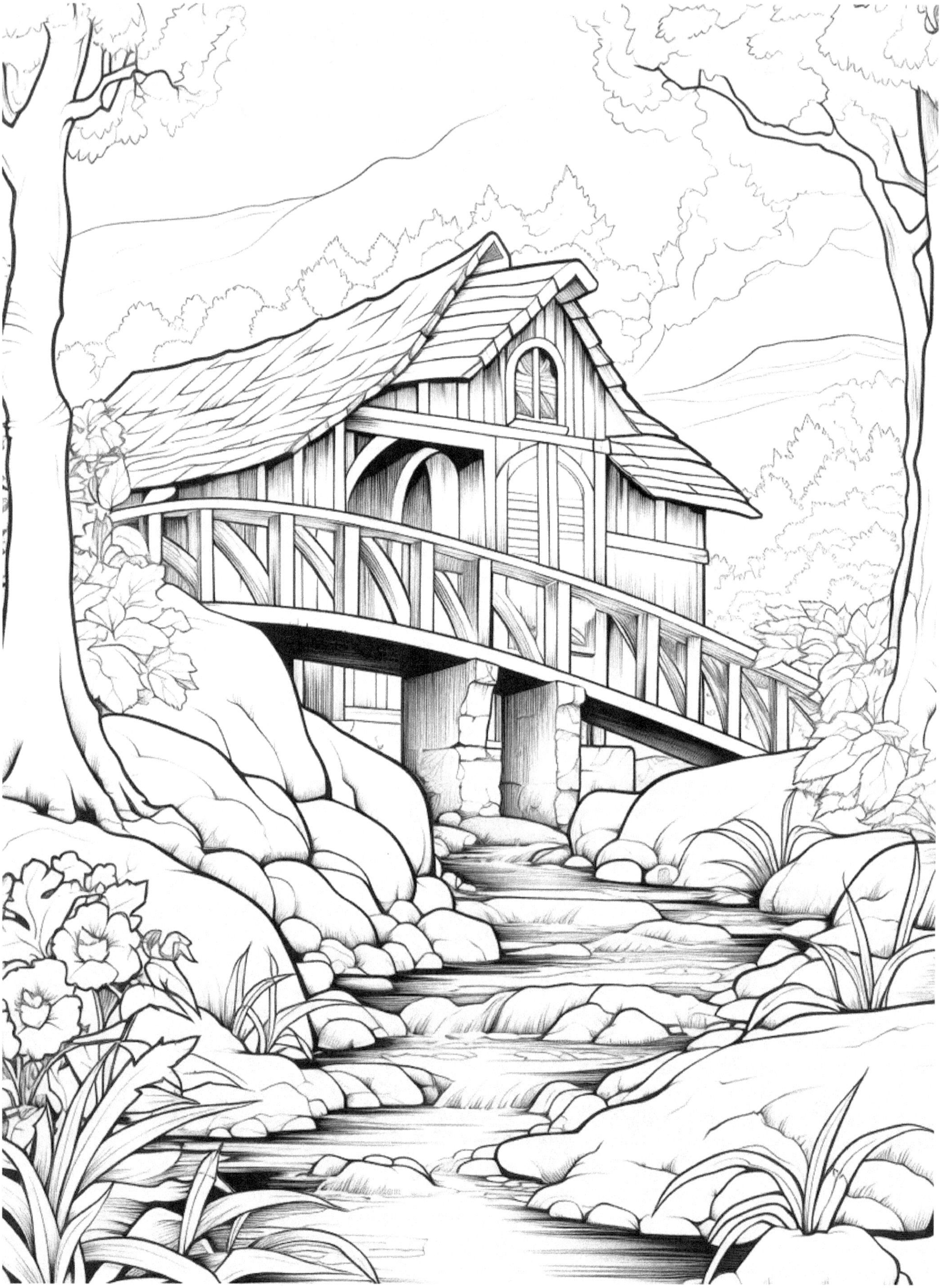

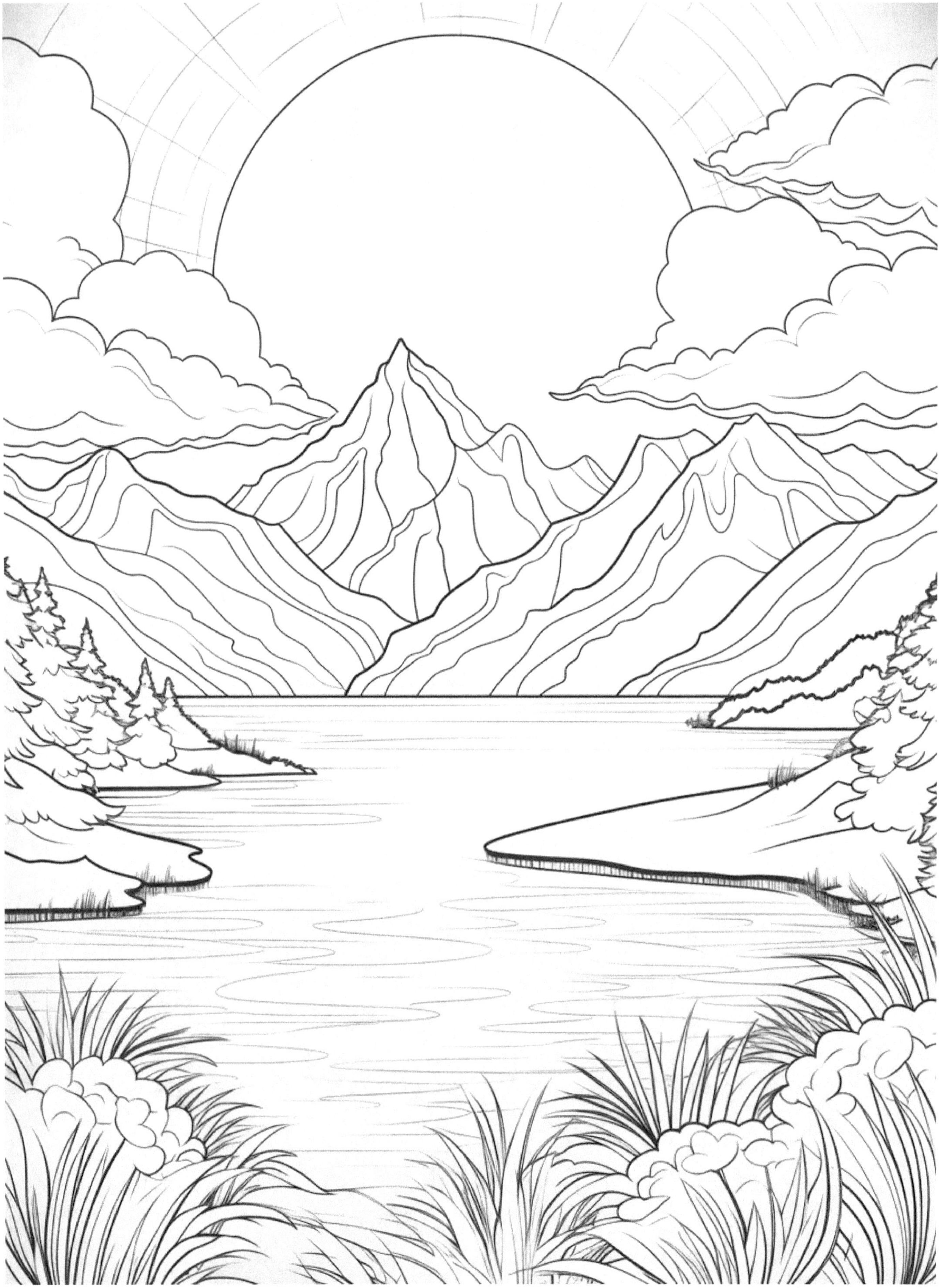

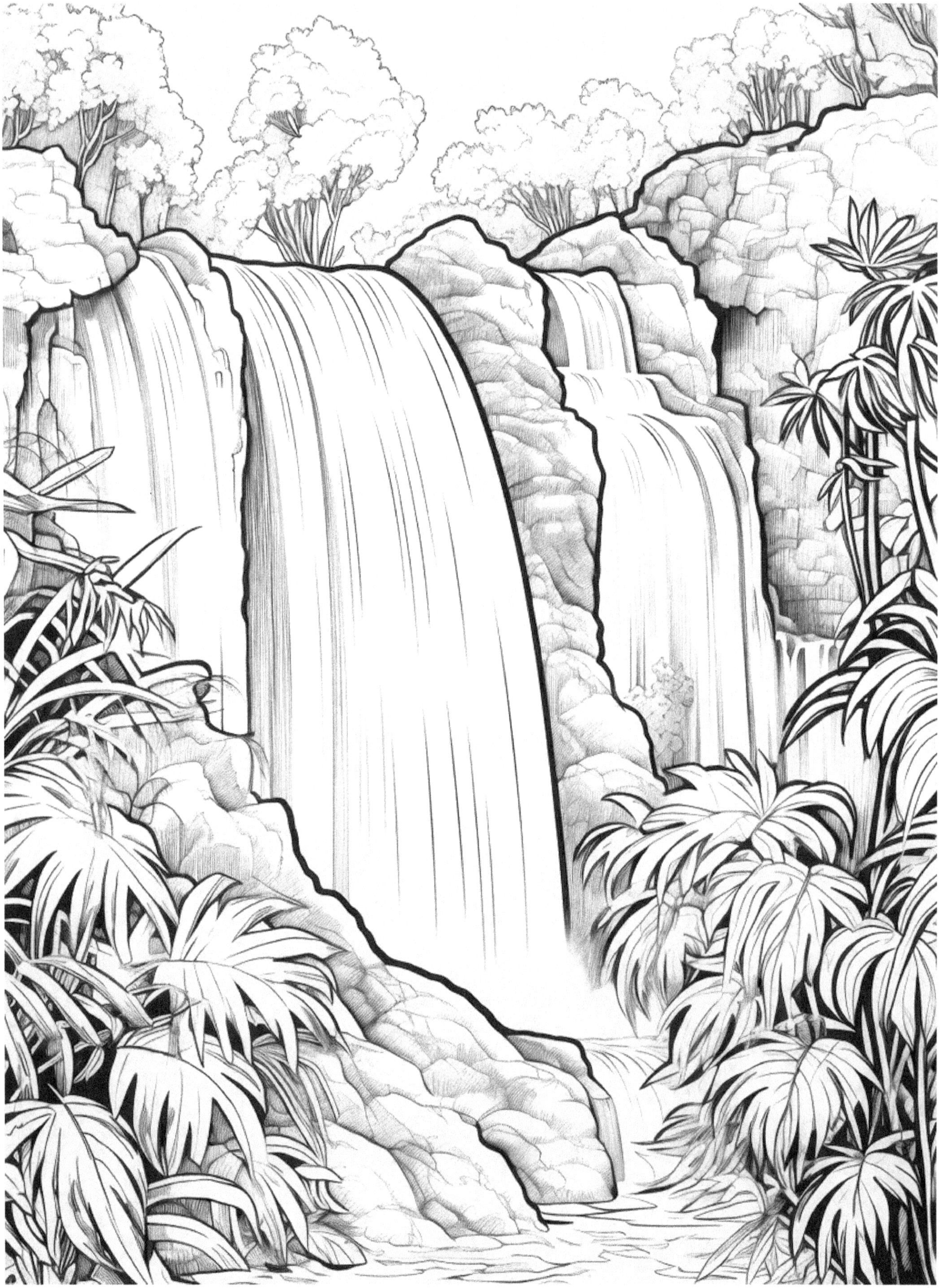

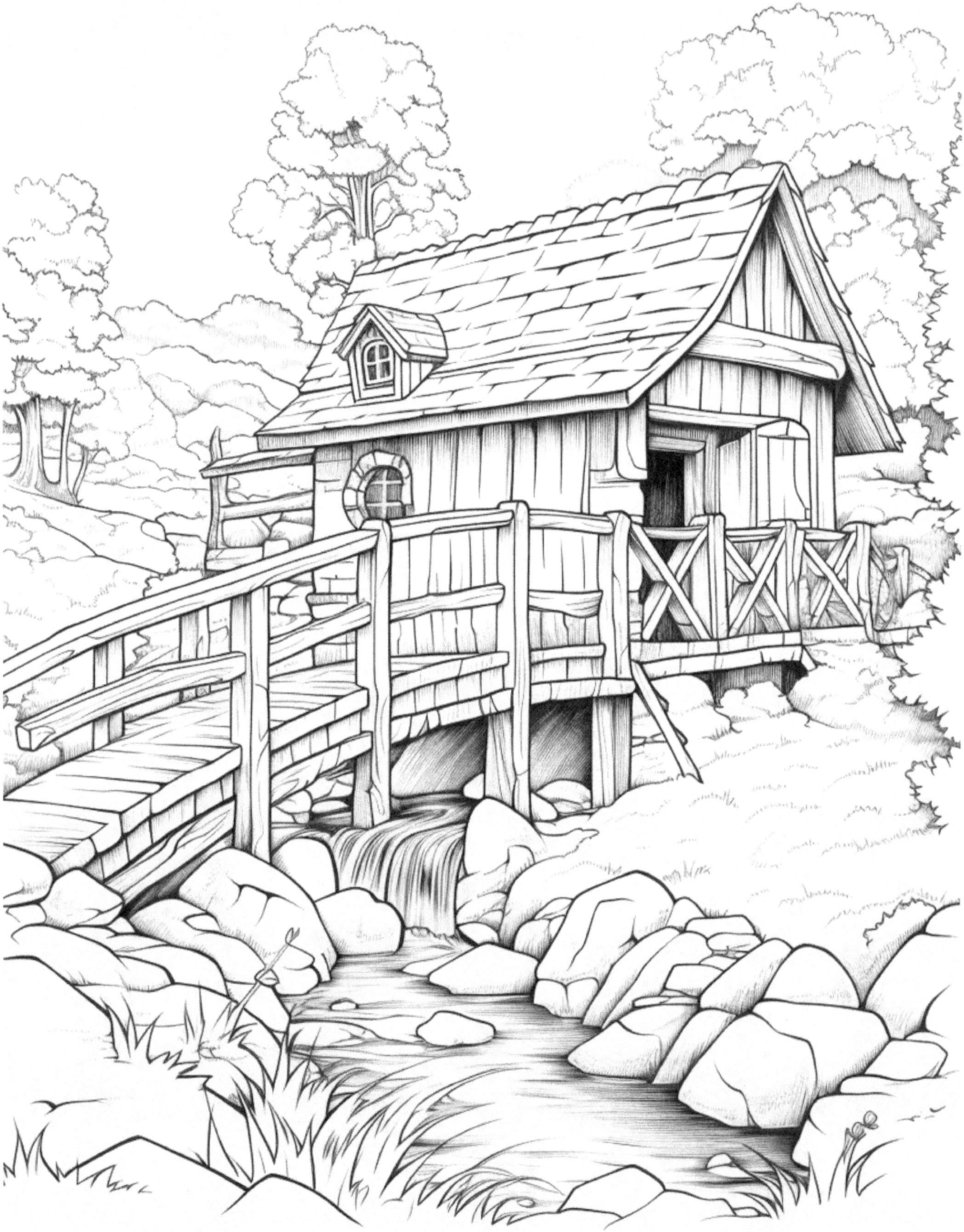

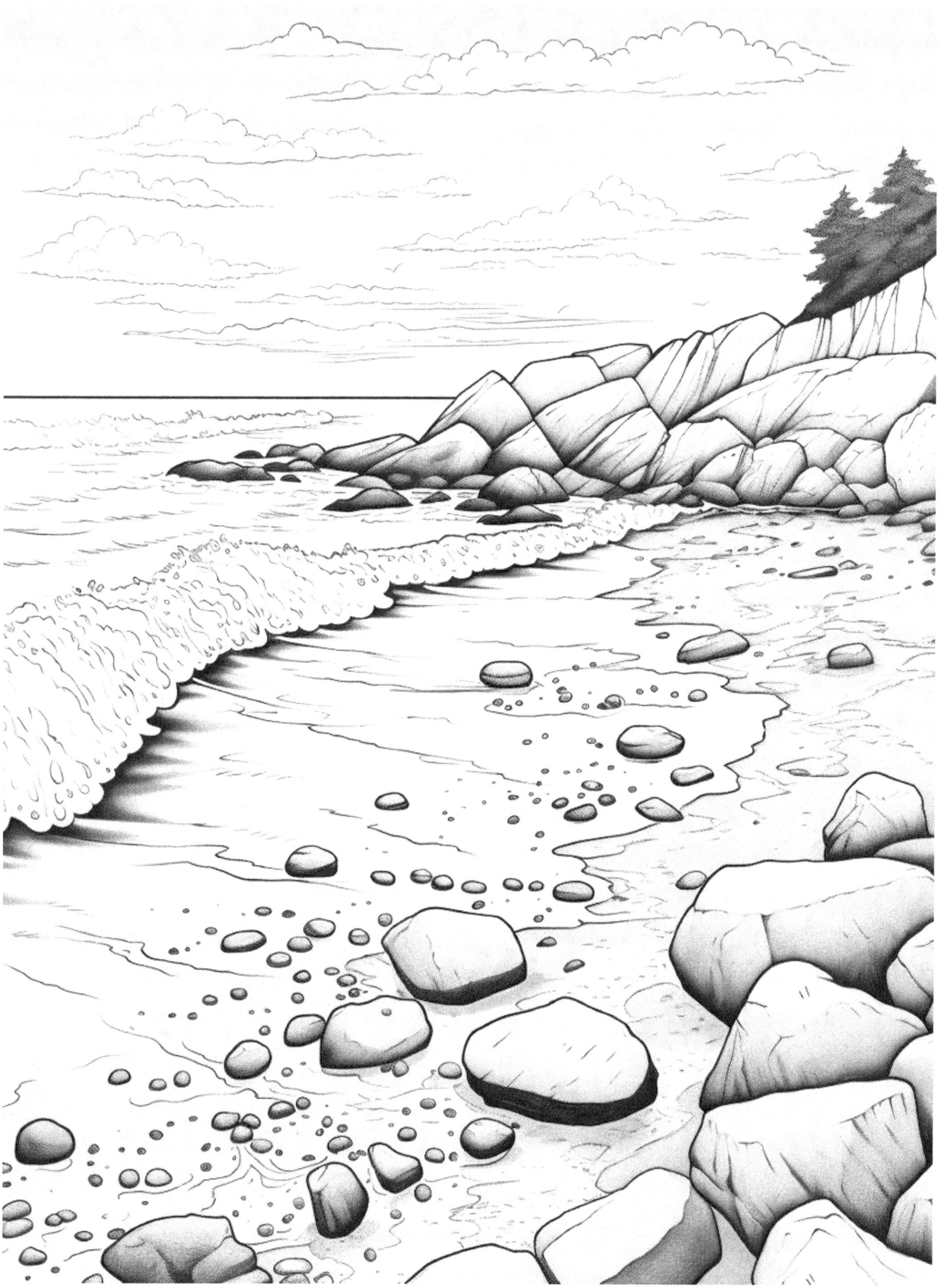

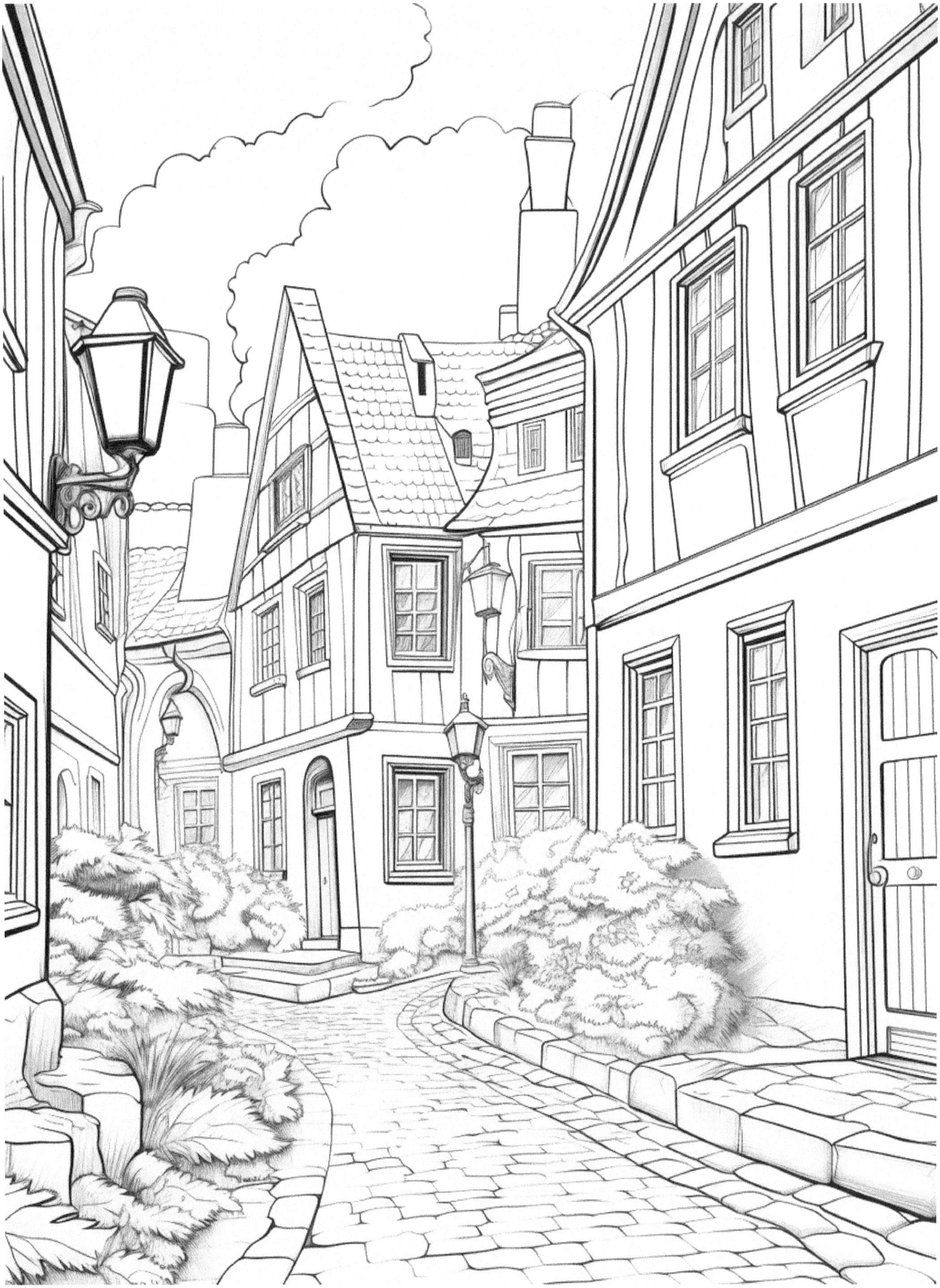

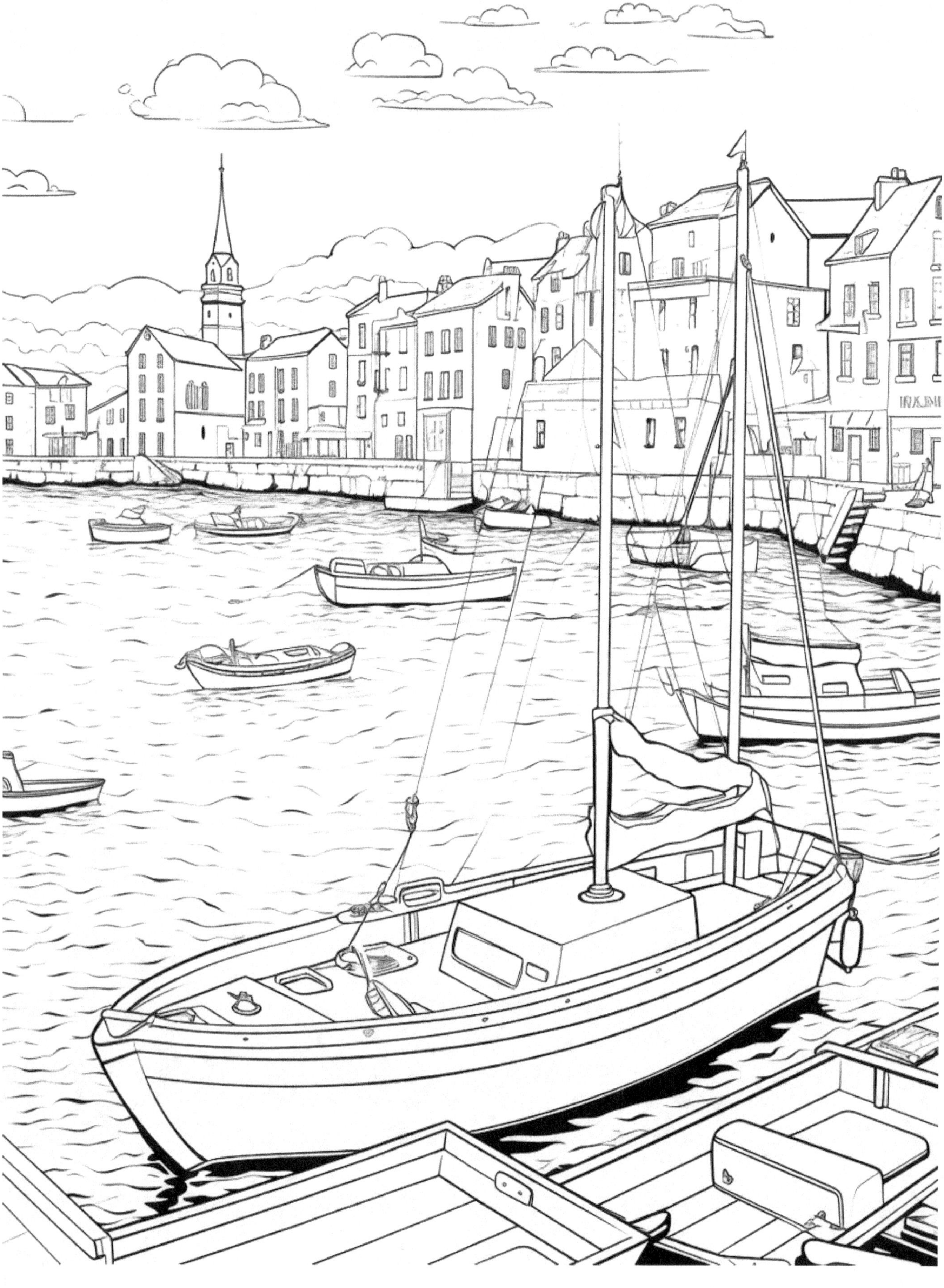

www.ingramcontent.com/pod-product-compliance
Lightning Source LLC
Chambersburg PA
CBHW062214220526
45471CB00009B/3197
* 9 7 9 8 3 2 3 7 5 8 9 7 5 *